D1590450

Named in remembrance of

the onetime *Antioch Review* editor

and longtime Bay Area resident,

the Lawrence Grauman, Jr. Fund

supports books that address

a wide range of human rights,

free speech, and social justice issues.

The publisher and the University of California Press Foundation gratefully acknowledge the generous support of the Lawrence Grauman, Jr. Fund.

Prison Truth

Prison Truth

THE STORY OF THE *SAN QUENTIN NEWS*

William J. Drummond

UNIVERSITY OF CALIFORNIA PRESS

University of California Press, one of the most distinguished university presses in the United States, enriches lives around the world by advancing scholarship in the humanities, social sciences, and natural sciences. Its activities are supported by the UC Press Foundation and by philanthropic contributions from individuals and institutions. For more information, visit www.ucpress.edu.

University of California Press
Oakland, California

Cataloging-in-Publication Data is on file at the Library of Congress.

ISBN 978-0-520-29836-1 (cloth : alk. paper)
ISBN 978-0-520-29837-8 (pbk. : alk. paper)
ISBN 978-0-520-97052-6 (ebook)

Manufactured in the United States of America

28 27 26 25 24 23 22 21 20
10 9 8 7 6 5 4 3 2 1

To Faith Fancher
(August 23, 1950–October 19, 2003)

I got a letter this mornin', how do you reckon it read?
It said, "Hurry, hurry, yeah, your love is dead."

Son House, "Death Letter"

Contents

Illustrations

Acknowledgments

When I began volunteering at the *San Quentin News* in 2012, I never considered writing a book about the experience. Arnulfo García, the inmate who was editor in chief, invited me to become an adviser to the *San Quentin News,* and the idea appealed to me. Bringing UC Berkeley students into the SQ newsroom, I reasoned, would be a way to strengthen the editing skills of aspiring Cal journalists. The University of California's School of Journalism had dropped editing as a separate course in the curriculum to make room for more emphasis on internet skills.

Maura Roessner of UC Press got in touch with me on September 8, 2015, and suggested I do a book. After some thought, I accepted. In retrospect, it proved to be a life-changing experience. Although I had been in journalism for half a century, this book was the first chance I had to reflect on many things that had happened in my career since I left graduate school in 1966. Maura was wonderfully supportive throughout the project, which proved to be an emotional roller-coaster at times.

Special thanks to Steve McNamara, Joan Lisetor, John Eagan, Lizzy Buchen, and Linda Xiques. As the original group of civilian advisers, they greeted me warmly when I first arrived in the SQ newsroom.

Arnulfo's brother, Nick, and Nick's wife, Monica, provided valuable details about the García family's early life in San Jose.

I want to give a big shout-out to all the Cal students who became *San Quentin News* volunteers and made regular visits to Bastille by the Bay, come rain or come shine. I had no idea how this experimental course would work, and it turned into one of the most rewarding teaching-learning experiences I've ever done.

My August 2012 pitch to recruit students read as follows: "You don't have to be a felon to write for the *San Quentin News*. But it helps. Otherwise, the *San Quentin News* wants a few good men and women to work as adjunct reporters and editors of the monthly newspaper." Slowly they answered the call. Since the advent of the SQ editing class, more than eighty UC students of all nationalities and ethnicities have participated: Knowles Adkisson, Brittany Barnes, Addie Baxter, Andrew Beale, Alessandra Bergamin, Gabby Bozmarova, Lucy Brennan, Laerke Cecilie, Grace Cha, Juan Marcos Martinez Chacon, Bonnie Chan, Jessica Chen, Noe-Marie Claraty, Abené Clayton, Marisa Conroy, Drew Costley, Adie Dinolfo, Trenise Ferreira, Fernando Gallo, Alissa Greenberg, Madeleine Gregory, Sara Grossman, Pendarvis Harshaw, Makaila Heifner, Meghan Herbst, Suhauna Hussain, Jacqui Ipp, Adam Iscoe, Charlotte Jacquemart, Soumya Karlamangla, Alex Kekauoha, Alexis Kenyon, Charlie Kidd, Ivy Kim, Laura Klivens, Bo Kovitz, Isara Krieger, Sara Lafleur-Vetter, Hannah Lawson, Cecilia Lei, Sasha Lekach, Cuong Phuoc Luu, Byrhonda Lyons, Allen Marshall, Anna Marsý, Dayton Martindale, Elena Mateus, Alex Leeds Matthews, Sam Karani Mbaabu, Lee G. Mengistu, Sophie Michielse, Salina Nasir, Jane Nho, Rose Oser, Tessa Paoli, Claire Perlman, Sonnet Phelps, Nicola Phillips, Fareed Abdul Rahman, Elizabeth Rainey, Danica Rodarmel, Gabriel Sanchez, Samantha Santamaria, Khaled Sayed, Elly Schmidt-Hopper, Emma Schwartz, Nate Sheidlower, Erin Shipstead, Meg Shutzer, Robin Simmonds, Brenna Smith, Daniel Steiner, Christian Gerard Stork, Ahna Kahealani Straube, Arielle Swedback, Amruta Manhohan Trivedi, Mara Van Ellis, Amina Waheed, Chloee Weiner, Spence Whitney, Byron Wilkes, Carla Williams, Kate Wolffe, Christopher Yee, S. Parker Yesko, and Jieqian Zhang. Most say they benefited. In addition, they helped make the *San Quentin News* a national leader in prison journalism, stemming the tide of mass incarceration.

Public information officer Sam Robinson's wise and firm leadership made the revived *San Quentin News* a success. Nobody would argue with that assertion, and Lieutenant Robinson supported the UC Berkeley collaboration from the beginning.

Raphaela Casale, a technician in the warden's office, handled the hundreds of clearance forms I submitted for students, volunteers, officials, and guest speakers over the years, and she did so with great skill and patience.

This book would never have come about had it not been for the support from the men in blue who made up the writing and editing staff of the *San Quentin News*. I learned more from them than they ever learned from me. After their parole Aly Tamboura and Richard Lindsey gave me valuable insights into how prisons work and helped shape my understanding of how journalism takes place behind bars.

My thanks to my Madrid journalist friend, Laura Rodriquez, who peppered me for months with the same Facebook message, *"¡Libro! ¡Libro!"*

Libby Rainey was an undergraduate at UC Berkeley when she joined the *San Quentin News* editing class in 2014. And she stayed involved with the San Quentin story after she had graduated and gone on to her career at *Democracy Now!* Libby shouldered the burden as my primary reader and conscience during the critical final months of churning out these chapters.

Thanks as well to Patricia LaHay, a graduate of the UC School of Journalism, for giving a read to the final product. Cathy Matthews and my daughter Tammerlin Drummond also looked over the manuscript and gave good advice.

Alex L. Weber provided invaluable assistance in finding forty-year-old articles from the *Los Angeles Times*.

Madison Wetzel of UC Press was kind and patient in helping me pull together all the details of preparing the manuscript and the attendant formalities.

Elisabeth Magnus, the UC Press copyeditor, did a superb job of tightening, sharpening, and clarifying my prose.

Of course, any lapses or errors are mine alone.

PART I   A Primer on Prison

1 Overview

"How many people are imprisoned, and how they are treated, has always been affected by much more than just recorded crime rates. Economics, political, legal and philosophical ideas and public opinion have all played roles," wrote Professor Alyson Brown of Edge Hill University in the United Kingdom.[1] Journalism, too, is a big factor in the treatment of incarcerated people because journalism ultimately shapes public opinion, which makes its way into politics and policy. Eventually, journalism affects the way the agencies of the state apply the rules of humanity to the people in prison. What you see on the prison yard is a reflection of what is going on in society. How closely does the truth of the media story reflect the lived experience of those behind bars who traveled through the criminal justice system? In the pages that follow, I will provide some answers to this question.

The book gives the reader a look inside a prison from a unique vantage point. Instead of seeing incarceration through a guard's eyes, it looks at imprisonment from within a newsroom that happens to be located inside a legendary prison.

California's oldest prison underwent dramatic change over the past three decades, and how those changes were witnessed and reported upon by inmate journalists is the subject of this book. San Quentin used to be a violent, dangerous human warehouse. It became instead a beacon for rehabilitation within the California Department of Corrections and Rehabilitation (CDCR).[2] I want to convince you that the *San Quentin News* played an important role in paving the way for that change because it helped shape public perception. I intend to lay out the history and context of the newspaper's rise to prominence since its founding in 1940, its struggle during the turmoil and shutdown in the 1980s, and its revival in 2008. Along the way I will explain the contributions of the core group who made the transformation happen. The pioneering 2008 inmates were a colorful and diverse collection. They consisted of a Los Angeles music mogul-cum-drug lord and some Three Strikes lifers, including a charismatic Chicano/Latino burglar, a bank robber, and a couple of men with murder convictions, all of whom were determined to become better men, and to do so through the unlikely medium of journalism!

The book also encompasses my own redemption, personally and professionally. After fifty years in journalism, I woke up one morning to discover that the news business had lost its way. Not only were newspapers collapsing financially, but the values that had attracted me to becoming a reporter were vanishing as well. Singer Gil Scott-Heron said his grandmother once told him, "If you don't stand for something, you'll fall for anything." Edward R. Murrow issued a warning years ago about television, a warning equally relevant today about our beloved digital devices: without values and a commitment to illumination and enlightenment, these gadgets are only "lights and wires in a box," and in the wrong hands they have proved to be pernicious.

The *San Quentin News* restored my faith in the craft of journalism by allowing me to work with writers who knowingly exposed themselves to losing privileges, being sent to the Hole, or risking ostracism by other inmates in order to tell their personal prison truth in a difficult, conflicted environment.

As a lifelong journalist, I had never noticed that my newsroom colleagues were transformed as human beings as a result of the job. Indeed, the many examples of alcohol abuse and divorce would indicate the opposite. Not so with the prisoners who became newsmen. For them journalism turned out to be something different, a path to personal redemption. Many prison newsmen found that the act of writing and reporting on the world around them opened the way to constructing a narrative about their own lives and making sense of the personal flaws that brought them to prison. There is social science research backing up my observation. In 2001 criminologist Shadd Maruna wrote that the construction of a new life story was the pathway for an offender to turn away from a life of crime. Maruna's observation illuminates one of the discoveries I made when researching this book: that journalism has proved to be a rehabilitation tool.[3] It is not just journalism. Writing in general has been widely accepted as a useful tool in rehabilitation. Just how this works will be explored in a later chapter. For now, I will just point out that the prison journalism model proved to be effective, so much so that, following the San Quentin success, half a dozen other California prisons explored ways to start their own inmate-run publications. But they discovered it was not so easy because San Quentin is unique, and the singularity is what the book is about.

RECALLED TO LIFE

The stars happened to align in 2008 at Point San Quentin overlooking San Francisco Bay. A group of inmates with no journalism training were given the opportunity to revive a newspaper that had been defunct since the 1980s. The offer came from a self-described maverick of a warden who was sure that his superiors would roll their eyes; later, despite budget cuts, an exceptional public information officer, who won the trust of the newspaper staff, kept the project afloat. They were aided and abetted by a handful of retired Marin County journalists who couldn't stay away from the allure of a newsroom. The secret of the success of the *San Quentin News* was that, beginning in 2008, a succession of wardens, the public information officer, and the newspaper staff and its supporters put together a pragmatic governance model based on mutual respect and trust. "This isn't your grandfather's prison," as one inmate remarked.[4]

And then, beginning in 2012, there was me. This calls for full disclosure. Early on in my career, I was taught to visualize professional journalism as a theater where I occupied a front-row seat. The action was to take place on the stage in front of me, and a transparent curtain would separate me from the actors on the stage. I had to sit front-row center: if I sat too far to the right or the left, my perspective might be biased. And I was not to go on stage and become a participant in the drama. But as you will see in the pages that follow, the story of San Quentin can be told fully only with reference to events beginning more than forty years ago, and I happened to be present for crucial parts of that evolving story. The drama plays out against the backdrop of racial conflict and a political backlash, not just in prison but in American society in general. I was a pioneering black man in the newsroom of the *Los Angeles Times,* the most influential newspaper in the state, and I seized on the prison unrest story from its beginnings. At that time the gap between prison truth and the truth that made its way to the printed page was huge, and I intend to explore the reasons why. On some occasions in these pages, I mount the stage and become a participant as I tell the saga of the *San Quentin News.* Prison, public opinion, and the press are engaged in a continuing dance, and I have waltzed with all three. That's why parts of this book unavoidably read like a memoir.

PERSONAL JOURNALISM

When I visited San Quentin in 2012, I came to teach fifteen weeks of an introductory journalism class to eighteen inmates and four auditors. My class was taught under the auspices of the Prison University Project, a nonprofit that offers college-level classes to San Quentin inmates free of charge. At that time, it was clear that American journalism was in deep trouble. Newsrooms were shrinking. Experienced journalists were taking buyouts, and to make rent many of them wound up in PR or tech jobs. The audience was turning to aggregators like Facebook and Google for their news. "Professionalism" was vanishing as journalism school graduates were absorbed into the "gig economy" instead of careers and the industry was "pivoting to video." I asked myself if there was any room left for old-fashioned journalism, beyond the content farming that had overwhelmed the media. My question was answered by the prison journalists with whom I worked. They replenished my enthusiasm. It was back to basics for all of us.

This book is meant to illuminate and supplement the many scholarly studies of incarceration. Because of my journalism training, I use a broad brush to paint a picture of many social and political trends converging over time. Personal journalism relies heavily on impressions, experiences, and judgments (much to the chagrin of many social scientists as well as "big data" journalists who like to rely on statistics). Even though I will rarely rely on numbers, I don't intend to make sweeping, unsubstantiated declarations. This study relies mostly on observation in true fly-on-the wall fashion. Rarely have I engaged in formal interviews with subjects. I never distributed any questionnaires. Much of the material came from overheard, informal conversations over a seven-year period. The book also relies on writings by the prisoners themselves in the prison newspaper, their personal journals, or their correspondence, as well as essays by my students from the University of California, Berkeley, who are a large part of this story. I also reference email correspondence with civilian advisers and others.

THE ROCK AND THE HARD PLACE

Another purely journalistic issue emerges in recounting the story of the *San Quentin News*. Ever since it resumed publication in 2008, its editors stated that the newspaper's mission was to inspire prisoners and give them hope, pointing the way for them to become "*desisters*" instead of recidivists.[5] In other words, its mission would be redemption. It would not be a traditional journalistic watchdog. "*San Quentin News* reports on rehabilitative efforts to increase public safety and achieve social justice." That's the newspaper's stated motto. It's even printed on the business cards.

A recent editor in chief, Richard (Bonaru) Richardson, summed up the editorial philosophy this way: "Many people believe the administration censors the content that goes in our newspaper, but that is not true. The *San Quentin News* staff makes the final decision on what goes on our website and the content that goes into the newspaper, and without our advisers, *San Quentin News* could not produce a quality newspaper every month. However, part of our goal is to build a better relationship with the California Department of Corrections and Rehabilitation because we both have a common goal: we all want to make it home safe and in one piece."[6]

Some journalism purists will argue that what the prisoners are writing is not really journalism at all but boosterism. That criticism deserves a thorough response. Every edition of the paper is submitted to officials of the CDCR for review before publication. Nevertheless, these officials would engage in censorship only at their peril legally. The courts in California have consistently held that inmate-written publications have some protections under the First Amendment so long as their content does not interfere with the lawful administration of the institution. Nevertheless, *San Quentin News* writers work under a regime of de facto self-censorship. Every story represents a judgment by the editors of the costs and benefits of the story. Stories that might reflect negatively on the San Quentin management or staff might have devastating consequences for the paper's relationship with the warden. That is a fact. The prisoners on the newspaper staff are reminded often enough. While the warden may not in the strictest sense censor the newspaper, he or she could shut it down, as has been done in the past. Conflicts have occurred. Nevertheless, in the last ten years, the leading editors, while pressing for a freer hand, have steered clear of investigative exposé pieces. Their pragmatism has been rewarded by gaining the support of the warden and the CDCR officials in Sacramento.

Former editor in chief Richardson wrote about the delicate balancing act of staying authentic in the eyes of the inmates while not antagonizing the warden. It could mean occasionally disappointing both sides. "Some inmates would call the *San Quentin News* a snitch paper, and some still do," he noted, but he also described being "told to 'piss off' when I tried to hand a newspaper to a correctional officer."[7]

All of this still begs the question of whether journalism can achieve meaningful reform without exposés that reveal shocking facts. Richard Hofstadter, the historian, once commented that "to an extraordinary degree the work of the Progressive movement rested upon its journalism. The fundamental cultural achievement of American Progressivism was the business of exposure, and journalism was the chief occupational source of its creative writers."[8] Exposure has been and still is nearly an article of faith among journalists. Certainly, since the Watergate revelations of the 1970s, exposé investigations have become the sine qua non of modern journalism. The *San Quentin News* took a different path, one that emphasized healing, reconciliation, and personal responsibility. I want to pose the question: Is the audience better off or worse off for that decision? What is the nature of prison truth?

2 Prison Voices Heard

When I showed up at the prison in June 2012, I watched the small, struggling *San Quentin News* operation slowly gain more support and recognition as the years went by. Nevertheless, I could not help but notice that the prison newspaper was slowly, almost imperceptibly, being swept along by a much larger and broader movement with profound implications beyond San Quentin and California. I sensed that something grander than the *San Quentin News* was affecting the way the public in general was thinking about the incarceration issue. When the presses began to roll out issues of the *San Quentin News,* its reappearance coincided with a sea change taking hold throughout the whole country in the way we see crime and punishment. Without this wind beneath its wings, the *San Quentin News* would not have succeeded in the way it did. The changing narrative about incarceration will also be explored in the pages that follow.

Skeptics would naturally ask how a feeble monthly publication of twenty-five thousand copies edited by inmates earning a dollar a day could affect the hearts and minds of a whole state and indeed a world at large. Answering that question is the second mission of this book. I want to demonstrate that, as virtually the only prison newspaper in the country, the *San Quentin News* was strategically in the right place at the right time. When the outside media wanted to seek a different narrative about what happened behind prison walls, the *San Quentin News* was there. It had become a reliable source and a trusted brand at a time when the news media, politicians, and vocal activist groups, relying on social media, had begun to push back against decades of mass incarceration. "We recognize that we are inmates, felons, convicted criminals and are being punished and isolated from society under the law," *San Quentin News* associate editor Juan Haines told the *Columbia Journalism Review* in January 2018. "It's different than mainstream media. But why not tell our positive stories in a place so dank?"[1] When those stories were told, they gained traction.

As mentioned, the *San Quentin News* resurgence took place against the backdrop of the shrinkage of newsrooms across California. The changes in the business model for advertising meant less money for specialized beat reporting and fewer reporters to watch prison affairs. Having reliable and resourceful prison journalists on the inside gave free-world publications an avenue to coverage, and it gave San Quentin editors and reporters access to publishing their own stories as well as enabling them to serve as tipsters to staff writers and freelancers on the outside. It had credibility. It established its own chapter of the Society of Professional Journalists. Prison writers at San Quentin found ready access to mainstream journalism. The access made the paper unique and gave some San Quentin journalists outsized influence in the larger world beyond prison walls.

The *San Quentin News* cannot say it's the most acclaimed inmate publication in the country. That honor must go to the *Angolite*, the award-winning inmate-written magazine published at the Louisiana State Prison at Angola. It established a reputation for investigative journalism under the leadership of its former editor Wilbert Rideau, who has visited San Quentin, and his example served as an inspiration to the *San Quentin News* staff. However, the *Angolite* magazine's location in rural Louisiana kept it isolated from mainstream journalism. It has not been a vocal player in the larger conversation about prison reform.

THE EMPATHY EXPLOSION

In June of 2013, a year almost to the day after I began as a volunteer at San Quentin, the comedy/drama *Orange Is the New Black* (*OITNB*) made its debut on Netflix. It was to run for seven seasons. Based on Piper Kerman's 2010 memoir about her year spent at the federal correctional institution at Danbury, the series was a critical and popular success. In its first season it won twelve Emmy Awards and became Netflix's most watched series. It also won a Peabody Award. "*Orange Is the New Black* has profoundly impacted popular culture worldwide," said Lionsgate Television Group Chairman Kevin Beggs.[2] *TV Guide* said six million viewers watched each of the first two episodes of *OITNB*.[3] *OITNB* focused on the plight of female prisoners, but it whetted an appetite for prison narratives from all prisoners, male, female, and trans. *OITNB* did not happen in a vacuum:

1. In 2010 Michelle Alexander's book *The New Jim Crow: Mass Incarceration in the Era of Color Blindness* hit the bookstores. It received immediate acclaim and went on to sell more than 750,000 copies. Alexander herself writes that ten years before writing *The New Jim Crow* she was unaware of the pervasive effects of incarceration. "Ten years ago, I would have argued strenuously against the central claim made here—namely, that something akin to a racial caste system currently exists in the United States."[4] Her eyes began to open, she wrote, when she saw a sign stapled on a Bay Area telephone pole proclaiming, "THE DRUG WAR IS THE NEW JIM CROW."

2. In January of 2012, Adam Gopnik, writing in the *New Yorker,* published an influential piece titled "The Caging of America."[5] He observed, "For a great many poor people in America, particularly poor black men, prison is a destination that braids through an ordinary life, much as high school and college do for rich white ones."[6] He followed up with another article on the exploding prison population.[7]

3. In 2014 the Marshall Project was founded by hedge fund entrepreneur Neil Barsky and former *New York Times* editor Bill Keller. Its focus was entirely on criminal justice. As of this writing, the Marshall Project had published seventy-seven first-person articles written by current or former prison inmates throughout the country, including a number from San Quentin.[8]

4. In October 2014 *This American Life,* a public radio program produced in Chicago, launched the *Serial* podcast, which

reinvestigated a 1999 murder case in Baltimore. Season 1 set podcast records. The series examining Adnan Syed's murder conviction eventually recorded more than three hundred million downloads, exposing the audience for the first time to details of the workings of the criminal justice system. The *Serial* podcast, produced by Julie Snyder, Ira Glass, and Sarah Koenig, began a third season in 2018 and spawned a blizzard of true crime programs.

5. On June 14, 2017, the first *Ear Hustle* podcast from San Quentin hit the internet. Having completed its third season, the podcast at the time of this writing has been downloaded more than fifteen million times, making it one of the most popular audio items on the internet. The brainchild of Sacramento State University professor Nigel Poor, it was cohosted with prisoner Earlonne Woods, and Antwan Williams, also an inmate, provided the sound design. The podcast was a popular and critical sensation. It won both a Webby and a Peabody Award.

PUBLIC OPINION SHIFTS

For thirty years the US public watched the TV show *Cops* on the Fox Network. It is one of the longest-running television programs in US history. Its companion in pulse-pounding reality programming, *America's Most Wanted*, helped set the stage for instilling deep-seated fears in the public about the residents of the other side of town. People in low-income neighborhoods were shown at their most distressed, while law enforcement was lionized. The message was clearly stated: underprivileged people are dysfunctional and dangerous.

The reality show *Lockup* picked up where *America's Most Wanted* left off. Since 2005, *Lockup* showed us what happened once the offenders were sentenced. Having filmed in more than thirty prisons, the program producer, Susan Carney, told MSNBC, "I have certainly become more aware of the inequities in our justice system since doing this program. I don't think it would surprise anyone to learn that socioeconomics and skin color can play big roles in who gets locked up and for how long."[9] But what was displayed on the TV screen was an unrelentingly threatening, dangerous, and hopeless environment in which black and brown people were the pitiful, the hapless, the "other."

By 2013 the reality shows had given way to something else. The public suddenly saw sympathetic stories about the plight of those same black and brown felons around the country. The creator of *OITNB* said she used a "Trojan Horse" approach to get America to hear the voices of the incarcerated. It could easily have been called a "bait and switch" approach. In an interview Jenji Kohan, the writer who adapted *OITNB* for Netflix, said,

> In a lot of ways Piper was my Trojan Horse. You're not going to go into a network and sell a show on really fascinating tales of black women, and Latina women, and old women and criminals. But if you take this white girl, this sort of fish out of water, and you follow her in, you can then expand your world and tell all of those other stories. But it's a hard sell to just go in and try to sell those stories initially. The girl next door, the cool blonde, is a very easy access point, and it's relatable for a lot of audiences and a lot of networks looking for a certain demographic. It's useful.[10]

Those story lines in the world of pop culture created an audience for nonfiction stories from entities like the *San Quentin News*. The newspaper helped serve the public's curiosity. Just how big of a role did the *San Quentin News* play? Although small, the prison newspaper was influential. Any reasonable person would have to admit that the landscape now in California public opinion no longer reflects the *Lockup* mentality. The punitive "throw away the key" stance does not play as well as it used to at the polls. The shift in sentiment has resulted in major changes in laws and policies. The California Legislature has backpedaled on many of the "tough on crime" measures that grew out of the 1980s and 1990s.[11] The *Sacramento Bee* praised Governor Brown for changing directions: "Gov. Jerry Brown deserves much of the credit for reform by admitting that the tough-on-crime laws he supported in his first go-round as governor from 1975 to 1983 went too far. To fix those mistakes, he has been willing to take on law enforcement and victims' groups."[12]

To understand the scope of change in the California prison system, one has to go back in time before Jerry Brown's first iteration as governor of California (1975–83). In the following chapter, I will explore the upheavals that first brought the California Department of Corrections to worldwide attention.

3 Soledad Brothers

Soledad Prison came to national attention on January 13, 1970, when Officer Opie G. Miller, a white California Department of Corrections (CDC) guard, opened fire on inmates during a racial brawl on the prison yard. Three black prisoners died of gunshot wounds. That event eventually brought the racialization of the prisons to public notice. Until that time, it's fair to say that most people in California were blissfully unaware that the inmate population of the state's prison system had changed from predominately white to a Third World majority. And it was the trouble at Soledad that brought me to San Quentin for the first time.

Those venerable movie melodramas about San Quentin beginning in 1937 almost always featured an all-white prison yard. *Duffy of San Quentin* (1954) did feature one black inmate. In 1950 blacks made up about 20 percent of the California inmate population (yet only 4.4 percent of the state population). By 1970 blacks made up around 30 percent of California's imprisoned population, so that African Americans and Latinos outnumbered whites in state penal institutions.[1] Nevertheless, the vintage *Dragnet* TV series (1951–58) never featured a black suspect in fifty-six episodes. One memorable episode did feature a Spanish-speaking Latino child. He had borrowed a statue of the baby Jesus from a Nativity scene at a Catholic church. It was a memorable Christmas program. Otherwise, *Dragnet* was white and Anglo. Until the 1960s the face of crime in the US was white. But that changed in a hurry.

A spike in the US crime rate beginning in the 1960s brought about a dramatic change in the American perception of who was committing crime and how the news media were reporting it. Cognitive science author Steven Pinker described the crime wave as a "decivilizing" spasm in our recent history. "Many criminologists have concluded that the 1960s crime surge cannot be explained by the usual socioeconomic variables but was caused in large part by a change in cultural norms," he wrote.[2] He goes on to describe a general loss of faith in the country's stabilizing institutions and the rise of the drug culture. "The decivilizing effects hit African American communities particularly hard. They started out with the historical disadvantages of second-class citizenship, which left many young people teetering between respectable and underclass lifestyles just when the new anti-establishment forces were pushing in the wrong direction," wrote Pinker.[3]

At the same time the "eyewitness news" format began to take over local television news. Portable equipment allowed cameras to venture easily into the field, and cheap crime and violence, most often in underprivileged neighborhoods, filled the evening local news.

Young blacks seeking the high life "by any means necessary" began filling up the prisons and jails. And they often brought with them a strong indoctrination in militancy. San Quentin's administration clashed with an influx of Black Muslim convicts, including Eldridge Cleaver, who figures prominently later on in these pages.[4] In January 1967 San Quentin had to quell a race riot on the yard. Officers fired live rounds to break up the fighting. A dozen inmates were reported injured. "In 1967–68 San Quentin would be a prison besieged from within and without," wrote Eric Cummins.[5] The face of crime in California had suddenly gone black.

SOLEDAD BROTHERS

Compared to San Quentin, Soledad was a wallflower. Soledad had no commanding vistas of the San Francisco Bay. It had never been a backdrop to a Hollywood movie. You could pass right by Soledad and not even know it was there. Located off Highway 101, near Salinas, Soledad in Spanish means "loneliness," and the prison is aptly named. Now called Salinas Valley State Prison, its three-story white concrete structures are barely visible from the highway, which winds through Castroville (the "Artichoke Capital of the World") and vast stretches of lettuce fields.

In retaliation for the death of the black inmates, correctional officer John Vincent Mills was murdered inside the prison, and his killers threw his body off a tier. Later another white Soledad correctional officer was found stabbed to death.

The Monterey County Grand Jury indicted three black inmates, Fleeta Drumgo, John Clutchette, and George Jackson, for the murder of Officer Mills. The "Soledad Brothers," as they were called, became a cause célèbre around the world. Supporters claimed that any retaliation against the Soledad guards was justified.

WITH MY OWN EYES

I visited Soledad Prison in the summer of 1970, several months after the murder of the prison guards. It was one stop on a grand tour I took researching an article on racial tensions throughout California prisons. My employer, the *Los Angeles Times*, had been running wire stories on the Soledad deaths. I convinced metropolitan editor William F. Thomas that it was a topic worth looking into in more depth. Thomas agreed. (More later on how I had earned Thomas's confidence.) I spent several weeks visiting prisons up and down the state, talking to officials and inmates about the role racial differences played in the day-to-day workings of the Department of Corrections.

Roy K. Procunier, then-director of the Department of Corrections, was a believer in opening up institutions to outside scrutiny by the news media. His office had called ahead, and each prison was expecting me, allowing me the run of the place and making available to me any inmates or staff I chose to talk to.

I didn't know then that the Soledad deaths would have a tremendous impact later on San Quentin.

The venue for George Jackson's murder trial in the Mills case had been changed from Monterey County to Marin County, and Jackson was housed in solitary confinement in San Quentin's Adjustment Center while he was awaiting trial.

THE SAN RAFAEL COURTHOUSE SHOOTING

While George Jackson awaited his day in court, his younger brother Jonathan Jackson, seventeen, entered a courtroom at the Marin County Civic Center on August 7, 1970. A criminal trial (unrelated to his brother's) was under way. A group of inmates from San Quentin Prison were in the courtroom to appear as witnesses.

Jonathan Jackson had a crudely simple plan. He would free the San Quentin inmates, take hostages, and attempt to negotiate the release of his brother. Armed with three guns registered in the name of author and former UCLA professor Angela Y. Davis, Jonathan Jackson attempted to flee the courtroom after seizing the judge, an assistant district attorney, and some jurors. Four people died in a shootout, including Jonathan and Superior Court Judge Harold Haley.

When the escape attempt took place, a draft of my story about racial tensions in prison was in my editor's hands. I was working nights in the *Los Angeles Times* city room the very Friday of the courthouse shooting. An early edition of the paper came up, and I read the AP story from San Francisco. One of the inmates who died in the courthouse shooting was identified as William Arthur Christmas. His age was listed as fifty-two.

I looked at the riveting pictures by San Raphael *Independent Journal* photographer Roger Bockrath.[6] I recognized Willie Christmas by his unmistakable short, muscular stature, dark complexion, and intense, expressive eyes. I knew him as one of my classmates from McClymonds High School in Oakland. Known as the "School of Champions," McClymonds had graduated a phenomenal number of famous athletes, including NBA great Bill Russell and Major League Baseball stars Frank Robinson, Vada Pinson, and Curt Flood. The same high school had also produced more than its fair share of CDC inmates. A couple of times I spotted familiar faces from the school grounds wearing blue denims on the prison grounds. That experience brought me closer to the prison story than any other newspaper stories I had covered.

Willie Christmas was about my age, twenty-six, and I knew that the age published in the paper had to be wrong. I explained this to the "slot man" on the copy desk, who queried the San Francisco AP Bureau. Later the correction was made.

Seeing a familiar face from high school and DeFremery Park in Oakland was unsettling for me.[7] Not for the first time, I thought to myself, "There but for the grace of God go I."

MY BIG SCOOP

Just two days after the courthouse shooting, the *Los Angeles Times* ran my investigative piece exploring racial tensions in California prisons on page 1. The timing was almost eerie. The story made the newspaper look prescient, and afterward my stock was high around the city room.

The story described in detail how the California correctional system had become racially polarized. I packed as much drama into the piece as the law would allow. The Soledad conflict led the story:

> Racial conflict has struck Soledad prison in recent months with as much heat and fury as the reckless winds that blow through the fertile lettuce bowl of the Salinas Valley. . . .
>
> Correctional officers there work in pairs now, after two white guards patrolling alone were killed. Their deaths came after another white guard shot three black prisoners to death during a racial fight last Jan. 13.
>
> A Times survey of the major state prisons—including Soledad, San Quentin, Vacaville, Chino and Deuel Vocational Institution near Tracy—found that a potential for racial violence boils just beneath a fragile surface. "What is surprising is that, in the long haul, it isn't worse than it is," said Charles W. Crary, head of the education program for inmates at Soledad. "Every one of us has prejudices. And men come to jail with them. But on the inside a lot of little things tend to rub raw nerves."
>
> A corrections counselor at Tracy remarked, "If we get into hassles on the outside, we can always find a place to run to. In the Joint, frustrations will build and there is always a residue of hurt feelings. Men retaliate out of proportion. I knew of a case of a man who was killed in the mess hall by an inmate who thought he was shorted on his sugar serving."[8]

A growing portion of the state's inmate population was black and Latino. The correctional staff and guards were predominately white. At the time, 631 staff and corrections officers were employed at San Quentin. Of that number only 41 were black and 17 were Mexican American. At Deuel Vocational Institute in Tracy inmates could buy suntan oil, but they could not buy special combs for natural hair or Mexican sweet rolls. Discrepancies like these further alienated the black and Latino inmates.

After my story on racial tension was published, I got a call from CDC director Procunier. He complimented me on the piece, saying it accurately reflected the problem. "We just have to do a better job," he said. Procunier was highly regarded and capable, but forces were at work beyond his control.

GEORGE JACKSON DIES

The violence was far from over. About a year later George Jackson was shot to death in an aborted attempt to escape from San Quentin's Adjustment Center in August 1971. He died shortly before his trial was scheduled to start for the murder of the correctional officer in Soledad.

The botched escape was one of the bloodiest events in San Quentin's notorious history.[9] Jackson's death received national attention and threw the CDC into a panic. In the weeks that followed, crowds of protesters pushed up against the San Quentin gates, sometimes chanting, "Three pigs is not enough." Correctional officers said they felt personally threatened, even in their own homes. One reported that his wife gave him an ultimatum: the job or me. He quit.

"A lieutenant with 18 years at 'Q' and regarded as one of the best officers ever to work there attempted to use his walkie-talkie, which had been in continual use, and found the batteries run down," read a 1971 *Los Angeles Times* piece on prison guards. "It was the last straw. Three more years and he would have retired, but he walked out of the gate."[10]

George Jackson's escape attempt and the upheaval that followed sent ripples throughout prisons around the country. While San Quentin was still reeling from Jackson's death, inmates at the Attica Correctional Facility in New York rioted on September 9, 1971. Guards suppressed the riot, in which thirty-three inmates died, along with ten civilians. New York's handling of the Attica uprising provoked an outcry and multiple investigations. To this day it stands as the bloodiest and most controversial prison riot in US history.

The rebellion of the prisoners, begun in California, had gone bicoastal. Alarm about violence in prison struck the media nationwide.

"Jackson's death led to inmate protests at multiple prisons," wrote Gretel Kauffman, a graduate student researcher at the University of Notre Dame. "On August 27 (1971), prisoners at Attica staged a silent protest over his death: nobody ate or spoke at breakfast that day." She said the protests showed the inmates' ability to "unite for a common cause."[11]

San Quentin's warden Louis (Red) Nelson was asked in the days following the Attica uprising if a similar rebellion were a possibility at San Quentin.[12]

"Absolutely. No question about it," the warden told reporters.

He was then asked, "If it did happen here, how would it be handled?"

"I'm sure we would do the same thing they did at Attica," said Nelson. "Regardless of the cost."

A San Quentin correctional officer jumped in: "But we'd do it quicker."

His comments reflected a new toughness in CDC management, a mentality that was to radiate outward into criminal justice circles, the legislature, and the governor's office. Prison administrators felt threatened by black militancy, gang-related threats, and racial violence. Meanwhile, they faced vocal anger and opposition from radical political groups outside the walls.

THE BACKLASH/CRACKDOWN

One San Quentin corrections officer told a reporter in 1971, "You know you got a rotten, dirty, low-paying job. But somebody's got to do it. So when you are challenged by the cons, you accept it—hell, you expect it. But when you are challenged by the people who are paying your salary and are asking you to do a job, for them . . . there's no way for you to win."[13] All that was to change in the decades to come.

California governor Ronald Reagan was a sympathetic listener to these complaints. And when he was succeeded by Jerry Brown, a Democrat, the tough-on-crime and incarceration trend began in earnest.

By fall 1971 the *San Quentin News* was allowed to publish again, but the news columns or editorial page made almost no mention of the events of the previous August when Jackson died. The effects of the crackdown were obliquely remarked upon in the pages of the *San Quentin News,* which noted that CDC director Procunier had decreed that "students are not to receive or have in their possession any of the following publications until further notice: The Berkeley Tribe, The Berkeley Barb, The Anvil, The Black Panther, The Great Speckled Bird and White Power."[14] The article quoted a memorandum from Sacramento saying, "These publications have characteristically incited murder, arson, riot and violent racism." In addition, San Quentin suspended the Inmate Activities Programs, everything from Alcoholics Anonymous to drug abuse groups, as well as Native American and Latino cultural awareness groups.

The newspaper's editor, Philip C. Clark, informed the readers that the Jackson death was off limits. He said he was not allowed to write about the event itself or about the aftermath and the many new security measures taken inside the prison. "Any editor who demands to work outside those guidelines will be replaced," he wrote.[15] He added, "That all is not well in our city is well known to the world and has been broadcast to that world through the media, all in gorgeous technicolor. Truth and distortion have walked hand in hand and I have no great interest in adding my voice to the confusion. This five-to-life is all I can handle, and I'm beginning to have some doubts about that."

A few months later in his "Bastille by the Bay" column, Clark wrote: "I look about me and see hate, fear, desolation, and a terrible wariness. . . . I have heard rumors of death, rumors of strife, rumors of riots, rumors of breaks, a black man called 'nigger,' a brown man called 'greaser,' and a white man called 'honkey.' Labels are the name of the game."[16] Clark was bemoaning the new racialized environment in the California prisons.

4 Kennedy to Cleaver

This is a difficult chapter to write, because it's principally about me. My personal tale eventually weaves itself into the San Quentin story line, as you will see. But I have to explain the steps that personally led me to visit a prison in the first place. Otherwise, the reader would be in the dark as to how the news media of the time would have missed the boat on the racial crisis that developed in the California prison system. The reader might assume that it was a routine newspaper assignment like any other. It wasn't just San Quentin that was racialized. It was the media, too. As I said in the beginning, this book is about prison, public opinion, and the press. I need to recreate the atmosphere as it prevailed an elite newsroom in the late 1960s. As far as I know, nobody has ever tried to piece these events together before.

"Oh, so you're going to Los Angeles," bubbled a young *Courier-Journal* executive's wife at a farewell party when I departed Louisville in 1967. "Tell me what you'll be doing, covering Watts?" Condescending though she was, she was not far off the mark. The 1,750 newspapers in America had virtually all-white newsrooms and executive suites. The numbers from that period paint a bleak picture. Between 1956 and 1966 the number of African

Figure 1. The *Los Angeles Times* staff that covered the 1965 Watts Riot. © 2012 Los Angeles Times. Used with permission.

Americans working on metropolitan daily newspapers rose from thirty-eight to sixty.[1] The de facto segregation in the newspaper industry did not stop most of nation's papers from campaigning through their editorial pages against racial discrimination and in favor of raising the level of the underprivileged. Internally, however, the term *diversity* had not yet been invented, or even the feel-good term *equal-opportunity employer.* Editors instead were still struggling to implement the more elementary concept of "desegregation."[2] "Along with the country as a whole, the press has too long basked in a white world," said the Kerner Commission report, "looking out of it, if at all, with white men's eyes and a white perspective."[3]

The *L.A. Times* fell into the "if at all" category—at least until the Watts Riot. What does the conspicuously homogeneous state of a Los Angeles newspaper staff have to do with California's prison situation? Discussing the state of journalism in detail would illuminate a lot about how the prison situation went from bad to worse without anybody—namely the Department of Corrections, a state agency that is supersensitive to publicity—doing anything.

Relative to today, America in the 1960s was an information desert. People could watch just a handful of television channels. Cable was struggling to get off the ground. There was as yet no NPR or PBS. Thus the power of print media in those days would be hard to exaggerate. And the

Los Angeles Times was the powerhouse in California. In size and prestige, the *L.A. Times* dwarfed its rivals in the Bay Area and San Diego. It was no contest. If you wanted to sell a car in Los Angeles, you had to use the *Los Angeles Times* classifieds. Same story with real estate. The US attorney in San Francisco, Cecil Poole, once confided to me that he would drive into the city of San Francisco from his suburban home on Sundays to get a copy of the *L.A. Times* to stay up with what he needed to know to do his job.

The editorial department I entered at the *L.A. Times* in 1967 was made up of well-meaning white men (almost no women). They knew almost nothing about the everyday lives of African Americans or Latinos. Media critics recognized this situation and raised objections. To their credit, the *L.A. Times* editors recognized the problem and took steps to bring new voices and viewpoints to the staff. The Watts Riots of 1965 jolted them into self-awareness.

When I joined the *Los Angeles Times*, it lagged way behind the *Washington Post* and *New York Times* in minority hires. The *L.A. Times* had won a Pulitzer Prize for its post-Watts coverage, which was carried out with exactly one black reporter. He had been working as a messenger in the classifieds department when the trouble broke out and was drafted into service, despite having zero journalism experience.

This was the heyday of the "instant Negro." With a degree from a classy university you were in management's embrace. The Negro in the newsroom was a source of never-ending curiosity, as I learned after my arrival in Los Angeles in 1967.

But as I also learned, editors often saw the black reporter as naturally suited to stories about the economically downtrodden, or as a foot soldier in the coverage of urban distress. You were considered an envoy to the underclass. If black people rioted or looted, naturally a colleague would approach you and ask, "What possessed them to do that?" as though you would know. Problem was, I'd answer anyway, often attempting some kind of half-baked apology!

AMONG FRIENDS

After a year at the paper, I had settled in and was feeling confident. I invited a few friends and colleagues from work over for dinner at my

Baldwin Hills apartment. Among them was *L.A. Times* writer Kenneth Reich, a legendary character in the newsroom. He was outspoken and passionate. Sometimes he would get so riled up you thought he might have a stroke. He often shouted into his telephone headset at his desk.

Ken and his date were the only Caucasians who showed up to the party. The other guests were all African Americans. In mid-1968, after the death of Martin Luther King Jr. in Memphis and the ensuing riots around the country, any conversations between whites and blacks were likely to be strained. Race was, to put it mildly, a dangerously touchy subject and a continuing national migraine that kept everybody on edge.

The dinner conversation began subdued and friendly. But as we settled into after-dinner drinks, Ken decided to become the provocateur. Wasn't it self-destructive for blacks to burn down their own neighborhoods? he asked. How was looting a political act?

To my horror, I watched as tempers and voices rose. It wasn't long before Ken was in a corner, surrounded by the other guests and engaged in a most uncongenial debate. Fortunately, everybody eventually got exhausted and went home.

I thought that Ken Reich would never speak to me again.

To my amazement, he called the next day thanking me for the invitation, saying that he found the whole group interesting and the discussion fascinating. He couldn't remember when he had been so stimulated. Insight No. 1 into Mr. Reich: he loved to be in the eye of controversy. I was Ken Reich's black friend. Reich's conversation at my home was probably a landmark event in his career up to that point. (He later went on to be the *L.A. Times* bureau chief in Atlanta and probably felt he had special insight into the black condition.)

A CAUSE OF URBAN UNREST

The black areas of town were terra incognita not just to Reich but to the whole city desk staff. The *Los Angeles Times* had covered the explosion of violence in Watts in 1965, but by 1967 things had settled back to "normal." That's another way of saying, "We covered that story. Now let's move on." It was the nature of daily journalism at that time. The big picture?

Somebody else's problem. Reporters in those days lacked the leeway to forecast or to do speculative analysis. Those pieces were scorned as "thumb-suckers" and often died on the desk. Only now, with the benefit of hindsight, do we see how clearly the "school-to-prison" pipeline in California was being constructed.

In Charles Dickens's time, prisons were open to public view. Reformers thought harsh penal conditions would serve as a crime deterrent if ordinary people could see what the jail looked like inside. But in modern penology it's the opposite. Prisons are run in deep secrecy. The walls and accordion wire keep inmates inside, but they also keep prying eyes out.

THE BLACK PANTHER

In 1968, I profiled Eldridge Cleaver, the Black Panther leader who had spent much of his young life in prison in California, for the *Los Angeles Times*. Much of Cleaver's thinking had been shaped by his experiences in prison. His best-selling book *Soul on Ice* is essentially a collection of his prison writings. Prison was an incubator at that time for black militancy. My profile made the case that the California Department of Corrections managed to take an inconsequential petty criminal from Watts and nurture him into the role of a charismatic leader of black power.

The Cleaver profile won praise and endeared me to my editors. Eventually, it opened the door for my several forays into the California prison system. In the ensuing months I visited major prisons in the state—Soledad, Vacaville, Chino, Tracy, San Luis Obispo, and, of course, San Quentin, the oldest and most notorious prison in California. I explored the connection between incarceration and racial tensions. By most measures I would have been considered too young and inexperienced to be allowed to do such a complex and sensitive story. But through complete accident I became a trusted reporter. Reliving that journey is worth exploring in detail because it illuminates the inner workings, especially regarding racial issues, of one of the great news organizations of its day, the *Los Angeles Times*.

5 The Primary Election

It was June 4, 1968. I was twenty-three years old, and I was completing my tenth month as a *Los Angeles Times* reporter. I worked the dreaded "lobster shift," for which I came to work in the gray, concrete, fortress-like *Times* building on First and Spring Streets at 7:00 p.m. and got off at 3:30 in the morning. With rare exceptions there was nothing interesting to do on the overnight shift. I'd write a few three-paragraph police shorts and check the papers for typographical errors when the early editions came up.

But June 4, 1968, was election night, and that promised to be exciting. Practically the whole staff worked late that night. Being young, new to L.A., and unfamiliar with Southern California politics, I had little to do with the main election coverage. I was assigned to write the results of an obscure congressional race in which a former lieutenant governor was waging a political comeback.

The polls closed at 8:00 p.m. in California. The first deadline was around 8:30 p.m. A copyboy (a generic term of art at the time, even though a few were female) would collect the ballot totals from an election central desk and distribute them around the newsroom to the reporters working on particular races. My plan was to write a noncommittal advance story

Figure 2. The author at his *L.A. Times* desk, 1968. Author's collection.

for the early edition and gradually update it with figures for each successive edition.

The great interest that night was the contest for the Democratic presidential nomination between Sen. Robert F. Kennedy and Sen. Eugene J. McCarthy, the peace candidate from Minnesota. The country was in turmoil. Martin Luther King had been assassinated in Memphis. The war in Vietnam had divided the country. President Lyndon B. Johnson had, on the eve of April Fool's Day 1968, announced that he would not run for reelection.

As the drama swirled around me, I was having trouble making sense of my congressional race in southern Los Angeles County. The ex-lieutenant governor, a Democrat, was trailing in the early totals, but the political savants in the office said he was certain to win. I had to write a story saying the guy was winning, despite totals that showed him losing. I was unsure of my footing.

The last home edition deadline was 12:30 a.m. Around midnight I polished off my last "new lead" and settled back with my feet (literally) on my desk. Around 12:15 a.m. the city editor asked me to take some dictation from another reporter, Daryl E. (Bud) Lembke, who was calling in from the Ambassador Hotel, where Kennedy had just given his victory speech.

"I'll just give you a few notes and you can write it the way you want," said Lembke, the *Times*'s San Francisco bureau chief who was covering RFK's California campaign. "Uhh, let me see, uhh, uhh," said Lembke, as he continued to fumble through his notes. I wished he would hurry up. I needed to keep an eye on my congressional race.

Suddenly, he said, "Wait just a minute. Something's going on here." Lembke, who was in a phone booth, dropped the receiver and ran off, but I could hear clearly the public address system in the background.

"Is there a doctor in the house?" Screams, shouts. "Is there a doctor in the house?" Through the phone I heard an uproar and screams from the crowd. Lembke came back on the line. "Kennedy's been shot—"

Instinctively, I shouted, "Kennedy's been shot—"

The city room, which had been filled with the hubbub of typewriters and conversation, fell silent. People froze in place, looking at me.

"—shot in the head."

My eyes locked on Metropolitan Editor William F. Thomas, forty-four, whose desk faced me about eight feet away. Thomas began sending reporters and photographers out. One crew went to the hotel, another to Central Receiving Hospital.

When Lembke came back to the phone, he gave me a few more details, which I typed up on newsprint scratch paper as colleagues gathered around my desk.

I handed the phone to the metro editor, who conferred with Lembke. I was momentarily bewildered. I expected Thomas to tell me to give my notes to one of the veteran reporters who would take over the most important news story in the world. Instead, Thomas told *me* to write the story, though I was just two years out of the Columbia School of Journalism.

Columbia's legendary irascible Professor John Hohenberg's mantra kicked in: "Go with what you've got." It was pitifully little at that point. In frustration, I punched my fist into my palm, and muttered, "Damn!" Bill Thomas was standing behind me looking over my shoulder. "Take it easy. You have all we need."

"Sen. Robert F. Kennedy was shot at 12:20 a.m. Wednesday at the Ambassador Hotel shortly after he had given his victory speech," I began, adding four or five short paragraphs of detail that Lembke had supplied.

Each time I banged out another page on my manual typewriter, Frank P. Haven, forty-six, the tall, sturdy managing editor with a distinctive bass voice (office wags nicknamed him "Lurch"), took the copy from my hand and walked it to the back shop in the bowels of the building so it could be set in type. Haven literally stopped the presses.[1]

The story was published for the final editions of the *Times*. It carried scant details, but it was as much as we knew.

A MANKIEWICZ MISTAKE

The idea of time "standing still" had never meant much to me until then. I had written the shooting of Robert Kennedy in ten minutes, from the moment he was shot until the final copy deadline. That historic story in the *L.A. Times* carried the lone byline of Daryl E. Lembke. Later Bud Lembke, an easygoing, pipe-smoking Quaker, came into the *Times* office and shook my hand. We both laughed. "I should put in for overtime," Lembke joked.

My story on the congressional race was a complete hash, but fortunately nobody noticed.

The very next night I came in to do my overnight shift as Kennedy lay mortally wounded in Good Samaritan Hospital in Santa Monica. Philip K. Fradkin was the *Times* reporter assigned to the hospital, and I was in the office doing the deathwatch.

Shortly after 1:00 a.m. Thursday morning, just half an hour before the final hundred thousand copies of the newspaper went to press, Frank Mankiewicz, Kennedy's press secretary, faced the reporters. Kennedy was dead.

Again, I was on the phone with the reporter on the scene. Fradkin dictated his notes. In another adrenalin rush, I wrote as though the weight of the world were on my shoulders. Once I sent the last page of the story off to the copy desk, I sat back to catch my breath.

Shortly afterward, a wizened, stooped figure wearing a printer's apron came into the newsroom, holding a mangled sheet of paper in his hand. It was a cut-up fragment of the copy I had written. "I sure hate to bother you, but are you sure this is right?" he asked, showing me the copy. I had erroneously identified Frank Mankiewicz, RFK's press secretary, as his uncle, film producer *Joseph* Mankiewicz (director of *All about Eve*)! If that blunder had gone into the paper, my journalism career would have been tarnished forever. I would never have lived it down. Instead, thanks to a printer who actually read the copy, I was saved a crushing embarrassment. (I never learned the name of that printer. I owed him a bottle of bourbon.)

The next day when I came to work, I got a hero's welcome.

GOLDEN CHILD

The Robert Kennedy assassination rocked the world. It also rocked my career. My work those two nights became the sensation of the office. But it still did not get me off the night shift!

Nevertheless, my stature and reputation around the office climbed. Editors at the time had generally restrained expectations of minority hires. The Bobby Kennedy assassination had allowed me to exceed expectations. If I had not hit home runs on those June nights, I might never have gained the confidence of my boss, Bill Thomas, who eventually gave me freer rein to explore areas of my interest. And it's quite likely I never would have worked the story of the trouble in California's prisons.

I was bursting with ambition and eager to make a name for myself. But as I remained the most junior person on the staff, page 1 stories were rarely handed to me. I bided my time.

THE NEXT BIG STEP

When I finally got off nights, I was able to move away from the routine story assignments. An elephant occupied the newsroom. It was race. African Americans live race every day. For whites it's an issue that comes up rarely. But black journalists often see racial undertones everywhere. This puts a black person in the newsroom in an awkward position. One would have to be cautious about getting labeled a firebrand or an "angry young man." Even though I went out of my way to be soft-spoken and discreet, I was introduced at lunch shortly after my arrival as "Bill Drummond, our angry young man." I didn't complain. It was a step up from what George Gill, the city editor in Louisville, called me: "Stokely."

When I arrived in August of 1967, the only other black person on the editorial staff was Ray Rogers, a quiet, engaging man from Washington, D.C., who had preceded me by several months.

THE DEMOCRATIC REPUBLIC OF BERKELEY

The late 1960s was a time of tremendous racial turmoil throughout the country. And in many ways California led the way. In 1964–65 as a senior at the University of California, Berkeley, I had witnessed firsthand the Free Speech Movement, which swept me into a path of radical politics that grabbed me and would not let go. Because I was only a few years out of school, my *L.A. Times* bosses would eventually send me up to the Bay Area to cover a range of left-wing issues, student protests, black power movements, and counterculture trends. I was the only reporter who maintained a subscription to the notorious *Berkeley Barb,* the underground newspaper that served as the publicist for radical politics. It thrived on a formula of left-wing politics and ads for sexual services. Fortunately for me, I had bonded with Bud Lembke, the *Times* bureau chief in San Francisco, during the Kennedy assassination story, and he never objected to my poaching on his territory.

As noted earlier, during the 1965 rioting in Watts the *Times* enlisted a black man working as a classified advertising messenger to help out on the coverage. I never met Robert Richardson, who by all accounts did a splendid job as a leg man.[2] He would go into the curfew area and phone in his observations back to the office. Many of Richardson's byline pieces were actually written by staff writer Jack McCurdy, the ginger-haired rewrite man. After the riots, management promoted Richardson to the reporting staff, but he left the paper shortly afterward. He died in 2000 of complications due to asthma. Kenneth Reich wrote his obituary.

It was a great time to be a reporter on a big, influential newspaper that was seeking greatness. For decades the *L.A. Times* under the conservative Chandler family had been synonymous with Republican politics and parochial news coverage. I arrived on the scene when Otis Chandler, then just thirty-nine years old, assumed the publisher's role, and he began hiring a first-rate editorial staff. The paper assembled a formidable Washington bureau and opened more than a dozen bureaus overseas. Nevertheless, big gaps existed in the quality of the coverage of Los Angeles as well as California in general.

HOMOGENEOUS NEWSROOM

Just thumbing through the greasy pages of the *Berkeley Barb,* I found numerous potential feature stories that nobody else on the paper wanted to touch. My *L.A. Times* colleagues were middle-aged, congenial white men with families living in the Southern California suburbs. (One female reporter, Dorothy Townsend Vanderveld, a soft-spoken devout Catholic, worked on the city desk as a reporter. She was usually stuck with talking to heartbroken families. This assignment was what came to be disparaged as the "sob sister" beat.) My colleagues were, for the most part, geographically and emotionally isolated from the turmoil of the inner cities and the angst of the Woodstock Generation. The city room also had an intolerant side to it, in no small part due to the legendary night city editor, Glen A. Binford, who reigned before political correctness had been invented.

THE NIGHT TRAIN

During the day shift, the *Times* city room was stodgy, businesslike, and subdued. People rarely raised their voices. Around six o'clock the top editors would leave to begin the drive home, and the night-side reporters and editors would roll in to finish the work for the next day's edition or to "put the newspaper to bed."

The night side was made up of older men on the way out of the business or young ones, like me, paying their dues. On this shift, Binford was the ringmaster for what was often an entertaining but profane circus. He raised cynicism to theater. He abhorred liberals, whom he called "limp-wrists," but his special wrath was directed at ethnicities of any stripe. The Irish, he quipped, would still be on all fours if they had not invented the wheelbarrow. Jews? He routinely called Beverley Hills the "Synagogue Hills." He relished clever insults. Scandinavians? "Square-heads." Catholics, "Mackerel Snappers." Any woman over fifty was "an old blister."

Not surprisingly, Binford viewed blacks and browns with particular annoyance. He referred to the do-rag (the scarf many black men wore as a head covering) as an "I-don't-want-to-work" hat. In dealings with me, however, he was always cordial, one might even say solicitous, occasionally offering to share his peanut-butter-and-jelly sandwich with me at dinnertime during the night shift. For all of his lapses into bad taste and misanthropy, he was one of the most entertaining people I have ever met. In addition, he was an excellent line editor, unsurpassed in his knowledge of the complicated geography of Southern California, and a resident historian concerning L.A. news events. He did not mind working nights. And so he endured. Many of my colleagues came to me privately and apologized for Binford's occasional bad behavior. The apologies were unnecessary because I never took any of it personally. I enjoyed working with him because he was an excellent newsman. His standards were strict for attribution, clean copy, and steering clear of ideological slant. Give us the facts, he would say. It's the reader's job to distort them.

Other notable members of the night-side crew were the burly Texan Dick (Night Train) Main, whose permanent assignment was the weather story. Southern California is obsessed with weather. The other fixture on the night side was T. O. (Ted) Thackrey Jr., chain-smoking, crew-cut, and a fountainhead of journalism wisdom. His father had been the longtime editor of the *New York Post*. Thackrey made a living as a ghostwriter, creating biographies for B-list Hollywood celebrities. Between Main, Thackrey, and Binford, they maintained a lively journalism seminar.

Meanwhile, my boss, metro editor Bill Thomas, was a trim, dapper man with formidable gold bridgework in his mouth. ("His smile is like a sunset," an office wag remarked.) He had hired me sight unseen from the *Louisville-Courier Journal* despite my scant experience and had given me my shot at the big show.

A NEWSPAPER ON THE MAKE

The *L.A. Times* in those days was not clogged with middle management, as unfortunately later came to be the case. I pitched my stories directly to Thomas. Most often, he said yes. Thomas, too, lived in the farthest reaches of the San Fernando Valley. Nevertheless, he had an open mind. I felt I would get a fair hearing from him.

After earning my stripes during Kennedy's assassination, I decided to go after a very big story happening in the Bay Area, which would acquaint me with the issue of prisons in California.

STALKING THE PANTHER

In 1968 the University of California at Berkeley was caught up in a political struggle between Gov. Ronald Reagan and the liberal faculty and radical students on campus. This crystallized when ex-convict Eldridge Cleaver, the fiery Black Panther Party minister of information, was invited to be a regular guest lecturer for ten meetings of an undergraduate class.

My mission was to profile Eldridge Cleaver. Thomas gave me the okay. I spent several days in late September and early October in the Bay Area gathering interviews from the principals.

I had shadowed Cleaver for several days. I watched him harangue Sproul Plaza crowds on the Berkeley campus, conveying visions of how dead bodies would litter the streets in a wave of racial warfare. In front of hundreds of young, radical admirers and thousands of more curious onlookers, Cleaver elicited giggles when he called Reagan a "punk, a sissy, and a coward" and the longtime Democratic Assembly speaker Jess M. Unruh "Big Mama Unruh." He led thousands of people in chants of "Fuck Ronald Reagan. Fuck Ronald Reagan." Unlike twenty-first century millennials, people in 1968 rarely used the f-word in public, let alone over a PA system. The behind-the-barn giggles I heard around me were revealing. The listeners were engaging in a rebellion—against the war in Vietnam, the university, the police, their parents. They stayed until the end of the rally just to hear the next outrageous utterance from the tall black man in the leather jacket at the microphone.

But to do a proper profile, I needed an interview alone with the man himself. The Black Panther Party headquarters was located in a ramshackle frame house south of the Berkeley campus. I paid it an unannounced visit one day and found Cleaver, relaxing in a chair against a wall, holding forth before six fellow Panthers and the same number of white radicals. Among them was Jerry Rubin, founder of the Vietnam Day Committee and the Yippies, and, later, one of the Chicago Seven defendants prosecuted after the rioting at the 1968 Democratic Convention in Chicago.

I was alone in the room with some pretty tough customers, but my youth was unrestrained by discretion. I asked Cleaver if he intended to instruct the students in his UC Berkeley class on the usefulness of violence.

"We are not going to be programming people to shoot Max Rafferty [then-state superintendent of public instruction and an outspoken Republican conservative]. But we are not going to impede anybody from doing it either. It will be their own inspiration," he said, eyeing me reproachfully. Then, visibly annoyed, he accused me of asking questions planted by "the racist pigs who control the mass media." His audience, black and white, nodded with approval and moved restlessly in their chairs. He demanded to be sent a copy of his comments and warned that if he were not pleased, he might come looking for me and kick my ass.

The moment ended as quickly as it had begun. Cleaver resumed his monologue with the Panthers and Yippies. He ignored me and then departed before I could call him aside. I left humiliated and deflated.

Some days passed before I approached Cleaver again. This time I called *Ramparts* magazine, where he worked, and first talked to his assistant, Kathy Stone. Finally, getting through to him, I asked for an interview, and after some verbal jousting on the phone he consented. I met him Monday, October 2, in his office on a crisp fall day at *Ramparts,* which was then located at 495 Beach Street in San Francisco, near Fort Mason. More than a little anxious, I entered the building at 10:30.

While I waited, I scribbled some notes with questions I intended to ask. His record included sexual assault. What was that all about? What did he think of James Baldwin? Had he ever read anything by Richard Wright? Finally I was ushered in, and I found Cleaver alone in his office with legal-sized yellow pads bearing scribbled notes spread out before him. Without an audience he had no need to be imperious or threatening. In fact, he was cordial, occasionally overly jocular, as though he regretted giving me such a hard time when we had last met at the Panthers HQ.

It dawned on me then that the Eldridge Cleaver in the macho leather jacket whipping up crowds with speeches that went beyond logic, propriety, or proportion might be a persona adopted for effect. He gave me answers without hesitation. They seemed rehearsed rather than original.

What was his program for his people?

Step one was to achieve a position of power, he said. "Once we have a solid organizational base, we can force concessions, we can take jobs, we can liberate the means of production."

As for himself, his goal was to "write a couple of novels," but he said his life was "given essentially to the struggle."

His doctrinaire answers were boring. I had learned my lesson from the first encounter and decided not to ask questions that would set him off. It did not matter. I had already spent many hours researching his background. I had talked to numerous people who had known him, including his Department of Corrections parole officer. I had gone over his prison record. I was awash in his past. For example, his full name was Leroy

Eldridge Cleaver. Why had he changed it? I could only surmise that "Leroy" just didn't cut it. The name had become almost a stereotype for a certain kind of commonplace Negro. No ghetto insurgency has ever been led by somebody named Leroy. But "Eldridge" was unique and memorable.

As preparation for the interview, I had brought a copy of Cleaver's book *Soul on Ice.*[3] I asked him to autograph it for me. Even militants succumb to flattery. "For William Drummond, A very persistent reporter who strikes me as a nice fellow, even if he does work for the L.A. Times. Eldridge Oct. 2, 1968."

When I came back to Los Angeles after the Cleaver interview, I returned to my general assignment duties, working on the profile in my spare time. I spent at least a month at a manual typewriter writing the profile. My tome was written on carbon paper "books." Each so-called book had four imbedded carbon sheets. The completed story had a considerable bulk, roughly the thickness of the Costa Mesa telephone directory.

The word around the office in Los Angeles about Eldridge Cleaver was that he was probably a psychopath and that the Black Panther Party was little more than a criminal gang. My colleagues gave me a hero's welcome for scoring an interview with Cleaver and living to tell the story. They seemed to think that I might get kidnapped and held for ransom. Their fear of the man and the movement was another example of the gulf between the races.

While writing the story, I was reminded constantly of the conservative center of gravity in the newsroom. Glen Binford's desk was immediately in front of mine, and whenever he looked up over his thick reading glasses, cigarette dangling from his lips, he was glancing in my direction.

STICKS AND STONES

Binford rarely worked quietly. He kept up a running commentary on whatever piece of copy he was editing. One would hear the occasional har-rumph, or an expletive ("shee-HUT!"), as he edited. On occasion I would hear him grumble, "Spear Chucker," "Jungle Bunny," or "Beaner."

When I finished the Cleaver story it went directly to metropolitan edi-tor Bill Thomas for approval. It took a week or so before Thomas called me into his private office. He had the pile of now dog-eared carbon books on his desk. I was braced to hear bad news.

"Cleaver sounds like an interesting guy," he said. "If that's the case, we have to report it." Momentarily stunned, I was at a loss for words. Thomas's instruction was simple. Don't soft-pedal Cleaver's criminal past or his more incendiary statements. Put them into some kind of context. Tell the reader that what he represents is a big deal.

I did one more rewrite. The story ran the day after Thanksgiving on page 1, with a picture of Cleaver that I had taken of him while he was autographing my copy of *Soul on Ice*.

> An 18-year-old from Watts stared across a table at his interrogators in February 1954.
>
> Young Eldridge Cleaver had been arrested by Los Angeles police in a vacant building with three pounds of marijuana in his possession and was facing his first felony charge. He protested his innocence. "'Who would believe me?" he asked a probation officer interviewing him. "You don't even believe me yourself!" Cleaver said that if he had to do any time, he did not want to go back to the California Youth Authority (his juvenile record began at age 12). He preferred the state prison because that was where the "men" go.
>
> A strapping youth, 6 feet tall and 160 pounds, Cleaver said he wanted to learn to box at the state prison.
>
> There was no indication at this point that the 18-year-old would become the personification of black militancy in the United States. Nor was there any indication that his presence would be desired in a classroom at UC Berkeley.

ONE SMALL STEP

The story, published November 29, 1968, proved to be a turning point for me as well as my newspaper.[4] It seemed to usher in a fresh attitude toward black militant movements in the newsroom in Los Angeles. Like them or not, they had to be taken seriously.

Some members of the UC Berkeley faculty told me later that they thought the Cleaver profile went a long way toward dampening the political fury about having an ex-convict in a UC classroom. The *Times* readers were not so sure, judging from some of the comments I received.

A woman who signed herself as "Subscriber, Lucille Glasscock" wrote me from Oxnard, a farming community north of Los Angeles, the day the story appeared. The letter was handwritten on simple drugstore-bought 6- by 9-inch lined paper, the kind of tablet my aunt used for her correspondence:

> I have been a daily subscriber to this paper since 1941. Today tho this paper you have floored me. Had the Pres of USA died—present or past—you would not have written as many columns, paragraphs or words about him as you did about one Eldridge Cleaver.
>
> Why did you decide to elaborately please him—not only him but all young black militants.
>
> Are you going to cut out the whole clipping and send it to him?[5]

Lucille Glasscock's shock at seeing the story in the *L.A. Times* was matched by the shock of many on the staff. It was not simply the subject matter. It was my illumination of an ex-convict's life and journey to transformation.

Stan Carter, Cleaver's Department of Corrections parole officer, whom I interviewed the day after talking to Eldridge himself, gave me the most unexpected quote for the article. "Cleaver is a very warm person, a very sensitive person," he said. "His talks of militancy are woven into a larger scheme."[6]

I asked Carter if he thought Cleaver was a safe parole risk. "I know that no one will agree with me. And maybe I'm in a minority, but Cleaver has a cause to work for and he is thinking seriously about it. He is not doing it for fun. . . . I don't think he would perform a senseless act of violence. . . . He is highly respected in the black community and his ideas are spreading and gaining worldwide attention."

Carter's advice was ominous. He said Cleaver was a moderate, compared to some of the militants. His advice was prophetic.

6 The Johnny Cash Myth

San Quentin's racial troubles, the furor over George Jackson's death, and the Soledad Brothers made headlines around the country, but the radical, progressive circles were the ones really in a rage. The Soledad Brothers barely made a ripple in Middle America. Prisons were not a big issue.

San Quentin did make a big splash in the American heartland in 1969 when Columbia Records released the album *Johnny Cash at San Quentin,* and it was an immediate hit. It was certified gold on August 12, 1969.[1] Millions of people listened to the recording of that concert and came away with a picture of what they took to be prison truth, but they were mistaken. They heard cheering and exuberance and thought it was celebration. It wasn't. It was more like a war whoop.

"Johnny Cash remembers the forgotten men," wrote a *Rolling Stone* magazine critic in a July 26, 1969, review of the album. "They love him. Singing inside a prison to men whose spirits are being destroyed by our mindless penal system is Johnny Cash's kind of revolution. Music becomes spirituality in the context of the prison. Music is inherently

Johnny Cash Arrested On Suspicion Of Drug Smuggling In Texas, 1965. "The Man in Black," musician Johnny Cash, also moved a little weight in his time. US narcotics officials raided his plane when he returned from touring Mexico, expecting to find heroin, but instead unearthing a massive stash of amphetamines and sedatives the musician hid in his guitar case. Cash had enough drugs to fill a legal prescription for a year or more.

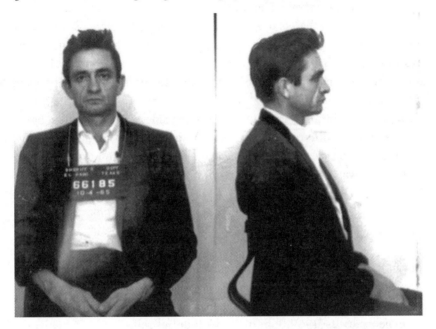

Figure 3. Johnny Cash on his arrest for suspected drug smuggling, Texas, 1965.

destructive of everything penology stands for. Music affirms. Music liberates."

The reviewer was enthusiastic and sympathetic to the prisoners, but the review had nothing to do with what was really happening on the ground in the prison. The writer simply echoed the romanticized view of prisoners popular in counterculture circles at the time. Eldridge Cleaver's presence in the radical movement was a powerful influence on the counterculture, which *Rolling Stone* helped propagate. Eric Cummins wrote that Cleaver was responsible for drawing many from the counterculture into the movement against California prisons: "Owing largely to this single charismatic convict, California became unique in the nation in the degree to which the prison movement came to dominate radical politics."[2] He added that Cleaver's writings "had confused these cultural radicals into thinking convicts, all convicts, were their soulmates and could be their leaders. For some extremists, the cons had become nature spirits, self-actualized, noble, violent, sexual primitives. Even some moderates on the Left idealized prisoners."

Another popular theme about prison life was deeply influential on the public at this time, thanks to several reform-minded movies about prison that trace their origins to the late 1930s.[3] Americans liked prison melodramas with no real bad guys, just good guys looking for redemption. Thanks to Hollywood movies dating back to 1937, up to an including the popular *Shawshank Redemption* (1994), the public saw cellblocks inhabited by a few hardened criminals who talked out of the side of their mouths, "See?" But the plot line often involved a mistakenly convicted hero confronting both sadistic guards and hard-core criminals. The romanticized prison of the matinee was a long way from describing San Quentin in 1969.

THE MAN IN BLACK

A close look at the *Johnny Cash at San Quentin* concert reveals that San Quentin was caught up in a powerful riptide of racial conflict that was gripping the country at that time.

On February 24, 1969, Johnny Cash's tour bus rolled up to San Quentin for what was to be a historic visit. After a successful 1968 live performance at Folsom Prison near Sacramento, Johnny Cash, his wife June Carter, and the rest of the Carter family, the Tennessee Three, and the Statler Brothers continued Cash's prison tour with a stop a hundred miles away toward the coast at San Quentin, the other walled, maximum-security lockup in Northern California. Folsom and San Quentin, the two oldest prisons in the state, were built when walls were synonymous with the harshest level of penology.

San Quentin's postcard vistas of the San Francisco Bay were a sharp contrast to the cultivated crops in the fields around Folsom. If San Quentin were not a prison, it would be the prime residential real estate of upscale Marin County. Instead, the stern, castle-like entrance greeted the Cash party. It was Cash's fourth visit to the prison. A cold rain was whipping when the troupe pulled up before the storied institution, home to

California's highest-security felons at the time, as well as the state's Death Row. Cash, sporting his signature pompadour hairstyle, wore a smart three-quarter-length tan leather overcoat. When he passed through the Count Gate, a correctional officer stamped the back of his right hand with an ink imprint that would identify him when the time came to depart the prison. Armed prison guards looked down from the gun towers and the catwalks as the musicians made their way to the dining hall.

To Europeans especially, San Quentin epitomized America's prison barbarity, so much so that London's Granada Television sent a film crew inside with Cash to shoot a documentary. The British producers saw Cash as a symbol of the American loner from the days of the lawless frontier, a kind of folk hero. They thought viewing him in the context of one of America's toughest real-life prisons might shed light on this country's fascination with violence.[4]

But what the cameras recorded was a glimpse of San Quentin at a unique moment of transition, a volcano just before the magma exploded into the stratosphere. The documentary was truer than the record album.

The Granada cameras captured onstage banter and shouts and approving howls from the inmates in the dining hall. Johnny Cash and June Carter talked to the men warmly and respectfully. The Man in Black, flashing his crooked smile, was at home in the mess hall filled mostly with white men. The Grenada TV footage captured few blacks or Latinos, even though they made up more than half of the inmate population. Cash told his audience, "The show is being recorded and televised for England, and they told me, they said you got to do this song, you got to do that song, you got to stand like this or act like this. They just don't get it, man, you know? I'm here to do what you want me to and what I want to do." He laughed along with the crowd. They shared jokes at the expense of the guards and the prison administrators.

At one point, Cash, sweating profusely, asked for a glass of water. When none appeared, the entire dining hall erupted in lusty boos. Finally, a correctional officer meekly offered a small metal cup to the singer. Cash sipped, eyed it warily, sniffed it, finally put it on the floor, and appeared to light it with a match and then stomp it. He was pretending the water was prison moonshine. It was an inside joke for all those inmates who sometimes brewed rotgut "pruno" in their cells.

THE CAMERA NEVER BLINKS

The Granada documentary was never shown in the US on TV, but the Columbia Records album was listened to by millions. Two generations of Americans would know San Quentin through the recording, which transports the listener inside that dining hall filled with a raucous, amped-up, seemingly good-humored bunch of convicts. But the listener is colorblind. It was nearly an all-white audience. It sounds like a USO audience of servicemen, celibate too long. June Carter, wearing a skirt hemmed well above her knees, actually did a suggestive hip wiggle or two during her duet performance of "Darling Companion," much to the men's delight. About the dress, Carter remarks to the men, "Since we're the only girls in the show, I don't know what kind of show you're expecting out of this. I've got one announcement. This is as sexy as I'm going to get."

Merle Haggard, who eventually became a country music star in his own right, credited seeing Cash perform at San Quentin with inspiring him to turn his life around. Haggard had been sentenced to fifteen years starting at age nineteen after a burglary conviction in Kern County.[5]

The reality of that dining hall performance was much different from what the *Rolling Stone* reviewer thought he was listening to. In the preceding decade the California prison population had gradually changed from predominately white to majority black and Latino. Inmates in prison at that time told me that the warden had done nothing to prevent blacks and Latinos from attending; nevertheless, the turnout for the concert eventually was almost all white. Why? Prison has many unwritten rules. Cash's reputation as a southerner and a country singer meant that the event was presumed to be the turf of the white prisoners. Cash mentioned in the performance that he was disappointed that not all of the prisoners were allowed to attend. Finding out why that happened is nearly impossible. It's worth stating that the prison authorities were ever mindful of clashes between racial groups. This possibility was certainly present at the time. The race riot of 1967 was no doubt fresh in the warden's mind. Racial tension, like the smell of the rancid cooking oil and Lysol in the mess hall, was an important nuance that the Columbia album was unable to transmit.

THE RACIAL DIVIDE

Black prisoners especially came to prison angry and militant. Because of their larger numbers, they asserted themselves, and they encountered white inmates who were used to running things their way.

Chuck EZ Williams, a white prisoner serving a life term at San Quentin during those days, later became editor of the *San Quentin News*. Williams recalled that racial tensions permeated even the musical events. As editor of the newspaper, Williams once had to assign a writer to cover a later concert that featured R&B legend James Brown, as well as white artists who also performed in the same event. Williams said of that concert: "It was understood I needed to send a Black reporter to cover him [James Brown]—as all the white boys would leave after the White performers were done. As I exited the East Block chow hall [concert venue], I walked right past JB, and didn't shake his hand or say hi or even acknowledge him. I wasn't racist when I went in; it was a game I knew I had to play, but over a short amount of time I became racist. (It took me a much longer period of time to get beyond it.)"[6]

DEFIANCE

Listeners to the Johnny Cash Columbia album mistook the full-throated cheering for delight, but it was mostly defiance. James M. Morris, author of *Prison Journalism: The Fourth Estate behind Bars,* told an interviewer, "The 1960s were turbulent throughout the United States and the prisons were not exempt. We were taking people off the streets of places like San Francisco and incarcerating them. And they were not going to shed the cultural changes that were occurring. The wardens were faced with tinderboxes, dangerous hard-to-control populations."[7]

The moment of truth arrived when Cash sang the song "San Quentin." Cash told the prisoners, "I was thinking about you guys yesterday. I've been here three times before, and I think I understand a little bit how you feel about some things. It's none of my business how you feel about some other things. And I don't give a damn about how you feel about some of the things.

"But anyways, I try to put myself in your place. And I believe this is the way that I would feel about San Quentin."

The song began, "San Quentin, I hate every inch of you."[8] Its blunt condemnation of California's oldest prison (founded in 1852, barely three years after California became a state) brought roars of approval after every verse. Words this harsh and explicit had never before been uttered at a sanctioned San Quentin event in more than a hundred years of the prison's existence.

Even in their letters home, San Quentin inmates were forbidden to criticize any law enforcement agency, government, or prison policy. Breaking this rule might have gotten a prisoner a disciplinary ticket or even a stay in administrative segregation (also known as the Hole). The prisoners nevertheless appeared nothing short of possessed when they heard Cash's words, according to *Johnny Cash: The Biography*, by Michael Streissguth.[9] The song validated their every complaint. They gave him a standing ovation. The song was so heartily received that the Man in Black did an encore. The musicians and technical crew appeared startled by the ferocity of the inmates' reaction. Cash later told his producer, "When I sang it again and all of a sudden, I looked around and I knew that if I wanted to let those people go, all I had to do was say 'The time is now.' And all those prisoners would've broken. I was tempted."

Rolling Stone reviewer Phil Marsh later wrote, "The concert is over, and those humans are still locked up on the other side of the Bay. The memory of Cash rapping with his hair-trigger audience stays with me. Where must Cash be *at* to relate so well to those we have put into our dungeons?"[10]

It was several months after the release of *Johnny Cash at San Quentin* that I began covering prison issues for the *Los Angeles Times,* and that is where the curtain goes up on my own personal story of involvement with the prison. When I visited San Quentin in 1970, it was run by the legendary warden Louis S. (Red) Nelson. Old-timers said he kept a gold record of *Johnny Cash at San Quentin* on display on his office wall.[11]

7 A West Oakland Murder

Our deaths illuminate our lives. If our deaths lack meaning,
our lives also lacked it. Therefore we are apt to say, when
somebody has died a violent death, "He got what he was
looking for." Each of us dies the death he is looking for, the
death he has made for himself.

Octavio Paz, *The Labyrinth of Solitude*

West Oakland echoed in my mind from the first visit I paid to San Quentin
in 1970. I had no idea that my prison odyssey would lead me to a painful
memory that I had kept buried inside me since I was twelve years old.

Looking inside California's prison system came easily to me. I was born
and raised in Oakland, a town that *Look* magazine once described as "the
terminal for the Negro exodus from the South since World War II." I grew
up in a black neighborhood in West Oakland. It was low income and had
its share of petty crime and occasional violence, but nothing to compare
with what one finds today. It had its own stable middle class made up of
Pullman porters, cooks on the Southern Pacific railroad, postal workers,
teachers, ministers, DMV clerks. Not many doctors or lawyers, however.

During my visits to prisons, I would occasionally meet inmates I recognized from the streets during my childhood. Some of them had attended
the same public schools as I had. Perhaps that was why I never felt afraid
when I walked among them. Because prisoners seemed normal to me, I
did not feel a need to romanticize them or to fear them. My older brother
had done a couple of stints in the juvie in Oakland.

My family was generally law abiding, although not necessarily church-
going. And this brings me to describing my family and my origins. Let's

start with the obvious. What do I look like? My complexion is dark. My eyes are dark brown and the flesh around them is puffy. In winter my color is an oily olive. In the summer sun it gets to be copper colored. I have always identified as colored, Negro, African American, black. I have been mistaken for everything from Mexican to Nepalese. I feel most at home on the streets of Honolulu, where tourists ask me for directions.

I've enrolled in the ancestry services of both *National Geographic* and 23andme. Both times the results I saw raised more questions than answers. Both services agreed, however, that Africa accounts for no more than 20 percent of my genetic makeup, proving once again that race is a social and not a biological construct.

Being racially ambiguous has been an advantage throughout my life. It gives me a ninety-second window of opportunity to establish myself to a stranger before a stereotype takes hold.

Growing up in West Oakland, I entirely fit in and was accepted by the black people around me. My father was a carpenter, and Mama was a punch-press operator in a factory that stamped out metal parts for everything from machinery to bridges. They both punched a clock, took their lunch in a bag or a lunch bucket, and got paid by the week. Neither had a proper bank account. They paid cash or, when necessary, bought a money order from the grocery store. They were union members and lifelong Democrats. They conscientiously voted.

To get a job, they both passed for white. They actually did not need to "pass." They would easily be mistaken for Italian or Greek. As an adult, when I obtained my birth certificate from the Alameda County Courthouse in order to get a passport, I found that my race was listed as "white." It was a shock, but it made sense. When I was born in 1944, my mother had a Jewish doctor who was on the staff of Peralta Hospital in Oakland. At the time Peralta Hospital was all white, and that's where my mother would deliver me. The physician and the clerks at Peralta never gave it a second thought. The Drummond woman in the maternity ward had to be white.

I won't apologize for my parents. Neither one was a role model for parenting. They did not get along. They argued often, and it was loud and disagreeable. On occasion the police were called. The old, rambling rooming house in which I lived with my parents and older brother was a hive of intrigues and affairs, drinking and loud partying and angry arguments. My mother divorced my father when I was ten.

My parents died within six months of each other, when I was twelve years old in 1957. My mother's death certificate said she had died of a "gunshot wound in the heart inflicted by a male." Three shots to be exact. Later—in court—they said four. But I heard three.

Driving across the Richmond-San Raphael Bridge in 1970, I caught sight of the mustard-colored buildings of San Quentin jutting out into San Francisco Bay. According to Catholic tradition, San Quentin was a Roman who went to Gaul and was eventually tortured and beheaded. But the Old Californians who named this piece of real estate had no idea it would become a prison where hundreds of people would be put to death.

As a kid, I had seen it from a distance, but this time I was actually going inside. The prison lies in the shadow of Mount Tamalpais (elevation 2,576 feet). At the end of Main Street is the East Gate, where I entered to begin three days of touring the most notorious prison in California. The director of the Department of Corrections, Raymond K. (Pro) Procunier, had instructed the prison to cooperate fully with me. I had the run of the institution, which was a level 4 (maximum-security) prison at the time. After a courtesy call on then-associate warden James W. L. Park, I was turned loose to talk to whomever I wished among inmates or staff.

Of course, I wanted to visit a cell block, and that's where I met with Wesley Robert Wells, sixty-one, the oldest black inmate in age and prison experience at San Quentin. He had been imprisoned for forty-two years, with one brief parole from 1941 to 1942. His offense: while in prison, he had thrown a cuspidor at a guard and injured him. He was serving life without parole. "Black prisoners have become aware," said Wells, and added, "They are more race conscious and have more race pride today, and there's a damn good reason to do so."

I asked Wells and other inmates if there was anybody on the prison staff they trusted. They were unanimous in naming Sam Hill Jr., a counselor at San Quentin. "There is only one man doing something about racism at San Quentin," one black inmate said. "It's that man there" (pointing to Hill).

Hill had a reputation for being a leader of the black staff and tried to clear up racial misunderstandings among correctional officers and officials. "When they see some guy clench his fist," said Hill, "this is misinterpreted to mean kill Whitey. They [black nationalists in prison] are not talking about that. Black consciousness is where they're headed, helping the less fortunate, not hate Whitey or shoot every white person."

I spent a considerable amount of time with Hill and grew to trust him. That is why I asked him if he would find out some details about what had become of the man who murdered my mother.

FLASHING BACK

It was Labor Day, 1957, a few weeks short of my twelfth birthday. I was watching *Kingdom of the Sea,* a TV program about sea creatures.

The gunshots were short and sharp. I was in a back bedroom. I ran to the front of the house to see. She was bent over the bed, her face buried in the covers. She was sliding face down, slowly, slowly. Gray and acrid smoke hung in the air, as if frozen. A man with terrible green eyes stood over her, a man with a grayish mustache and coffee-and-cream-colored face, a man named Jimmy. In his hand was a gray Colt .32-caliber automatic pistol. Mama's back was bloody. She slid to the floor hunched up in a perfect prenatal position.

Jimmy turned on me. "Go on back!" he ordered, as he turned the Colt pistol around. "Yeah, I killed her. She was nothing but a whore." I knew I needed to run, to run fast, anywhere. I ran back to the kitchen. I grabbed the extension phone and heard the dial tone. The child in me can never erase the memory:

"Operator," I whispered, still afraid Jimmy would appear at any moment. "Send help—"

I heard the front door close. I slammed down the receiver and ran to the front bedroom. She lay helpless. She lay still. I grasped the extension phone. Dial tone. Operator. Police, operator, please, a man just shot my mother. She's wiggling: I think she's dead. She's breathing so hoarse. Try to feel her heart. Her arms are doubled up over her belly. It's bleeding too. I stick in my hand to feel her heart. I feel blood, warm, thick, sticky.

"Is there anything I can do?" says a woman's voice over the phone. "Do you want me to stay on the line?" Yes, but hurry, please, quick! Ambulance! God, what's taking them so long? She's wiggling. Spasms, maybe. Now she's still again. Jimmy did it. Jimmy, her boyfriend. Why did you do it? You must have loved her too. Why? Hurry, please, hurry. Somebody's at the door. I feel sick. Poor Mama. She wasn't a churchgoer. She'll go to hell, I bet. Like the Jehovah's Witnesses say. Oh, Mama! Policemen. "Come on, Joe," he yells outside. "I think we got a D.O.A."

At the trial I testified. I took time off from school. In preparation for my testimony, the prosecutor (who later became a judge) showed me pictures of my mother's body taken on the slab in the morgue. She was thirty-five years old. The trial went on for two weeks. During my testimony, the prosecutor wanted me to view the morgue pictures again, but the judge pulled him up short. "Not necessary. Proceed." Finally, the judge sentenced James S. Dobson to a term of five years to life in the state prison. He walked out of my life that day, but the memories of what had happened that Labor Day were indelible, along with my curiosity about what had happened to my mother's killer.

Sam Hill, the San Quentin counselor, was one of the few people to whom I ever confided my secret. My mother had been shot to death by a jealous boyfriend. She died in my arms. I testified at the trial of the perpetrator, James S. Dobson, who went off to prison. What had happened to him? Was he perhaps at San Quentin? I had this conversation with Hill in a nondescript records room full of gray-green filing cabinets at San Quentin. Hill listened without showing any expression. I asked if he could find out anything. He said he would look. He disappeared and came back about twenty-five minutes later and said cryptically, "No, he's not here."

Jimmy Dobson was no stranger to me. We had gone fishing and hunting together. He had taught me to play poker. I had admired him in many ways. Even after what he had done, I was unable to demonize him. And there the trail of his whereabouts ended for me. I had no chance to try out the concept of restorative justice.

When somebody you love dies a violent death, you grieve and eventually you move on. It helps if you reconcile your grief with the perpetrator. That is what restorative justice does. Without that, you always walk with an emotional limp.

Nevertheless, by coming to San Quentin I had faced the fact of her murder. My request of Sam Hill was not easy. It was made out of curiosity mostly, to want to know if the story had an ending. I overcame my years-long fear of facing her murderer, but the trail was cold. Still, I was a step closer to a resolution.

I've always wondered why the law places special penalties on hate crimes. Love crimes are just as deadly, and much more common.

THE SAME PRISON, FORTY YEARS ON

In 2012 I found myself once again inside the walls of San Quentin, only this time in an entirely different role. No longer a young reporter for the *Los Angeles Times,* I was a senior professor of journalism at UC Berkeley, having left full-time journalism for academia in 1983. "Bastille by the Bay" was the name given the prison by an inmate columnist in the early days. The *San Francisco Chronicle's* iconic columnist Herb Caen used the same snappy moniker, which added some class to a dreary setting. The weather-beaten collection of buildings was the same, but San Quentin was a vastly different place. No longer maximum security, San Quentin was stepped down to level 2, which is minimum security, for its mainline population. The Department of Corrections even had a different name. The legislature in 2004 had added "rehabilitation" to its title: the California Department of Corrections and Rehabilitation. All the staff members and inmates from my first visit in 1970 had moved on, to release, retirement, or Boot Hill, the nickname for the cemetery overlooking the prison grounds.

8 The Lee Commission and the "Tough-on-Crime" Era

THE COMMISSION ON THE STATUS OF AFRICAN-AMERICAN MALES

In the first chapter, I pointed out that what you see on the prison yard is a reflection of what is going on out in the streets. Now I want to provide the reader with some observations of what was going on in California when turmoil struck the prisons and how the news and entertainment media were portraying the lived experiences of blacks and Latinos.

Before becoming a member of the US Congress, Oakland political leader US Rep. Barbara Lee was a member of the California State Senate. In the fall of 1996, then-state senator Lee asked me to write a chapter for a special legislative report she was preparing for the California Commission on the Status of African-American Males. The study would cover critical topics including health, education, and social services. My chapter would examine media portrayals of African American males.

Senator Lee turned to me because I had had a long career in journalism (*L.A. Times* and NPR) and had moved into academia at Berkeley. Also, I was available and had something to say. The things that I had witnessed in my career had convinced me that news media representations were a strong influence on the way the racial crisis was unfolding in the United States. I was one of the few black people who had had the vantage point of being an eyewitness to history. By 1996 the Kerner Commission Report was already nearly thirty years old.[1] Its warnings about the negligent behavior of news organizations had gone largely unheeded and are unheeded to this day. At Berkeley I taught courses on race and media, and they convinced me even more that nothing had changed. The Rodney King beating and the riots that followed the acquittals of the police officers proved that point: we were still two societies, separate and unequal, one black and one white.

When my career began, the news media had plunged into a daring tryst with tokenism. I was the second African American reporter at the *Courier-Journal* in Louisville, where I worked from 1966 to 1967. And when I joined the *Los Angeles Times* in 1967, I was the third black reporter in the iconic fortress at First and Spring Streets. In that role I was not just another employee. I would become one of the few black colleagues the crew in the editorial department would have. More particularly, I would be one of the few black people with whom they would have a serious conversation.

I was deeply troubled about the role into which I had stumbled at the *L.A. Times*. I had certainly found a career niche, but I worried that I was an imposter. My bosses and my colleagues looked at me and decided, "We've got this race thing covered. We have Drummond." But I was not representative of anything. That's the trouble with being a token. As I noted earlier, in Louisville the city editor, as a good-natured joke, called me Stokely, a reference to SNCC militant Stokely Carmichael, and in Los Angeles an assistant city editor called me the "angry young man." Really? Was I inadvertently pretending to be something I was not? This predicament bothered me so much that I wrote an article for the *Columbia Journalism Review* about it:

> It is understandable that any Negro hired onto a big daily will consider himself lucky and will not complain if he gets the race beat. One reason for the silence is that racial coverage is an important assignment in which there is a great deal of interest and thus a guarantee to the reporter of plentiful exposure. Another reason is that a Negro reporter doubtless feels secure with the race beat because, by dint of his birth, he is an expert, or should be, and he

will have easy rapport with his sources, who are either Negroes or persons used to dealing with them. Third, behind all is a feeling of protectiveness: No white man could possibly give us as sympathetic treatment as I can; he just would not understand.

Nevertheless, the terms of the arrangement are a limitation on editor and reporter alike, but especially on the reporter. The suspicion that an editor's interest lies in the external man, rather than in the whole man, could prevent a reporter from keeping the faith with his profession.[2]

The thirty years that passed between my 1968 *CJR* piece and my study for Barbara Lee were not kind to black people in the news and entertainment media. To begin with, the 1970s ushered in the "blaxploitation" movie genre. These motion pictures featured funk and soul soundtracks, employed talented black actors, and portrayed inner-city stories of discontent and injustice. But their content was often violent and upsetting. The movies exploited racial stereotypes, sexism, violence, and profanity for profits.[3]

Variety credits *Sweet Sweetback's Baadasssss Song* and *Shaft*, both released in 1971, as the pioneers in this brand of cinema, which was pitched primarily to African American audiences. At least fifty different iterations were released, until in 1988 the genre was put to rest with a comedy spoof titled *I'm Gonna Get You Sucka*.[4]

Against this backdrop I undertook the study of black portrayals in the media. I wrote this summation for the Lee report:

> The news media and the entertainment media in this regard are nearly indistinguishable. Occasionally, one finds a storyline based on African American males who are decent, responsible and hardworking, or who hold non-traditional jobs, or espouse unexpected beliefs, but more often, the African American male intrudes into the public consciousness in handcuffs, bent over the hood of a police vehicle. He is a symbol of failure, of the unraveling of family, respect and values.
>
> We know him only in the abstract (more African American males in jail than in higher education, for example).[5] The nameless "looter" from a burned-out inner-city neighborhood, Rodney King, the gangsta rapper, O.J. Simpson, and hundreds of other standard images from the media are similarly opaque and threatening. They are African American males, whose motivations cannot be understood, whose intentions can never be trusted. They lie outside the pale of the respectable community.[6]

Such was the dominant media narrative about the African American male, but even more so about the African American felon in those turbulent years of the 1960s until the present day.

"Black pathology is big business," wrote Ishmael Reed, Oakland poet and chair of PEN's Oakland media committee, in a November 20, 1989, article for the *Nation*.[7] "News producers have found a lucrative market in exhibiting black pathology, while coverage of pathologies such as drug addiction, child abuse, spousal battering and crime among whites and their 'model minorities' is negligible. According to the news shows, you'd conclude that that two black gangs, the Crips and the Bloods, are both the cause and the result of the nation's drug problem, even though this country was high long before these children were born."

By the time Reed wrote, the "black pathology biz" had been thriving for decades. The stage had been set by Daniel Patrick Moynihan in 1965, when he blamed African American male unemployment on "the deterioration of the Negro family," a phenomenon he attributed to slavery.[8] "It was by destroying the Negro family that white America broke the will of the Negro people," wrote Moynihan, who coined the phrase a "tangle of pathology."[9]

The generation of black men coming of age in the sixties, seventies, and eighties were constantly receiving this message from the news and entertainment media. And it had a pernicious effect: to some extent many internalized it, seeing lived experiences of disruption and trouble in their families and communities in the context of omnipresent narratives of racial pathology and restricting their aspirations to what the media represented for them.

Dr. Grace Carol Massey, an educational psychologist at the University of California at Berkeley, told me, "If people believe a lie, they act like it's the truth for all practical purposes."[10] Massey said her greatest fear was that the steady drumbeat about African American pathology in the news created a self-fulfilling prophecy for youngsters, whose limits of achievement, she said, could be predetermined for them by suggestions in narratives they found in the media.

From Eldridge Cleaver to Huey P. Newton and George Jackson, the lives and expectations of black men were profoundly influenced by the fifty years of media narratives of pathology and failure. Before the advent of the internet, television was the single biggest factor in shaping people's view of the world and of themselves. But TV was disproportionately influential among young blacks, who spent more time watching television than their white counterparts.

A 1972 study found that 83 percent of black boys between the ages of eleven and fourteen spent more than three hours a day watching television, compared to 51 percent of white boys the same age. "Television Violence and Deviant Behavior," a report by Jennie J. McIntyre and James J. Teevan, reported a similar disparity for black girls.[11]

News programming at this time was especially biased against African Americans. This was before *The Bill Cosby Show*, the NBC program that was hailed as a big breakthrough in positive portrayals of blacks. This was the heyday of "eyewitness news." "If it bleeds, it leads" was the mantra of news programming. Flashing lights, yellow tape, cheap crime, and violence were staples of local news programming. Inner-city disenfranchised people were more likely to wind up in the television police blotter evening dramas.

The Radio-Television News Directors Association reported in 1996 that just 1 percent of TV news directors were black. Although blacks were seen on TV as anchors and reporters, they rarely had a hand in determining news policy. The impressionable African American viewer was indoctrinated in racial alienation, misunderstanding, fear, and antagonism. It was expected that he would engage in aggressiveness, lawlessness, and violence. Is it any wonder that the most influential black musical innovation of this period, hip-hop, often celebrates violence, exploitation, sexism, and greed? As Caliban, the half-beast, complains in Shakespeare's *The Tempest*, "You taught me language and my profit on't is I know how to curse."[12]

TOUGH-ON-CRIME POLICY AND ITS CONSEQUENCES

The dominant narrative correlated almost perfectly to a "tough-on-crime" policy that swept the state. California's prison population had been stable through the 1960s and '70s. Even after the San Quentin violence surrounding George Jackson's death, CDC director Procunier sounded optimistic at the end of 1971. "The population of prisons has gone down substantially. The prison return rate [recidivism] held at an all-time low," he wrote. And he said new changes in the parole regulations meant men would go home sooner.[13]

His predictions were flat wrong.

There were eight male prisons in the state in 1970 when I made my grand tour. But in the ensuing decades, the state of California led a building boom. By 2018 California had brought the number of prisons to thirty-five. Dozens of small towns in the Central Valley became the sites of penitentiaries, far away from the urban population centers that fed the great majority of felons into the system. Corrections became a growth industry, a rural development program based on confining urban offenders (blacks and Latinos) hundreds of miles away from their families. Incarceration developed a life of its own. California's prison population ballooned from 25,000 in 1970 to more than 160,000 by 2016. California had more prison guards by 2018 than it had prisoners in 1970.[14] Today it is the third-largest police agency in the country, next to the New York Police Department and the US Customs and Border Patrol.[15]

"By the early 1990s," wrote Steven Pinker in 2011, "Americans had gotten sick of the muggers, vandals, and drive-by shootings, and the country beefed up the criminal justice system in several ways. The most effective was also the crudest: putting more men behind bars for longer stretches of time. The rate of imprisonment in the United States was pretty much flat from the 1920s to the early 1960s, and it even declined a bit until the early 1970s. But then it shot up almost fivefold, and today more than two million Americans are in jail, the highest incarceration rate on the planet."[16]

This kind of dramatic public policy shift could not have taken place without compliant and docile public opinion. And that is where the insistent drumbeat of news media messages took its toll.

In 1971 the Nixon administration began to expand the size and powers of the federal drug control agencies and push for mandatory minimum sentencing laws for drug offenses. This effort, which became the notorious War on Drugs, would greatly escalate rates of arrest and incarceration throughout the United States.

In California from 1970 to 2008 a succession of governors—Democrats and Republicans—adopted a tough-on-crime stance. Republican governor Pete Wilson's address to the legislature in 1994 was the high-water mark. He embraced the idea of throwing away the key:

> To make our streets safe again, we must target the most vicious criminals. Research shows us that most serious crimes are committed by relatively few habitual criminals.
> Richard Allen Davis is the most recent example. Davis has confessed to the tragic murder of little Polly Klaas. Davis is a repeat felon, a career criminal with a long, long record of habitual sordid crimes and violence. This animal should have never been let loose.
> Last year, in California more than four hundred children were murdered.
> Our streets are being stained with the blood of our children—and damn it, it's got to stop. It has got to stop.
> So I ask you, please, to work with me to pass tougher laws. We know what California needs to make our cities, our suburbs, and our small towns safe again. . . .
> Yes, these reforms will mean building more prisons, and hiring more correctional officers. There's no getting around that fact. But that's a price we've got to pay. As governor, I've opened five new prisons and tonight I propose we offer $2 billion worth of bonds to build six more.
> There will be those who protest such costs. They'll complain that they would prefer to spend the money on higher education rather than more prisons. Well, so would I. But this is not a matter of choice. The cost of California's failure to keep Richard Allen Davis behind bars was paid by little Polly Klaas. Does anyone want to tell me how much a child's life is worth? Does anyone want to assign a dollar value to 400 murdered children?[17]

Wilson's successor as governor, Gray Davis, a Democrat, prided himself in rejecting parole for felons who had been sentenced to a life term. It did not matter that the parole boards had found the prisoner suitable for parole.

In 1996, the time of the Lee Commission's report, California's mass incarceration boom was in full swing. Some pertinent statistics gleaned from the criminal justice section of the Lee report and elsewhere reveal who paid the price for the incarceration push in the 1990s:

- African American males accounted for about 3.7 percent of the statewide population but over 35 percent of the arrestee and inmate populations.
- Two-thirds of the men of color in California had been arrested at least once between the ages of eighteen and thirty.

- Under California's "Three Strikes and You're Out" law, African Americans were charged for felonies at 4.7 times the rate of whites and were imprisoned for a third "strike" at 13.3 times the rate of whites.

- The Lee report cited the finding from a 1990 *Sacramento Bee* article that while 78 percent of drug users in Sacramento County were white, only 34 percent of those arrested for narcotics offenses were white. Conversely, 52 percent of those arrested for drug offenses in Sacramento were African American, even though African Americans made up only 12 percent of the county's drug users.[18]

- African American males accounted for 43 percent of felony narcotics arrests.

- While one out of every three African American males in their twenties were under some form of criminal justice control, the figure was even higher for California: nearly four in ten young African American males were in prison or jail, or on probation or parole. The comparable rate for young white males was one in 20.[19]

The seeds of mass incarceration had been planted in the late 1960s. It was a story I stumbled upon almost by accident. "LA Crime Rate Could Collapse Justice System, Computer Says," reads the headline on a page 1 story that I wrote for the *Los Angeles Times* on September 13, 1970.[20] The story went on:

> About six months ago a USC research team began feeding a computer information on the trends in major crimes in Los Angeles County from 1960 to 1968 and estimates of the county's population growth to the year 2000.
>
> They asked the computer what was going to happen to the criminal justice system in the county during the next 30 years, assuming the 1960–68 crime rates continue and assuming there is no change in the handling of offenders.
>
> Inspired by the motion picture "2001: A Space Odyssey," the team from Public Systems Research Institute subtitled the study "1970 to 2000: A Crime Odyssey."
>
> There were no grandiose musical overtures when the IBM 1130 spoke. It simply rattled off a series of numbers.
>
> What these numbers describe is a scenario beginning when the phone rings in the chambers of the presiding judge of the Superior Court of Los Angeles County.

> The caller will be the sheriff: "I don't know how to say this, but we've got no place else to put 'em. We're full up. We can't take any more prisoners."
>
> This call is perhaps six years away, according to the computer. It will represent the first sign of the collapse of the criminal justice system.

The prediction was alarming, but it failed to gain any traction in official circles in the state. The inertia was largely due to what was termed criminal justice "provincialism," meaning the uncoordinated actions of various agencies. Law enforcement agencies were arresting more people, and courts were sentencing more people, but nobody was taking into account what would happen to those convicted defendants.

Criminologists remark that the only thing worse than not catching a criminal is catching one. Thereupon, the criminal must be processed through a complaint, a court disposition, and, in the case of a conviction, confinement, a fine, or probation. With each arrest, the workload up the line increases.

The end of the line in the criminal justice pipeline is the state prison system. California eventually responded with an expensive, unprecedented prison-building program.

But as computer analysis had predicted in my story on the potential collapse of the justice system, something would eventually have to give. In 2011 mass incarceration received a check in the federal courts' decision that overcrowding in the CDC amounted to "cruel and unusual punishment." A trickle of releases on parole began.

Governor Davis, who had unilaterally rejected any parole for felons, was eventually recalled from office in October 2003 for reasons other than criminal justice, with 55 percent of the electorate wanting him gone. When he left, he had allowed just two lifers to get parole. But by that point his tough stance on parole was not enough to save him politically. His successor, Republican Arnold Schwarzenegger, approved 557 lifers for parole in six years. Gov. Jerry Brown, Schwarzenegger's successor, approved parole for more than 2,000 lifers, more than four previous governors put together.[21]

By 2017, the fever for mass incarceration had apparently broken. The public's mood had evidently cooled. The courts had become alarmed about the human rights infringements inherent in mass incarceration. And seemingly out of nowhere, a vocal coalition appeared, supporting prison reform and sending prisoners home.

Inside the dingy confines of the newsroom at San Quentin, a dozen or so convict journalists played a significant role in changing the narrative about prisoners and the way we think about all the people in the penitentiary. How did that happen?

9 The *San Quentin News*

San Quentin warden Clinton T. Duffy wanted to quell rumors in the cell-blocks, so he had the prison create its own newspaper. The first edition of the *San Quentin News* was published on December 10, 1940. Duffy wrote: "The first edition of the *San Quentin News*, hand-set and printed on gaudy green paper, was . . . not exactly a sensation, but it was a revelation to the permanent tenants who thought they had seen everything in prison. Those first issues were tough in spots, full of slang and even a little bawdy at times. We printed poetry, quizzes, cartoons, short stories, gags, and news."[1]

Duffy, who died in 1982, is rightly referred to as legendary: he was even the subject of a 1954 Hollywood movie. The newspapers of that era described him as a reformer and credited him with cleaning up a particularly corrupt and brutal prison administration when he took over. He changed the public face of the institution from punishment to "treatment" and pioneered psychology-based group counseling. Nevertheless, during his tenure, he executed eighty-eight men and two women; in fact, *88 Men and 2 Women* is the title of his 1962 memoir. His public relations campaign

65

succeeded, but behind the walls San Quentin remained a grim and bizarrely cruel place.

Clinton Duffy wasn't the only prison administrator to give the newspaper idea a try. Dozens of other penitentiaries around the country began their own internal newspapers. Some prisons funded the papers as vocational training. Other papers were paid for out of the various inmate welfare funds. Most of the content was routine. Sports reporting was a staple. VIP visits were highlighted. Profiles were done on prison staff members. The warden would often contribute a column. The paper would keep track of arrival and departure statistics within the Department of Corrections. Columns were written about colorful prisoners and eulogies were written for dedicated staff members who died.

James Park, a clinical psychologist in the CDC in the 1950s who later became associate warden at San Quentin in the 1960s, handled most of the contacts with the press. He called San Quentin "a fairly brutal, old-fashioned behind the times system" under the celebrated Duffy. Author Eric Cummins quoted Park as saying that Duffy "got an awful lot of publicity, [but] people were still being beaten to death under Duffy's regime. He was not the great fucking savior that his own press agent built him up to be."[2]

Nevertheless, San Quentin kept the lid on through the 1950s and 1960s, and it stayed out of the news, except for the occasional visit from a celebrity, ranging from evangelist Billy Graham to singer Eartha Kitt.

FREEDOM OF THE PRISON PRESS

During the 1970s and 1980s inmate journalists repeatedly clashed with the CDC. These conflicts had profound First Amendment implications.

The conflicts became especially acute during the turmoil of the changing racial demographics within the CDC and the polarized politics that created tensions between inmate journalists and the warden's office. Black inmates and radical whites sought, in the best progressive tradition, to expose harsh and possibly illegal prison conditions. Wardens and superintendents felt themselves besieged and wanted to keep the lid on.

The conflicts were not unique to San Quentin. Most California prisons at that time had newspapers as well. Not all of the papers were set in type and professionally printed on a letterpress. Some, such as the *Vacavalley Star,* published at the California Medical Facility at Vacaville, were mimeographed inside the prison. The CMF housed inmates needing psychiatric care and was the home for years of the cult leader Charles Manson. Seven of the eight male California prisons had newspapers of one sort or another. The three main protagonists in the conflicts with the CDC were the *San Quentin News,* the *Vacavalley Star,* and the *Soledad Star News,* published at the state prison in Monterey County. They all had their issues with prison management.

"For over four years in the late 1970s, inmate-journalists had squabbled with prison authorities over what they considered excessive censorship," James McGarth Morris wrote.[3] [3]"The stubborn refusal of California corrections officials to grant their inmate newspapers freedom like that given to the *Angolite* in Louisiana had brought the conflict into the courtroom."

The *Angolite,* a magazine produced at Angola State Prison, won national awards under the leadership of Wilbert Rideau, a convicted murderer who took over the magazine as editor in 1975. Rideau and his staff enjoyed remarkable editorial freedom. California prison publications were not so lucky.

The wardens and superintendents for the CDC were wary that things written in the newspapers might touch off a riot. Prison management was also concerned that any dysfunctional conditions on the inside would be exposed to the outside world, especially to the governor or to the legislature. Although the prison publications had small circulations, journalists in the free world were among their most avid readers.

Mainstream journalism had long ignored or neglected prison conditions because gaining access was so difficult. Editors also had a mind-set that excused harsh prison conditions, on the assumption that prisoners should suffer for their crimes.

Conditions in the San Quentin mess hall were a source of great unhappiness. Over the years, inmate complaints brought no improvement. Eventually the *San Quentin News* produced a well-researched investigative report accompanied by photographs.

The February 5, 1980, issue included photographs of bird droppings in the mess hall. That was the last straw for prison management. The warden fired everybody on the newspaper who had anything to do with the story.

Later Mike Madding, the prison's public information officer, told the *San Francisco Chronicle*, "The warden feels that it didn't give both sides of the story—and that it violated his agreement with the *San Quentin News* staff. . . . We've got a provocative situation here, and we're not going to fuel it." He didn't dispute the existence of the bird droppings. Madding said the birds had come inside the mess hall through some broken windows, but he refused to let the *San Francisco Chronicle* reporter visit the mess hall.[4] The conflict wound up in court, and the judge sided with the inmate journalists. Superior Court judge Joseph Wilson ordered the warden to show cause why the inmate staff should not be reinstated, and publication of the newspaper resumed. "This is an ordinary news story I don't see anything horrendous about it. . . . I can't imagine how the warden could say this is unfair."[5]

Following the bird droppings incident, the warden announced that in the future the *San Quentin News* would be published by the Men's Advisory Council, a body the administration thought it could better control. Marvin Mutch, who came to prison in 1975 on a murder conviction, was a member of the Men's Advisory Council at San Quentin and eventually became its chairman. But he was hardly an administration pushover. Mutch had been active in trying to organize a statewide prisoners union. In an interview, Mutch told me he had abandoned the idea of a union in 1977 because of tensions and disagreements between men behind bars and "organizers" for the union in the streets. Mutch said the organizers outside were collecting dues and trying to turn the union into a for-profit operation. So, Mutch said, he had instead pressed for a statewide, elected inmate "Prisoners Council" that would engage in collective bargaining with the CDC about pressing issues. But that effort fell apart. Early in 1980 the San Quentin newspaper was added to Mutch's portfolio at the Men's Advisory Council.

The *San Quentin News* in those days was like a small-town newspaper, devoting space and coverage to sports, legislative developments, and "police blotter" incidents at the prison, such as stabbings, assaults, and disruptions. Mutch said reporting on "police blotter" events made the administration uncomfortable. Ostensibly the warden wanted facts to be reported that would curtail rumors, he but disliked seeing reports in print of the sordid details of inmate clashes. The CDC spokesman at the time was Phil Guthrie, who was usually sanguine and unflappable. Nevertheless, Guthrie warned that all prison newspapers had to be under the control of the local wardens, and he warned "if the courts decided something other than that, we won't have them [newspapers] anymore."[6]

The power of the wardens and superintendents to control the free expression of California prisoners was frequently put to the test in the courts. Recall that when Johnny Cash played San Quentin in 1969 California, inmates were forbidden to criticize any law enforcement agency, any government, or any prison policy even in a letter home, let alone a publication.

When an inmate challenged the correspondence policy in court, the result was a groundbreaking decision by the US Supreme Court in *Procunier v. Martinez* issued in April 29, 1974. Roy K. Procunier was the director of the Department of Corrections, and Robert Martinez was a San Quentin inmate. The prison authorities were attempting to enforce a regulation allowing officials to censor correspondence between the inmate and members of his legal team. The Supreme Court, under Chief Justice Warren Burger, ruled unanimously against Procunier. The court said that censorship of private mail was a breach of the First Amendment. Justice Lewis F. Powell Jr. wrote the majority opinion: "The censorship of direct personal correspondence involves incidental restrictions on the right to free speech of both prisoners and their correspondents, and is justified if the following criteria are met: (1) it must further one or more of the important and substantial governmental interests of security, order, and the rehabilitation of inmates, and (2) it must be no greater than is necessary to further the legitimate governmental interest involved."[7] Powell noted that the federal courts had traditionally taken a hands-off policy in dealing with prison administration but asserted that the regulations in question did not meet the criteria to allow for censorship and thus "unduly burden[ed] the right of free speech."

Justice Thurgood Marshall, however, wrote a separate opinion that drew broader conclusions, and Justice William O. Douglas joined him. "The First Amendment serves not only the needs of the polity, but also those of the human spirit—a spirit that demands self-expression," wrote Justice Marshall. "Such expression is an integral part of the development of ideas and a sense of identity. To suppress expression is to reject the basic human desire for recognition and affront the individual's worth and dignity."[8]

The case involved only correspondence between an inmate and his defense team. But Justice Marshall took a giant step beyond the subject of correspondence. He continued:

> When the prison gates slam behind an inmate, he does not lose his human quality; his mind does not become closed to ideas; his intellect does not cease to feed on a free and open interchange of opinions; his yearning for self-respect does not end; nor is his quest for self-realization concluded. If anything, the needs for identity and self-respect are more compelling in the dehumanizing prison environment. Whether an O. Henry writing his short stories in a jail cell or a frightened young inmate writing his family, a prisoner needs a medium for self-expression. It is the role of the First Amendment and this Court to protect those precious personal rights by which we satisfy such basic yearnings of the human spirit.[9]

Largely because of a misunderstanding, the decision in *Procunier v. Martinez* fanned the flames of free expression inside the prison system. Many people read the Marshall opinion and assumed that the Supreme Court was stating those views. Many prison journalists and their supporters read the news stories about the decision and decided that the court had loosened the regulations on prison newspapers. They figured, wrongly, that wardens were forbidden to censor prison newspapers. In response, the *San Quentin News* took ever more bold steps.

THE FINAL BATTLES

In its May 7, 1982, issue, the *San Quentin News* was prohibited from running an editorial written by inmates opposing the death penalty. Incensed, the staff left a blank space in the print edition where the article would have been. The word *censored* appeared in large font across the blank space. Some five thousand copies of the issue were confiscated. The editor at the time was Charles EZ Williams. He filed suit against the Department of Corrections for the confiscation and won.

Later that year, the California Supreme Court upheld a complaint by inmate journalists at Soledad State Prison, where the superintendent had blocked publication of two stories. In *Bailey v. Loggins,* the state supreme court upheld a lower court ruling ordering the CDC to permit publication of

Figure 4. San Quentin cell, 1982. Charles EZ Williams, then editor of the *San Quentin News*, is in the foreground. Courtesy of Charles EZ Williams.

the two disputed articles in the Soledad prison newspaper, the *Star News*, and to formulate guidelines limiting administrative censorship of the newspaper to matters that "would reasonably be deemed a threat to institutional security or which described the making of a weapon or other dangerous device." The ruling also ordered the CDC "to formulate regulations for expeditious review of controversies concerning inmate articles."[10]

Phil Guthrie, the CDC spokesman, complained in 1984, "We were losing control of the content of the newspapers by virtue of the court cases. Inmates wanted to play investigative journalist in what was essentially a house organ."[11]

Without the ability to control what inmates wrote and published, the wardens in California took matters in hand. Williams was transferred from San Quentin. His replacement, Elmo Chattman Jr., said that the administrators perceived him and the paper's four reporters as "troublemakers," adding: "The administration believes they can censor anything they seem to find offensive, libelous, embarrassing, or editorial statements which fail to include their side of the story."[12] Shortly thereafter, in 1982, the *San Quentin News* went on a twenty-year hiatus.

With few exceptions prison newspapers were all shut down. Journalism behind bars virtually ceased to exist by 1990. Rideau, the former editor of the *Angolite*, coauthored an article in the *Nation* in 2014, writing, "From a high of 250 in 1959, prison newspapers and magazines today number less than a dozen."[13] At one time prison publications were so numerous that they even had their own journalism association, which eventually went dark. The American Penal Press stopped giving out awards in 1990. Rideau's award-winning *Angolite,* however, remained active. The *San Quentin News* was the last of the seven sanctioned California publications to stop printing.

OUTLAW AND RESTORATION OF THE *SAN QUENTIN NEWS*

Despite the shutdowns and the reassignment of activist inmates, prison journalists refused to go away. Underground newspapers sporadically appeared inside San Quentin. The most notorious was titled *Outlaw.* It was secretly run off on a mimeograph machine in a prison office, said Mutch. *Outlaw* was passed around discreetly among inmates and smuggled out, to appear in the pages of the *Berkeley Barb,* the radical newspaper published in the East Bay. Procunier, the CDC director, had banned the *Barb* in October 1971.[14]

Outlaw was considered contraband. Inmates found in possession of it were subject to discipline.

According to Mutch, prison officials eventually had about enough of the underground prison journalism. Mutch said that in 2008 the warden at San Quentin, Robert L. Ayers Jr., decided to turn the institution upside down and put a stop to the *Outlaw.* Correctional officers carried out a thorough search and found the rogue mimeograph machine and the typewriter that cut the stencils. In addition, the officers located stashes of vintage copies of the *San Quentin News,* which were hidden away among the personal property of some inmates. The correctional officers presented the contraband "evidence" to the warden.

Warden Ayers reportedly looked over the yellowed, dog-eared copies of the papers and was intrigued, according to Mutch's account. "These are not so bad," Ayers said. The warden had begun his career at San Quentin as a correctional officer in 1968 and he was working there during the time of the iconic Johnny Cash concert. Ayers, a Republican, came back as warden in 2006 and stayed until his retirement at the end of 2008. Dapper, compact, and trim, he often dressed like a latter-day George Raft and had a reputation for following his own lights. "When I came back here, I was

Figure 5. Richard (Bonaru) Richardson, Warden Robert Ayers Jr., and Arnulfo García. Photo by Lt. Sam Robinson.

looking for various things that would rekindle some pride, some dignity to both the staff and the inmate population," he later said of his return.[15]

To the consternation of some officials in Sacramento, Ayers decided in his final year on the job to bring back the *San Quentin News*. The choice made him a folk hero to the prisoners. After his retirement, Ayers wrote in a *San Quentin News* editorial that he had no regrets about his decision:

> I must admit that there was a bit of "eye rolling" when I decided to resurrect the *San Quentin News* (Oh gawd! He's at it again!!!!!!). It wasn't an easy sale to the Education Department, which is where I believed the paper should be administered. But, the Vocational Print Shop was game to try it and when I mentioned the thought to some in the inmate population I received enthusiastic responses. Indeed, the first two members of the *News* staff, Kenny Brydon and Michael Harris, were beyond eager to send the first edition to print. A seasoned and highly professional advisory staff took that raw talent and guided it to the first publication in 2008.[16]

Mutch was chairman of the Men's Advisory Council when Warden Ayers made his historic decision. Mutch recommended Kenny Brydon, a white inmate serving a life sentence, to be the first editor in chief of the revived newspaper. He took the job. Brydon was widely respected and was not identified with any factions or interest groups in the prison. "Prison is an angry place. You learn to carry yourself with a degree of diplomacy," Brydon told an interviewer at the time.[17]

In June 2008, he and four other inmates produced the first edition of the reborn *San Quentin News*. Five thousand copies were printed. Each copy was four pages long, and each copy was printed in black ink on gold-colored paper. The news staff hand-delivered copies to the cellblocks inside the prison.

Aly Tamboura, a former businessman/engineer from Santa Clara County who would serve nearly sixteen years in prison before his parole in 2017 and who would then go to work for a philanthropic venture run by Facebook founder Mark Zuckerberg's wife, was one of the original inmates on the newspaper staff. "The feedback we get from the paper, it varies," Tamboura said in 2008. "In the beginning it was pretty much all bad." The inmates wanted the paper to expose conditions in the prison. "What about the cold showers? What about the horrible food? What are you guys writing about? What's wrong with you guys?"[18]

In late 2018 Brydon walked out of San Quentin having served a thirty-nine-year sentence. In an email to me, Brydon reflected on his experience as editor in chief of the revived newspaper: "We had been given a difficult task, getting the paper going, and it would require acceptance on the part of some who wouldn't necessarily want it. It was deemed a joke by many, and not-so-subtle threats of having it shut down were a common issue. We were given access where it wasn't welcome, and the ability to be a resource of information wasn't necessarily 'good news' to those who didn't want another perspective."[19]

Brydon added, "While we had our limits, there were occasions when we went to the point of issues as they were directly impacting prisoners." For example, one of the writers did a story describing conditions in the Adjustment Center, also known as the Hole.

> The story, written by Jeff Brooks, was about the poor conditions in Ad Seg [administrative segregation]. How this article differed from informal gripes was that it was common knowledge, and the writer had set it forth as to why you would not wish to go there. Technically, Warden Ayers made the final decision to print Jeff's story, but that did not stop the demands that we print written rebuttals (which didn't deny that the situation was true), and brought the anger of Administration on many fronts to both the San

Quentin News and myself. *But things improved in the Hole . . .* [emphasis Brydon's]. When change begins, it typically is with the recognition from those who one would expect to be completely in support of the status quo. People were being neglected, CDCR had become a behemoth with so much neglect happening that it could not be denied.[20]

In the very first edition with Brydon at the helm the newspaper reported on the topic of integration in assigning cellmates. The CDCR was contemplating a policy change that inmates saw as coercive. Sharing the 9-x-4-foot space a prisoner calls home is a touchy subject, as Brydon wrote to me. "Integration was a matter of choice or forced sharing of space in a place and a manner that would put individuals in harm's way. It was not only a question of race, but of age, and ideology. If an elderly individual was forced to live with an aggressive younger person from another race, that alone could result in racial tensions escalating. The policy lacked in addressing many issues which should have been answered prior to the attempt. . . . It wasn't implemented."[21]

The approach of Brydon and his successors was one of caution. The activist passion of the 1970s and 1980s was conspicuously absent in the revived San Quentin newsroom. The new staff of the paper was more than willing to stay within the boundaries of the rules laid down by Warden Ayers.

This attitude was a sharp contrast to the stance of the inmate editors of the 1980s. Elmo Chattman, the last editor of the *San Quentin News* before it was shut down, talked to MediaFile about his time at the paper:

All I wanted to do was to remain true to the basic ethos of journalism . . . to write the objective truth. Of course, in a correctional setting, "my" objective truth amounts to a biased condemnation of "the system" and, moreover, of the employees who serve that institution. All in all . . . the *News* was a great experience for me. Taught me how important it is to stand up and speak my personal truth, the truth of those without a voice, and even the truth of those w/ whom I do not agree. Taught me the truth & importance of objectivity . . . and the point of view of others.[22]

By 2008 the *San Quentin News* was being run under a different philosophy. "You have to be responsible and educated journalists," Ayers told the prison newsmen. "You have to learn that craft. You have to learn how to do this, and you have to understand what you say and if it causes the governor to call the director of corrections and say, 'Shut that damned thing down,' then you will have failed in what you're trying to do. You don't want to be a failure."[23]

Ayers issued each prison journalist a yellow laminated card that said, "Press Pass." It stated, "The bearer of this card along with his CDCR ID has access to locations inside the perimeter of San Quentin State Prison. Approved. Robert L. Ayers Jr., Warden."

Dave Marsh, an inmate journalist in the original crew, said some guards were astonished when he showed his press pass. "I tell 'em it's pretty self-explanatory. If you read it, it kind of says it all."[24]

THE *SAN QUENTIN NEWS* TODAY

The setting was the airy, well-lit Protestant chapel at San Quentin on September 29, 2016.

When it comes to religion, San Quentin is ecumenical if nothing else. Besides the Protestant chapel, it has a Catholic chapel. In an adjacent room Jews and the Muslims collegially share the same space on alternate days, and the arrangement works fine. Buddhists dressed in black gather in that same room on Sunday evenings for their services, while next door the strains of a gospel choir spill out into the night. Native Americans and Native Hawaiians have their own space.

The special September event was the first awards ceremony for the *San Quentin News* since its founding in 1940 by Warden Duffy. But now it was the only prison newspaper in the state. The *San Quentin News* had come back from more than twenty years in oblivion in 2008 and had been publishing monthly ever since. This was a cause for celebration, which attracted dozens of civilian volunteers and supporters of the newspaper, as well as inmates in freshly pressed prison denim.

Lt. Sam Robinson of the CDCR was in the audience. His role was probably unique in the world of corrections: as public information officer, he served as de facto publisher of the newspaper.

The *San Quentin News,* because of its peculiar evolution, was an administrative anomaly within the prison system. Though in 2008 it was first placed under the supervision of the Vocational Print Shop, shortly afterward budget cuts eliminated the print shop, leaving the newspaper as an administrative orphan. The prison's Audio/Visual Department took over the paper, but it was not a good fit. So the publication was eventually added to the PIO's portfolio.

This situation turned out to be a blessing in disguise. The newspaper would never have developed beyond an inoffensive newsletter if it had been assigned to the education department. It would have had to fit into a teaching curriculum with preset learning outcomes, reading lists, and assigned units and would have to administer examinations. Instructors or principals would be able to kill stories on a whim. That would not be how newsrooms should run. Instead, the reborn *San Quentin News* had come back to life in a spirited, altered format. The awards ceremony for the paper marked eight years of increasing recognition, expansion, and partnerships with groups and programs beyond the prison walls.

10 The Founding Fathers

Kenny Brydon stepped down as editor of the *San Quentin News* in 2010. During his tenure, he said, he had walked a fine line:

> Was I Threatened?
>
> That's a yes and a no. No one came at me with a knife in their hand and threatened to assault me, and it was more coming from those who believed that we "should" be this expose of all the corruption and evil that is a part of the system.
>
> They would throw out vague comments that people weren't happy with it, but, when I told these individuals to send them to me directly, no one showed their face.
>
> I did have a staff member in my face demanding that I print his story. We'd had some encounters prior to the Paper, and he thought I wouldn't publish him because of this. He wrote a good story on Warden Duffy which was published.[1]

Brydon's successor was Michael "Harry O" Harris, cofounder, with Suge Knight, of Death Row Records. (Knight himself was convicted of murder charges in 2018.) Harris was from Los Angeles and was serving twenty-eight years on a conspiracy to commit murder charge and drug trafficking.

His business enterprises, including the drug trade, had allowed him to accumulate considerable personal wealth. How much? In 2005 Harris and his wife divided $107 million in Monterey Superior Court in their divorce settlement. Lydia Harris had received the colossal judgment from Suge Knight in a civil suit in Los Angeles County.[2]

When the CDCR cut the prison budget and eliminated the funding for San Quentin's Vocational Print Shop shortly after the *San Quentin News* resumed production, the *San Quentin News* could no longer be published at state expense. It published the last edition on the Heidelberg offset letterpress inside the prison print shop in February 2010.

"How I feel about it? Actually I'm disappointed, you know," said Richard (Bonaru) Richardson, who worked on the printing press. "They say they offering rehabilitation programs but yet, they taking them. So, they leave us in a situation where we're just sitting around the yard and don't have really nothing to do."[3]

The story of the newspaper's revival might have ended right there. Instead, the story took another unexpected turn.

ENTER THE CIVILIAN ADVISERS

One of the first things Ayers did when he restarted the paper was to recruit a handful of civilian advisers, all former journalists, to help launch the newspaper. Ayers recruited John C. Eagan, a longtime AP reporter; Joan Lisetor, a Marin County journalist who had been involved with the paper before the shutdown in the 1980s; and Steve McNamara, former publisher of a weekly newspaper, the *Pacific Sun*. The move was a practical necessity. The initial staff of inmate writers and reporters had no experience whatsoever in journalism. In the early days, the advisers *were* the staff. They made all the editorial decisions, edited the copy, laid out the paper, wrote the headlines, and called the shots.

The assembled group of civilian advisers was formidable. Besides his work with the Associated Press, Eagen was a former editor of the *Novato Advance* and *Petaluma Argus Courier* and was the former publisher of the Marinscope Community Newspapers; Lisetor was a former writer for the

Marin Independent Journal and a previous adviser to the *San Quentin News* during the 1980s when it was judged the best prison newspaper in the United States; McNamara, besides being former owner, editor, and publisher of the *Pacific Sun,* was a former writer and editor for the *Winston-Salem Journal,* the *Miami Herald,* and the *San Francisco Examiner,* and was a former president of the California Society of Newspaper Editors, former director of the California Newspaper Publishers Association, and founding president of both the National Association of Alternative Newsweeklies and the California Association of Alternative Newsweeklies; Linda Xiques was former managing editor of the *Pacific Sun;* Jan Perry was a former copy editor at the *Pacific Sun;* and Nikki Meredith was a former reporter for the *Pacific Sun.*

The prisoners worked on the paper more than sixty hours per week. They were in the newsroom from the time it opened until it closed, and they returned to their cells, except for their meal breaks or to attend rehab programs or education classes. García and Juan Haines were paid $57 per month by the CDCR, while the remaining staff were paid $48 each per month. But none of the men received all their pay because 55 percent to 75 percent of their wages was garnished by the state for restitution and victim services.

From its inception the revived *San Quentin News* was boldly middle-of-the-road. It embraced many of the values of the original set of advisers, who were older, white Marin County homeowners. They read the *Marin Independent Journal.* They were comfortable in legacy journalism's worldview. The paper would embody an upbeat, optimistic viewpoint, stressing hopeful stories of reconciliation and success. The reader would not find impassioned screeds attacking institutional racism or mass incarceration. Former editor Elmo Chattman's idea of "my truth" would have no place in the new paper. But as the inmate staff became more self-confident, the newspaper began to develop its own, distinctive voice. It was a long way from Eldridge Cleaver, but neither did it reflect the positions of Supreme Court Justice Clarence Thomas.

Editor in chief Harris and the team of advisers set about coping with the financial crisis. Adviser McNamara, who had been the owner of Pacific Sun Printing in San Raphael, worked out a deal with the new owners to produce the newspaper at cost.

Convicted drug dealer and editor Harris paid the invoices from Marin Sun Printing out of his own pocket. The irony was lost on nobody that funds possibly derived from cocaine sales in Los Angeles in the 1970s went toward publishing a prison newspaper in 2010.

Shortly afterward Harris completed his sentence and walked out of San Quentin, taking his checkbook with him. US marshals were awaiting him and took him to another penitentiary to begin serving a term for a federal conviction, where he remained in 2019.

McNamara, the civilian adviser, created the nonprofit Prison Media Project and applied to the Marin Community Foundation to fund the paper. Grants also came in from the Annenberg Foundation and Columbia Foundation. The resurrection was under way.

FIRMLY REESTABLISHED

At the September 2016 awards event, Arnulfo García, editor in chief for six years, wearing a freshly pressed powder-blue prison-issue shirt and creased denim pants and white sneakers, walked to the podium. He was especially careful about his appearance. The prison blue does not allow for much variety, but García made sure his was neat. One of the prize perks of working for the newspaper was that the office had its own electric iron. And García noticed the dress of others, often stopping in midconversation to pay a compliment about an item of clothing. "Welcome everyone to the *San Quentin News* first award ceremony. My name is Arnulfo García. I'm the executive editor for the SQN editorial board."

That night was probably Arnulfo García's proudest moment. He was the third executive editor to hold that position in the revived newspaper, following in the footsteps of Brydon and Harris. And he had presided over a breathtaking period of expansion and recognition.

"I've been at *SQ* since 2008 and I was assigned to the print shop," said García. "A week later, I was called into the office and told to find another job because I didn't even know how to turn a computer on. Friends of mine knew that I liked to write, so they spoke to instructor John Wilkerson and promised that they would help me learn how to operate a computer. I was called back into the office and told that I would be given a chance, but

I was to only do print shop work and that I would not be able to work or write for the *San Quentin News*."

In 2008 and in characteristic fashion García brushed aside all the discouraging comments. Instead, he mastered the computer. In addition, he joined the *San Quentin News* Journalism Guild. It was a journalist-in-training program for aspiring prison writers. Adviser John Eagen put the men through a kind of Journalism 101 course, teaching them the essentials of reporting, the AP Stylebook, and the good old inverted pyramid style of newspaper writing.

García was an apt pupil, and he proved himself to be a popular leader. He was elected chairman of the Journalism Guild by a "landslide," as he described it to the audience.

"When the print shop closed in 2010, my boss Mr. John Wilkerson gave me a laudatory chrono," he said, referring to his performance evaluation, "and said I was the best clerk he ever had." That was an important turnaround. But another big one was in store.

> Just before Michael Harris was to depart, he called me to his cell and said I was going to be the next editor in chief. I said, "But there are others more qualified than I, like Aly Tamboura." He [Harris] said, "You're the one, and all the advisers have approved it." I would serve as editor in chief for the next five years, and I step aside to pursue another dream: *San Quentin News*'s first magazine. At this time I would like to give special thanks to those who have contributed to *San Quentin News* while I was editor in chief.

ENTER UC BERKELEY'S BUSINESS SCHOOL

2/12/13

Dear Dean Lyons,

Here's the deal. The *San Quentin News* is the only inmate-produced newspaper in the country. I teach a class in the Journalism School in which Berkeley students work with inmates to produce the newspaper, which circulates mostly among the 4,000 or so inmates in the prison.

The inmate editors are ambitious, however. They've secured modest foundation funding. They want to increase their press run and become the newspaper of record for the whole California prison system and its 120,000 or so inmates in more than 30 institutions.

They need help with their business model and with managing their growth. These skills are beyond my pay grade and my competence.

Do you see a possibility for collaboration?

Thank you.
Bill Drummond

Thanks, Bill, for reaching out. Yes, I think we can help. Nora Silver runs our Non-Profit and Public Leadership Center and has a program called Social Sector Solutions that does work along these lines. I'll let you two connect directly.

Rich

Bill, FYI, my wife Jen teaches at the prison and may be able to help Nora and the MBA team.

It was strictly a shot in the dark when I emailed Rich Lyons, then dean of UC Berkeley's Haas School of Business, in February of 2013. His encouraging response caught me by surprise. But it began to make sense. Jen Lyons, the dean's wife, taught basic literacy and math classes in San Quentin's Prison University Project (PUP) and was a regular volunteer at the prison.

This connection with Rich and Jen Lyons was a vivid example of the ecology of rehabilitation in the Bay Area that winds up beneficial to prisoners. San Quentin is the only prison located in a major metropolitan area in California. It has more than three hundred ongoing programs and more than two thousand volunteers serving an inmate population of around four thousand as of 2018, primarily the approximately two thousand "mainline" prisoners (the others are Death Row, with about 750 souls; the Adjustment Center, where prisoners are held as punishment or in protective custody; and the Reception Center, where recently sentenced prisoners from the counties are sorted out before going off to their eventual assignment). Prisons located in remote areas of California are lucky to have ten programs.

I made an appointment to see Professor Nora Silver the next day at 3:00 p.m. in her office in the sprawling Haas complex across from the

Memorial Stadium on the far eastern edge of the Berkeley campus. Arriving early, I sat on a bench in the corridor outside her office. Frankly, I thought it would be a reach to get Haas involved, solely on the basis of my assumption about what business schools actually do, namely train people to make profits. Prisons do turn profits, but not for inmates.

Silver welcomed me warmly into her office and listened intently as I explained about how my involvement with the prison newspaper had come about. I told her about Arnulfo García's ambitious plans for expansion and described how well the editing relationship with UC Berkeley students was going. She was enthusiastic. Silver explained how her center worked. The *San Quentin News* would have to apply formally for assistance.

If the paper was selected, Haas would provide more than seven hundred hours of consultation support prepared by MBA students. The goal would be creation of a detailed business plan. The program was officially known as the Haas-Bridgespan Consulting Teams. Each team consisted of five MBAs and other students assigned to a given project. For the Haas students this would be an "experiential learning course" under the direction of the Bridgespan Group, a nonprofit consulting company. Don Howard, a partner in Bridgespan, and Silver, who holds a PhD, taught the course.

Silver sent me the application form. It was daunting. It envisioned clients as being proper agencies that had offices, cubicles, copy machines, coffee breaks, internet connections. Bridgespan had never contemplated a prison—the open latrines, the Hole, occasional stabbings, and catwalks with armed correctional officers on the Lower Yard at San Quentin.

Nevertheless, I reported back to the editors at the prison on my conversation with Silver. It all came as music to the ears of García, Haines, and the other editors. Their previous campaign had raised around $60,000, and the costs of printing and distributing the paper ran around $5,000 a month. So they were burning through their nest egg fast. A legitimate business plan from the Haas Business School would be a launching pad from which the paper could build a new fund-raising campaign that would allow the *San Quentin News* not only to endure but to thrive.

BUSINESS SCHOOL MEETS THE PRISONERS

4/18/13

Dear Nora,

The *San Quentin News* editors have hammered out their proposal. The question is how should the application be delivered to you? They can print out hard copy, which I would be happy to bring to you. Or, they can copy it to a thumb drive, and I can forward the digital version to you in email.

In addition, I would like to suggest that you pay a visit to the SQ News offices at the prison. You would benefit from meeting the people behind the project. If this appeals to you, you can be cleared for entry into the prison. You would have to provide me with your date of birth, CA drivers license number and social security number. I will pass these along to the warden. It normally takes about a week to obtain clearance.

I make the visit to the prison three times per week, Tuesday evening, Wednesday morning and Friday afternoon. Would be happy to provide transportation.

Thank you.
Bill Drummond

Clearing Silver into San Quentin was not a problem. Assuming the visitor had a clean record (including no DUIs), he or she would be permitted to enter the prison under escort by another civilian who had a special Brown or Green Card clearance. Silver and I spoke first in February, but it was June before she was able to visit. Part of the delay was due to San Quentin being locked down for a period because of a virus outbreak.

It was not until Monday, June 24, 2013, at 5:15 p.m. that I picked up Professor Silver and drove her across the Richmond-San Raphael Bridge to San Quentin to meet García and the other prison editors so she could get an idea of what she might be getting herself into.

Nothing I could say would have prepared her for this experience. Walking through the clanking, interlocking gates and finally emerging in the quiet, manicured gardens of the plaza outside the religious buildings often confuses the visitor. The elaborate security measures vanish once the visitor walks from the Count Gate into the plaza with its Lincoln roses. At first glance, it looks like a public park. But then one walks down a gentle slope beneath an observation post manned by an armed correctional officer and on the left is the "dungeon," made of roughly hewn concrete blocks with an iron gate, a relic of nineteenth-century penology, more suited to *The Count of Monte Cristo*. The dungeon is preserved as a museum piece, visited only by the occasional prison tour. Winding left around another corner, the visitor looks down upon the sunken four-acre expanse of the Lower Yard.

When you turn around the corner beneath a gun tower, it's as though a curtain has been raised on an opera. The yard is filled with prisoners engaged in all matter of athletic pursuits—jogging around the track, playing tennis, punching an Everlast heavy bag, shooting hoops.

As Silver and I descended into the Lower Yard, inmates were drifting back to the recreation area after having dined in the mess hall. As usual, they stared at the strangers. They meant no harm; nevertheless, they presented a formidable and daunting spectacle. Their clothing was made up of all manner of baggy denim, stenciled in bold yellow letters "CDCR PRISONER." Even though prisoner garb is state-issue and intended to be uniform, every inmate has, in one way or another, managed to create his own distinctive look, whether it is hair, tattoos, head gear, pants, or shirt.

On the sixty-degree June evening, a handful of inmates were stripped to the waist. Many had uncommonly huge upper-body muscles. Twenty years ago, the CDCR banned the weight piles from all the state prisons. But the ruling did not affect pull-up bars, heavy bags, dip bars, or sit-up boards. Determined inmates are probably more buffed now than they were before the weight-pile ban.

Many inmates displayed complex, alarmingly vivid tattoos. Tattooing is another practice that's officially banned but thrives.

A crowd of men, predominately African American and Latino, turned around to check us out. A couple of correctional officers standing around a small wooden hut, their hands in their utility belts, were all the law enforcement in evidence on the Lower Yard.

Professor Silver looked down on picnic tables and a tennis court on one end of a scraggly dirt athletic field, populated by year-round Canada geese. Arrayed on the left side of the playing field is a group of one-story portable buildings that make up the education complex. The *San Quentin News* made its home in those days in what had once been a classroom.

Along the way we passed three sets of open latrines. The word *noncha-lant* describes Professor Silver's reaction.

A SUMMIT MEETING

The *San Quentin News* crew were all on hand to greet Silver and pay her the respect befitting a VIP visitor. Friendly and charming as usual, García briefed her on how the newspaper did business and his ambitious plans for expansion. They seemed to hit it off famously. Silver's questions went into some detail about the publishing procedures, discussing the nuts and bolts of the business operations. We were in the prison for about an hour.

On the drive back to Berkeley Silver was already thinking of ways to put the newspaper on a more businesslike footing. She said, for example, that UPS had a foundation and that perhaps it might be persuaded to underwrite some of the costs of distributing the newspapers to some of the other prisons in the state. All the while the application for support from Silver's center was still under review, but I suspected then that it was a done deal.

After the meeting, I wrote to Jen Lyons:

Arnulfo and Juan did a clear and forceful outline of their ambitions for the paper. They handled Nora's probing questions well. She gave a necessary tone of practical expectations, and they listened.

This was her first prison visit, and she went through all the usual stages, apprehension, nervousness, curiosity, confusion, and finally an "ah-ha" experience. I think on balance she decided that this was a project worthy of Haas. On the ride back, she was making a number of great suggestions about implementing the study.

Shortly afterward, I received this message from Professor Silver:

Bill and Jen,

I want to thank you both for helping prepare us for our work with *San Quentin News,* and for offering to help our student team in their consultation with Arnulfo and Juan to expand distribution of the newspaper beyond San Quentin.

Please be sure to mark the following two dates on your calendars, to represent *San Quentin News* at the Social Sector Solutions kick-off and finale, when we bring together all teams, clients and coaches to present the scope of the work and brief the teams on the project, client context and logistics (kick-off); and de-brief the results, learnings and effectiveness of the consultations (finale).

Kick-off
Friday, August 30, 2013, 3–5pm
Office of FSG, 123 Mission Street, Floor 8 SF (Embarcadero BART)

Finale
Friday, December 6, 2013, 3–5pm
Office of FSG, 123 Mission Street, Floor 8 SF (Embarcadero BART)

Sincere thanks to you for helping make this partnership possible. With the difficult logistical, communications and political challenges, we simply could not do this without you.

All best
Nora

The Haas Social Sector program came with a price: $10,000. Any agencies selected to participate would agree to pay the fee once the project was completed. This payment would later become a bone of contention between adviser Steve McNamara, who acted as treasurer, and the inmate editors. More on that later.

THE HAAS TEAM ARRIVES

On August 29, 2013, I sent in the paperwork to clear the Haas team to visit the *San Quentin News* for the next twelve months. The team consisted of six members: Jon Michael Spurlock, Shilpa Grover, Glen Ottinger, Virginia Anne Zimpel, Laura Tilghman, and Robert Todd Brantley. Rarely have I seen a more impressive collection of résumés. Spurlock was an ex-naval officer with a splendid academic record, and he also ran marathons. He would stay deeply involved with the newspaper even after the formal Haas project had ended.

The Haas team had great credentials, but San Quentin was still a prison. Even though Haas accepted the newspaper for the consultation arrangement, the question remained in my mind whether the prison authorities would allow this partnership to take place. In California, as nearly as I could learn, there was no precedent for an inmate organization contracting with an outside consulting agency.

Here is where García's immense political and diplomatic skills came into play. It was his job to sell the Haas partnership to the warden's office. In his mind there was never a question. He said, "I'll handle that. It'll be okay. This is the way it's going to be." He was in the "shot caller" mode as the man who could make things happen.

At this point I was slowly becoming a believer. I had doubted that the inmates would be able to create a credible application. I had doubted that the Social Sector Center would accept the prison newspaper as a suitable partner. I had doubted that the MBA students would provide anything useful as far as putting the *San Quentin News* on a more businesslike footing. And I had doubted that the warden would permit the project to get off the ground.

In each case, I was proved wrong, especially with regard to how the MBA students would react to working with prisoners. Just like Silver, the Haas crew went through the same emotional waypoints when they first went through the prison gates, namely apprehension, nervousness, curiosity, confusion, and finally an "ah-ha" experience.

The informed consent document the prison distributes has a warning:

No Hostage Policy

Familiarize yourself with the following statute taken from California Code of Regulations, Title 15, Section 3304, Hostages:

> "Employees must not permit inmates or others to use hostages to escape from custody or otherwise interfere with orderly institutional operations. Hostages will not be recognized for bargaining purposes. All inmates, visitors, and staff will be informed of this regulation."

In other words, you are on your own. This warning alone would cause a reasonable person to have misgivings. And the long walk through the Lower Yard past the intense stares from the inmates does little to relieve one's anxieties. But the first face-to-face encounters invariably put the guest's mind at ease.

Perhaps fifteen minutes or so into the visit, the guest no longer notices the blue denims. The conversations usually reveal that the prisoner is way more intelligent than one might expect. He is often better informed about current affairs than the average person, especially about criminal justice issues. Prisoners read everything they can get their hands on, newspapers, magazines, as well as books.

11 Media Recognition

11/2/13

Dear Professor Drummond,

My name is Melissa and I am a reporter from the *Daily Californian*. I am writing an article about the *San Quentin News*, and would love to speak to you about your involvement with the newspaper. Would you be willing to talk to me sometime in the next few days?

   Thank you for your time!

Best,
Melissa

The email from UC Berkeley student Melissa Wen, then a reporter for the campus newspaper, was the first step in gaining recognition for the reborn *San Quentin News*. Wen's interest came about because several of the students enrolled in my UC class to help edit the newspaper talked up their experience with their friends. Attention to the prison newspaper spread first through word of mouth in a college newsroom. A story in the college newspaper was a modest enough start, but I had no idea where it would lead.

   The involvement of the Haas Business School in the project was the new angle. Until that time coverage of the *San Quentin News* was confined

mainly to the Marin *Independent Journal,* for whom the prison had always
been a local story on account of its location nearby in Marin County.
Melissa Wen did her homework and interviewed members of the Haas
team. When she spoke with them, they were just a couple of weeks away
from presenting their final report and their business plan. Her extensive
and timely story was published December 3, 2013:

> This semester, six UC Berkeley graduate students hatched a business plan
> that led them to prison. It is their clients, however, who are wearing the blue
> uniforms. The business and policy students, who enrolled in a UC Berkeley
> Haas School of Business class that provides guidance to nonprofits, arrived
> at prison to assist the only inmate-run newspaper in California, the *San
> Quentin News.* A little more than a dozen felons write, edit and design from
> behind the walls of San Quentin State Prison in Marin County. "They are, in
> my mind, serious journalists," said Bill Drummond, a UC Berkeley journal-
> ism professor and an adviser for the newspaper.

The *Daily Cal* story falls in the category of "one small step for a man,
one giant leap for mankind." The day after the story ran, I brought a copy
into the newsroom in the prison. The men were proud and abashedly
pleased that they would be featured in the *Daily Caliornian.*

I sent Melissa Wen an email: "Visited SQ yesterday. Editors thank you
for the story. Arnulfo said it was the first time he was portrayed in a positive light in a newspaper. He plans to show a copy to his daughter."

The *Daily Cal* story took off in the prestige media on the outside. In the
ensuing weeks major publications in the country did feature stories portraying the newspaper in a positive light. On January 1, 2014, Chris Magerian of
the *Los Angeles Times* published this story about the *San Quentin News:*

> The paper typically has an aspirational tone, emphasizing uplifting stories
> about inmates improving their lives and taking advantage of education pro-
> grams. Headlines refer to prisoners who "promise to work for peace" or go
> from "criminal life to positive futures."
>
> Staffers say their work can induce soul-searching, that telling other peo-
> ple's stories helps them explore their own lives. And it can be a source of
> pride.
>
> Rahsaan Thomas, a convicted killer, mailed his mother a copy of the
> October issue, where he appeared in a front-page photo of a basketball
> game.

"It was the first time I was in the paper and nobody got shot," said Thomas, 43, the sports editor.

Before they reached San Quentin, many of the editors' only brush with journalism was as subjects of articles about the crimes that put them behind bars. Each issue of the monthly *San Quentin News* is a reminder that their lives did not end when they were locked up.

The Haas team delivered its fifty-seven-page report and business plan in December 2013. It was an impressive and well-written document. "This report presents the detailed conclusions and recommendations from our project with *San Quentin News* conducted as part of the UC Berkeley-Haas 'Social Sector Solutions: Social Enterprises' course. It provides a business plan that will allow the *San Quentin News* enterprise to meet its stated primary goal of newspaper circulation to every prisoner in the California Department of Corrections and Rehabilitation (CDCR). It also addresses how to meet this goal while ensuring long-term financial and organizational sustainability."

If you looked closely, you would see that it was student work, for a class. But it had the credibility of a respected business school, and the MBA students had done their homework. Their work was replete with charts, graphs, tables, and numbers. The Haas Plan gave the prison journalists the legitimacy they so eagerly sought. The executive summary was the essence of Arnulfo Garcia's vision:

> Reaching all 120,000 California prisoners plus external audiences with *San Quentin News* will require scaling to over 10 times its current circulation. This very large circulation growth will require significant increases in funding and transformative increases in organizational capacity (i.e., the activity level supported by SQN staff and supporters) and basic business functions like marketing and operations (e.g., printing and distribution). Successfully reaching the goal will also require a high level of discipline in planning and execution by SQN and its supporters. We believe SQN can expand to reach every prisoner on an aggressive but still reasonable timeframe of 12 years. As a stretch goal, if all activity goes exactly according to plan and no unforeseen challenges emerge, SQN may be able to reach its goal in as little as 10 years. On the other hand, reaching the goal in 15 years would still be considered a very successful expansion.
>
> As expected, SQN's ability to grow depends foremost on its ability to secure the funding required to fuel that growth. This funding will have to

come from both unearned (e.g., grants) and earned (e.g., subscriptions) revenue sources, at least until goal attainment. Specifically, we recommend that SQN should expand prisoner circulation to 120,000 no faster than it achieves 10,000 paying subscriptions. In turn, obtaining grant funding and subscriptions requires effective marketing and continuous improvement of the paper to meet the needs of all key audiences. Finally, executing all aspects will require additional organizational support, business function specialization, and a transition to an operational model that can support the printing and distribution of 120,000 papers per month.

The ink on the Haas plan was not dry when disaster struck. The warden, Kevin Chappelle, suspended the newspaper for forty-five days. Despite all the recognition and accolades, the *San Quentin News* was suddenly out of business. Here is how it all went down, based on interviews with several people with firsthand knowledge.

The December 2013 issue contained "disapproved content," according to public information officer Sam Robinson. He said the inmates had "circumvented the editorial process."[1] These terms had a disturbingly familiar ring. These were the very words the wardens had used in the disputes back in the early 1980s that had led to the twenty-year shutdown.

The five thousand or so copies containing the disapproved content were destroyed. A whole new press run was done and distributed.

This incident represented my initiation into the delicate politics of prisons. The warden never specified what the "disapproved content" might have been. What the offense involved was a photograph taken during a Shakespeare production of *The Merchant of Venice* that took place in the Protestant Chapel.[2] The Marin Shakespeare Company had been staging productions for nearly fifteen years at the prison, casting inmates as well as actors from outside.

Several inmate staff members told me that after the page proofs were submitted to Lieutenant Robinson for approval, the design editor noticed that one photograph would not reproduce. So he substituted another photograph, which depicted prisoners and an actress lying down. According to a prisoner familiar with the incident, someone with a prurient disposition could imagine that the prisoner and actress were "spooning," but it would have been a stretch. The prisoners later ruefully referred to the photo of the recumbent figures as the "yoga photo."

The design editor, Richard (Bonaru) Richardson, did not inform the PIO of the substituted picture. Robinson told the paper's staff that the editors had not followed "journalistic standards and a checks and balances system where copy, photographs, graphics and other content goes through an editing process."Any suggestion of sexuality in a prison publication is out of bounds, no matter how benign. In this case, "the yoga photo" failed the "zero-tolerance" test.

Obviously, however, more was at play in the incident than the substitution of one innocuous picture for another. A number of issues below the surface may have played a role in the forty-five-day suspension. The prison officials and some civilian advisers were unhappy with a *San Quentin News* Facebook page, which the authorities accused of bias and editorializing. That page was shortly afterward taken down. The civilian volunteer who managed the Facebook page was subsequently "excommunicated": that is, she had her access privileges to the prison withdrawn.

When the *Independent Journal* interviewed me, I said, "The picture in question has no salacious content. The picture they published was the same content [as the picture that was approved, a depiction of an inmate and volunteer]. It's an unfortunate and unhappy incident." I described the warden's action as "overkill" and said it had had a devastating effect on morale.

My comments did not go over well in the warden's office, as I soon found out. When I visited the prison in February 2014 after the *Independent Journal* story ran, editor in chief García was waiting for me. Though his countenance was normally sunny, he had a pained expression. "I need to talk to you," he said, and we walked out to the Lower Yard.

García let me know that the suspension was really unfair and "really messed up" but said there was nothing we could do about it. With every phrase in which he, in effect, reprimanded me, he would flash a quick smile. Arnulfo and I were friends, but as a UC professor I enjoyed a huge advantage over him in power. Yet he played his hand confidently and deftly. It was a plea I could not refuse. I had to make things right with Lieutenant Robinson.

This conversation forced me to see the *San Quentin News* from a different standpoint. The issue meant something different to García than it did to me. As a journalist, I saw the warden's suspension as a brute abuse of power. In court the suspension would not stand up. It was a rank violation of the First Amendment. Yet although I might be right, my continuing vocal resistance would have been disastrous to the newspaper. The warden always has the nuclear option. He or she can shut the paper down, as was done in the 1980s. The fact was that my comments to the *Independent Journal* had embarrassed the warden and reflected badly on the PIO. Robinson had most likely come to García, the shot-caller, to make things right. I was expected to acknowledge my error and promise to steer clear of criticizing the San Quentin administration. And I'm sure Arnulfo said, "I'll take care of it."

I imagined the final scene from the Roman Polanski film *Chinatown*. The detective looks into the eyes of the Jack Nicholson character and says, "Forget it, Jake. It's Chinatown."

And so I did something I have rarely done. I apologized.

2/28/2014

Dear Sam,

Arnulfo talked to me yesterday about the problems my statements in the media caused. I apologized to him, and I now would like to apologize to you.

In the future, I won't take it upon myself to speak for the advisors. I look forward to a long and productive partnership.

Yours,
Bill

The newspaper resumed normal operations in March 2014. The inmate staff had stayed in touch, even though they were locked out of the newsroom.

"For the forty-five days that we were shut down it didn't stop the *San Quentin News* from reporting," said Richard (Bonaru) Richardson, who had succeeded García as editor in chief of the paper. "We met on the yard in the dugout and sometimes in someone's cell to discuss the upcoming events that needed to be covered. Every event that took place in SQ, one of our staff was there with a Neo." If you've ever seen a TRS-80, you'll recognize a Neo. It's a dumb laptop. It does word processing, but has no internet access. The *San Quentin News* had dozens of these devices. The Neo could be connected to a PC and its files and folders downloaded.

"Thanks to donors we were able to get enough Neos for the whole staff," said Richardson. "Thanks to the Nolan and Barton law firm for donating over fifty Neos to the *SQ News.*" The Nolan and Barton firm had represented Arnulfo García for more than fifteen years. "Of course the editor in chief, Arnulfo, wanted to take full responsibility for the paper being shut down," Richardson said, "but in all actuality, it was my fault for switching a picture at the last minute. Even though I still believe I was right and the administration was wrong, I will accept the responsibility because they didn't approve of it. I have great sources, and I don't think anything was wrong with my judgment."

Ironically, the suspension proved to be the best thing that could ever have happened to the newspaper. It spurred controversy and media attention across the country. The forty-five-day shutdown gave the *San Quentin News* a giant dose of credibility in the eyes of the outside media world. Suddenly in the estimation of big media around the country, the motley crew had become a beleaguered bunch of prisoner/journalists standing up for the First Amendment.

On March 20, 2014, the *San Quentin News* was honored by the Northern California chapter of the Society of Professional Journalists at a sold-out banquet in San Francisco. The paper received the Annual James Madison Freedom of Information Award for excellence in journalism because of its efforts to inform the public about mass incarceration in California.

Winning this award gave a big boost to the morale of the prison journalists, still wincing from the forty-five-day suspension. Of course, they were not allowed to attend the banquet. But through the miracle of video, a UC Berkeley graduate student, Sarah La Fleur Vetter, was able to get all the men in front of a camera, while García read an acceptance message, which was shown on a projector to the SPJ audience. García expressed appreciation for the award and thanked the SPJ. He also thanked the volunteers from the UC Berkeley School of Journalism, the Haas School of Business and the civilian advisers, and all of the volunteers who had helped the newspaper achieve its goals.

Former *San Quentin News* editor Richard Lindsey, paroled in 2013 having served his sentence on a murder conviction, accepted the award on behalf of the newspaper staff. Lindsey had spent twenty-six years in prison. While behind bars, he also facilitated the creation of the Victim Offender Education Group. Since his parole, Lindsey had worked as an electrician in San Francisco.

"It feels awesome for this recognition to be given," Lindsey said. "To be sitting in a room with some of the highest-ranking journalists of our time. Sitting in the room with them and to be recognized by them as their peers; it feels awesome."[3]

Another honoree at the banquet was then-state senator Leland Yee, a champion of prison reform. In 2018 Yee want off to federal prison for five years after his conviction on bribery and arms trafficking charges. He was arrested just days after the banquet.

Sam Robinson later told the *Los Angeles Times* that the award to the *San Quentin News* was "well deserved."[4] "The *San Quentin News* is published because CDCR allows, encourages and dedicates resources to it," he said. "It is a rehabilitative program that prepares inmates for their release to society."

Thomas Peele, an investigative reporter for the Bay Area News Group and the cochair of the committee honoring the *San Quentin News*, said, "If there was indeed no security risk, this type of suspension certainly underscores the types of difficulties these prison journalists face in publishing their newspaper." And he added: "We recognized the newspaper because of the inherent difficulties the journalists there face in doing their work."

The suspension had another unexpected outcome. Heretofore, decisions on the newspaper content had been the preserve of the San Quentin warden and his designee, the local public information officer. But CDCR officials in Sacramento decided that the newspaper was too important to be left up to the local San Quentin administration.

After the paper resumed normal operations, it received a delegation from the CDCR public affairs office in Sacramento. "The CDCR sent three staff members from its press office to meet with the *News*. At the time, we thought we were going to get shut down for good," said Richardson. "But the CDCR's objective was far from closing or controlling the newspaper. In their words, they wanted to 'make it better.'"

The two sides struck a bargain. Sacramento would make a public affairs professional available to copy-read and fact-check each edition of the paper. That was no small commitment of staff time: the paper is published once a month, and each edition is more than eighteen thousand words (twenty pages). But Sacramento figured that since the paper was getting so much attention, it needed to look more professional and be more reliable.

"After all the writing, editing, and proofing is done," said Richardson, "the CDCR public information officer II, Krissi Khokhobashvili, reviews every article, holding her office to its word to make the paper better. This process takes place before our supervisor, San Quentin public information officer Lt. Sam Robinson reviews the paper before it goes to press."

Krissi, as she's known because her Georgian last name is unpronounceable, joined CDCR in March 2014 after a career as a journalist at publications in California's Central Valley. She holds a bachelor of arts degree in journalism from the University of Montana. After a story is finished in the newsroom and the local editors sign off on it, the story goes to Krissi by email. She reviews it and sends it back. Thereupon the completed paper goes to Robinson for final clearance.

Almost all of Krissi's corrections are grammar, punctuation, or style changes. Once in a while, however, she might challenge a story on policy grounds. The agreement with the prisoners is that the writers and editors include any such objection as a quote in the story. The result would be a story with more authority than it might otherwise have. Here is a sample of her work from October 27, 2017:[5]

> Here are some of the things I caught:
>
> *Page 1*
>
> Population: 3,989
> Sidebar: Take out comma after "Mexican music"
> Change "self awareness" to "self-awareness"
> Change to "Counselors recognized"
> Beauty: There's a space missing between the comma and Marleny in the cutline
> There's a space missing between "Beauty" and "on" in the jump line
>
> *Page 2*
> Arnulfo: Arnulfo's name misspelled in cutline
> Pull quote should read "More than 300 people chanted 'I am Arnulfo Garcia'"
> Nane Alejandrez's name misspelled in cutline

Krissi's are not the only eyes that review *San Quentin News* copy. Before she sees them the stories have been read carefully by any of around a dozen civilian editors and roughly a dozen visiting editors from UC

Berkeley. The *San Quentin News* is perhaps the most intensively edited newspaper in the state.

The appointment of a higher-level public affairs professional has enabled Sacramento to keep a watchful, if seemingly benign, eye over the paper's content. It has also provided political cover for the newsroom, because if Sacramento approves a story and controversy ensues, the inmate editors and writers will be off the hook. They will not likely be fired or shipped off to another prison, as happened on occasion in the 1980s.

Nevertheless, writers and editors feel vulnerable and they heed the Ayers dictum that they don't want to do something that would get the paper shut down. They tread softly around any stories they know would create controversy either for San Quentin locally or the CDCR systemwide.

The outcome of the review arrangement with Sacramento was a smoother flow of copy and a much more reliable vetting system.

The most notable exception occurred about six months after the "yoga picture" controversy. The story involved a San Quentin correctional officer who underwent gender reassignment. Hired as Michael Hauwert, Mandi Camille Hauwert, then thirty-four, told her story to the *San Quentin News* in 2014.

When I came into the newsroom one day, I noticed Officer Hauwert sitting talking to a group of writers. The story about her transition was up on a computer screen. The talk was friendly and congenial. The story was ready to go, but it did not run for another couple of months. Finally it appeared on November 30, 2014.

> Seven years ago, M. Hauwert was hired as a male correctional officer at San Quentin State Prison. Now Officer Hauwert is transitioning to a female identity.
>
> "I'm hoping that someday it'll get to the point where we don't need to make gender identification an issue," Hauwert said in an interview.
>
> Hauwert, who is 34, began her transition by first growing her hair out and using bobby pins. She later started using makeup. A year before she came out, she got her ears pierced. However, male officers cannot wear earrings, so Hauwert wore Band-Aids over her ears. Since then, Hauwert has legally changed her name and her birth certificate now declares that she is a female.
>
> "At first, I was a transgender woman who was cross-dressing," Hauwert said. "Then I began experimenting with makeup and clothes for my body type. Some of the outfits were horrendous!"

She first decided to identify as transsexual at age 23, while still in the Navy. Military records show that Hauwert served for eight years and received an honorable discharge from the Navy.[6]

The stonewalling in Sacramento came against a background of legal issues involving trans prisoners. Several inmates went to court to demand that the state pay for their gender reassignment surgery. The courts eventually sided with the inmates. The CDCR apparently saw the Hauwert story as compromising its position in court. If the state would pay for a sex change operation for a correctional officer, then why not for an inmate?[7]

The Hauwert scoop generated a cascade of stories in the mainstream media about the correctional officer's remarkable journey. And it wasn't long afterward that more stories appeared about the *San Quentin News*. One was a *New York Times* story, written on May 20, 2014, by Patricia Leigh Brown, that described how, in a notorious prison best known for its death row, the men are committed to what Juan Haines, the 56-year-old managing editor, who is serving 55 years to life for that 1996 bank robbery, calls 'boots on the ground' journalism, accomplished without cellphones or direct Internet access. 'It's about being heard in a place that's literally shut off from the world,' he said."

That piece inspired Mark Berman of the *Washington Post* a few day later to write a story titled, "Five Things I Learned Reading the *San Quentin News*." He lists stories on a prison art exhibit, a forum with the Santa Clara County district attorney, the decline in public support for capital punishment, a historian writing on San Quentin, and sports at San Quentin.[8]

The story of the forty-five-day suspension and the controversy over the "yoga picture" shows that the journalism produced inside the prison is there because the warden allows it. And on a larger scale the history of the *San Quentin News* has proved that hard-hitting investigative work that points out lapses in administration or staff misfeasance is likely to be suppressed. Everybody in the newsroom knows that. It goes back to Warden Ayers's admonition in 2008. If the governor or the director of corrections were to call and say, 'Shut that damn thing down,' the editors and reporters would have failed. And as in 1984, the courts would be unwilling to intervene if the newspaper were simply to cease operations.

By definition, the *San Quentin News* operates under a regime of self-censorship. It is by no means the only media organization to do so.

But within its own limitations the reborn newspaper has been surprisingly effective in ways most people do not appreciate. Its most important contribution to combating mass incarceration is that it has helped to change the narrative about prisoners and ex-convicts. In the words of the *L.A. Times* article, its emphasis on "uplifting stories about inmates improving their lives and taking advantage of education programs has been an antidote to the decades of get-tough-on-crime stories." It is a story line that not only has proved acceptable to the warden and to Sacramento but also has found a following in the wider world.

12 Sam Robinson

García's tenure as editor in chief ran smoothly. Considering how ambitiously he pushed out the boundaries of what the newspaper was doing, he encountered surprising little resistance. He had a mix of personal charm and political savvy. He kept the various interest groups on the paper working together. But most important, he had a great working relationship with the man at the top of the pyramid. That was public information officer Sam Robinson, to whom a succession of wardens had assigned the oversight of the newspaper.

A twenty-year veteran of CDCR, Robinson was a black correctional lieutenant who was de facto publisher of the newspaper. His was the final call on what would go into the paper. Beyond that he was the person to whom they would go to clear any new project or to discuss any possibly contentious or controversial story. Robinson was not a participant in the many newsroom dramas as much as he was an overarching, reasonable presence. He would rarely visit the newsroom, but he was usually available by phone. He was responsive to my emergency texts, when, for example, I was stalled at the East Gate because of some glitch in the clearance processing.

Sam Robinson had a unique management style that's not taught in business school. It was based on a hearty laugh, which he delivered in his deep, rich, baritone voice. If you asked for something that he opposed, he would simply fold his arms, rear back, and give a hearty laugh. And that was the end of that. He was a man of few words. His texts were notoriously brief—for example, "Gotcha."

Robinson was thoroughly professional. He was a buffer between the warden and the paper. And he knew when to be firm. Juan Haines, arguably the best reporter on the staff, on occasion would become too assertive or outspoken, and Robinson would hand him a furlough, or a time-out, to give him a chance to work on his anger issues. Chastened, Haines would return to his reporting job after cooling off.

The PIO also maintained a sense of humor. He could take it, and he could dish it out. Aly Tamboura, one of the 2008 original staff members, who had been paroled in 2017, returned to the newsroom on March 11, 2018, for a meeting with local law enforcement officials, all but one of whom was black. The police officials were planning an event with the editors and writers. Robinson sat next to Tamboura, who had served a sixteen-year sentence for making criminal threats against his wife. Asked to introduce himself, the parolee said straight-faced, "I'm Aly Tamboura. I used to be Sam Robinson's supervisor." They all laughed. They were a bunch of black forty-year-old guys, making sport of each other. I tried to imagine that scenario with a white PIO, and I just could not.

When California's DMV issued the vintage black-and-gold license plates, I ordered a vanity set. It was not cheap, seventy dollars. "SQNEWS" adorned the front and back of my 2015 Prius. When I was driving through the East Gate one afternoon, Robinson was assembling a tour group of a dozen visitors. He approached me on the driver's side and said, "I want you to name me in your will so I can get those plates." A morbid suggestion, but we both laughed.

One of Robinson's duties was to conduct regular tours of the historic prison. He was no mere docent. Instead, he was a consummate storyteller. He also relied on the inmates to fill out the tour. Robinson had some of the more colorful inmates tag along and impart their experiences. No two tours were alike. Sometimes they would go on for three hours or more. Sometimes the visitors passed by some of San Quentin's inmate celebrities. One tour in 2016 ran into Death Row murderer Scott Peterson from Modesto, who was out for his daily exercise in one of the special outdoor cages. He had been convicted of killing his wife and unborn child. A regular participant on the prison tour was Curtis (Wall Street) Carroll, convicted of a double murder in Oakland, who had made himself into a commentator on financial markets and had done TED Talks on the subject. The tours were not for the general public. Robinson confined them to correctional personnel, law students, volunteers, and others from allied organizations.

Robinson told me once that when he graduated from Saint Elizabeth's High School in Oakland he had been admitted to UC Berkeley but chose to go to San Jose State instead. That decision did not surprise me. In my thirty-plus years at UC I had witnessed Berkeley's failure to provide a welcoming atmosphere for gifted and talented black students. Robinson obtained his degree in 1996 from San Jose State and went to work for the Department of Corrections right away. Four years later he made sergeant, and five years after that he made lieutenant.

He spent ten years working on Death Row. Those ten years were formative for him. Working the condemned row requires a heightened sense of awareness. The more than 750 residents in that cellblock have nothing to lose. Robinson is compact and muscular but hardly a bruiser. He once related a story to me about accidentally dropping a ballpoint pen in front of a Death Row inmate and realizing that the prisoner might seize it and turn it into a stabbing weapon. He and the condemned prisoner stared knowingly into each other's eyes, each one thinking the same thing. The inmate did not like the odds and backed off. He decided to die another day.

In an *Ear Hustle* podcast Robinson told the story of escorting a muscular Aryan Brotherhood character into the Adjustment Center (a.k.a. the Hole). The towering prisoner looked down menacingly at him and said, "Robinson, you're a good little cop. I been checking you out. But if I get out of here, I'll kill you."

"You better bring some of your friends," Robinson replied. His dauntless David-to-Goliath response defused the situation, and the big Aryan gave him no more problems.[1]

Robinson became PIO in 2008. He became so well known around the prison at all levels that he was referred to just by his first name. In one instance he had to handle the press preparations for an execution. It was

2010. Albert Greenwood Brown, a black inmate convicted of the rape and murder of a Riverside county teenager, had exhausted his appeals.

Once the date was set, Robinson began preparing a press release containing information such as where the condemned inmate was from, where and when the inmate committed the crime. After it was sent out, he responded to dozens of reporters' questions and requests to interview the inmate, visit the institution, and obtain stock 1M footage of the prison and the execution chambers. The execution was ultimately halted by a California Supreme Court decision, but that didn't change the amount of work Robinson did in anticipation of the newsworthy event.

"It's certainly the most challenging job in my life," Robinson said of his PIO position, "but it's an honor that I get to represent a flagship of CDCR."[2]

When *Ear Hustle* was born in 2017, the highly successful podcast brought Robinson's congenial basso profundo voice and presence to hundreds of thousands of listeners in the free world. He was integrated into the production in a curious way: he signed off every podcast with "I'm Lieutenant Sam Robinson and I approve this story." The signoff actually represented his censorship authority over the stories, but it sounded like ordinary programming. The podcast hosts Earlonne Woods and Nigel Poor would engage in some happy talk and then go to Robinson's signoff. It was a disarmingly normal exchange, considering the three participants occupied vastly different spaces in prison life.

Robinson deserved recognition for making the newspaper and the other media initiatives successful. García would go out of his way to praise Robinson at every opportunity. It was hard to judge how Robinson's work played within the CDCR. But the people inside the CDCR had to appreciate what he had done at San Quentin. Given his track record, Sam Robinson appeared to be headed for a promotion to captain in the near future, and eventually he would probably be a warden at some institution, either in California or elsewhere. Replacing him would not be easy. His reputation for fairness, intelligence, and firmness helped defuse whatever tensions, racial or otherwise, might have emerged in the newsroom.

13   Race in the Prison Newsroom

Jesse Vasquez, then-managing editor of the *San Quentin News,* wrote that he got his first lesson in prison race relations when, as a teenager, he began serving a life sentence at the maximum-security prison at Calipatria, California.

> An older Mexican dude with the signature handlebar mustache told me, in that Hollywood stereotyped Mexican whisper, "Hey homie, we don't associate with *llantas* (literally "tires," shorthand for African Americans) around here. The *animales* (animals) have their own rules, we follow ours, so don't talk to them too much because someone might feel disrespected and you're going to get dealt with."[1]

The older "homie" warned Vasquez that he risked a beating or worse if he fraternized with those of another race. That meant no exchanging toiletry products or food, no using the phone on the "wrong side" of the day room, and no hanging out with other races. "If a black so much as raised his voice, I was supposed to punch him in the mouth even if it started a riot."

Jesse Vasquez obediently learned this lesson: "I was only 18-years-old and the only way I knew how was to conform. I absorbed the racist rhetoric of the older generation of Mexicans that had fought in the prison gang and race wars of the past." Later, as a prisoner at Ironwood State Prison, Vasquez would take pride in standing sentry duty over "property" on the yard that was claimed by the Mexicans. Blacks and Mexicans were willing to go to war over a concrete bench. "Our stare down got the yard shut down. I stressed all night because I knew that the Mexicans were willing to riot for the picnic table," wrote Vasquez.

The customary picture of California prisons that the public sees is a collection of race-based gangs. It's largely accurate, if exaggerated. In California's prisons racial antagonisms are a factor in everything and sometimes turn deadly. In prison, gang activity keeps the general population under constant pressure to conform to the prescribed rules of behavior, and the most influential, problematic, and violent gangs in prison are usually Latino, as they try to hold on to their identity—linguistic, cultural, geographical.[2] Black militant gangs in prison are largely a thing of the past, although prison officials still punish prisoners for alleged membership in such defunct groups as the Black Guerrilla Family. White "skinhead" gangs are a small but violent reality. There are so few Asians in California prisons that they can hardly support formation of an actual gang.

On the outside gang members can stick with their buddies. In the free world they have plenty of room to avoid a rival group's territory. However, prisons are hothouses for gang violence because the men are crammed together in a confined space. They live in a racial pressure cooker, where blacks, Latinos and whites vie for supremacy.

At San Quentin, the mainline prison population (excluding Death Row, the Adjustment Center, and the Reception Center) is diverse: roughly 33 percent white, 33 percent Hispanic, and 28 percent black. That leaves around 5 percent as "other," including Asians, Pacific Islanders, Arabs, even Armenians![3] Yet Vasquez, like dozens of other inmates I have known since 2012, say that they felt gang and race pressures almost disappear when they were transferred to San Quentin. San Quentin is unique, according to the longtime inmates, in that the gang influence there is minimal. You hear a mention now and again of "shot-callers," the nickname given to prison gang leaders. But they don't seem to command the allegiance they do at other institutions. The level of inmate-on-inmate violence is low.

Certain areas of the Lower Yard are still informally segregated by race. After dark Latinos congregate around a picnic table and sing while somebody plays the guitar. Black inmates shoot hoops on the basketball court. At the far end, white inmates punch the heavy bag or play tennis. But the race lines are hardly rigid. Blacks, whites, Latinos, and Asians talk and work together with no evident signs of the friction that Jesse Vasquez described at Calpatria.

San Quentin Prison, and its journalism program in particular, escaped this cycle, and the question is, how? In this chapter I will try to give some reasons for how the men avoided putting race above reason.

Despite its storied past, San Quentin now has a reputation as a prison that will help you go home. It is known for its many self-help programs, which are essential for parole. Nearly everybody in the mainline population is enrolled in these programs, including education.

The inmates of San Quentin are usually older and have already had their tickets punched at the "gladiator schools." Before arriving at San Quentin most worked hard keeping their records clean so they could be transferred to Bastille by the Bay. In making that choice, they took a big step away from their gang allegiances.

Once Jesse Vasquez realized that San Quentin did not feature the racial gang pressures to self-segregate that he had experienced in other prisons, he was able to begin making connections across racial lines and finding a commonality of experience. When he joined a self-help group of men of different races who shared their stories, he discovered that "our pasts were similar, full of pain, regret and remorse." The next step would be his joining the staff at the *San Quentin News*.

BONDING ACROSS RACE IN THE NEWSROOM

Before his parole in early 2019, Jesse Vasquez had become editor in chief, and he presided over a San Quentin newsroom that was not only the most racially diverse in the country but also probably the most racially harmonious. Blacks, whites, Latinos, and Asians getting along had been a signature feature of the *San Quentin News* since the newspaper returned from the twenty-year shutdown in 2008, and that phenomenon needs to be explained. It played a role in the newspaper's success. Despite racial differences, the men built a genuine camaraderie. It lasted even after some left prison on parole.

The newspaper staff was made up mostly of blacks. A small contingent of Asians and Hispanics on the staff always outnumbered white prisoners. The newspaper staff customarily had only a few whites after resuming operations in 2008. Richard Lindsey, a white prisoner who paroled in 2013 after serving his time on a homicide conviction, was a fixture as layout and design editor and continued to work as an outside researcher for the paper through 2018. After he left, the only whites on the staff were Theodore Swain (securities fraud), Dwane Boatwright (gross vehicular manslaughter), and Wesley Eisiminger (1999 homicide in Orange County). Swain transferred to Chino in 2014.

The core group of civilian advisers remained predominately white, except for Yukari Kane (Japanese American) and me. And as mentioned before, the white civilian advisers were the core of the editing infrastructure. Their dedication was demonstrated by the hours they spent in the newsroom. April 2017 was a representative month. In that time Linda Xiques logged twenty-nine hours and Jan Perry twenty-six hours in the newsroom. (I had a meager eleven!). For just that April the civilian advisers, including UC Berkeley students, accounted for nearly 190 hours of volunteer time.

One day I walked into the newsroom, and three writers were seated in front of a computer discussing a story. Tare Beltranchue was Latino, Marcus (Wali) Henderson was black, and David Le was Asian. "Is this a meeting of the Third World Liberation Front?" I asked. They roared with laughter. They saw the 1970s Third World Liberation trope as ridiculously irrelevant to prison.

But the two-thirds of San Quentin's mainline prison population who are people of color have much in common. Listening to their testimonials about their lives, one hears a familiar refrain: neglect or abuse as a child, resort to violence as a defense, followed by run-ins with the law. This was the pattern followed by the García brothers and the other Latinos. Blacks told much the same story.

The Southeast Asians wound up in the United States because of troubles in the land of their birth. Many were destitute when they landed in small towns in the Central Valley or in violent inner cities, where they were subject to threats and attacks by local gangs. Clashes ensued; often somebody got killed, and somebody else went to prison for life.

Joining the newspaper staff was a process of self-selection. The men were attracted to joining an endeavor where they would find kindred spirits, even though they were from another race. They shared a common traumatic experience, imprisonment. They were like veterans of war. They had bonded, most particularly the lifers. They wanted a way to demonstrate that the confinement had not broken them.

White staff member Tommy Winfrey recounted the change in his own racial attitudes that the *San Quentin News* had been especially instrumental in creating. "I was a white kid in one of the most violent jails in the nation (LA County Jail), where everyone practically hated the 'white man.' Most of the Sheriffs where white and they were abusing everyone they could. It was a war, and it didn't matter that I was wearing blue, because I was white," he wrote, recalling his thoughts when he began his twenty-five-to-life sentence for murder.[4]

He was nineteen when he killed a man over drugs and his odyssey in the prison began. He went from LA County to North Kern State Prison, and then to Susanville, and to San Luis Obispo and eventually to San Quentin. In other words, he spent most of his sentence in "gladiator school," just hoping to survive.

Winfrey survived the violence of North Kern and Susanville. San Luis Obispo was somewhat more civilized. But His arrival at San Quentin proved to be his rescue. He immersed himself in education programs at the Prison University Program. He also discovered the *San Quentin News*.

"I met the Managing Editor Juan Haines in an English class we were both enrolled in," Winfrey wrote. "He worked with the paper, and I was curious about how I could write for it. One day I approached him and gave him the article I wrote. From that day forward we were friends. Our bond started over my writing."

Winfrey became the arts writer and began to hone his own skills as an artist. He valued his special relationship with the short black man with the gravelly voice. When he left prison in 2017 after nearly two decades as an inmate he would describe it as "a place I grew up and built friendships and did all the normal things in life . . . in a space the size of a parking lot."[5]

For Vasquez, the newsroom turned out to be a place where the old, deadly racial barriers did not exist and where he could free himself from the prejudices and defense mechanisms he had been forced to adopt during the seventeen years he was confined to California' prison gladiator schools. Although at the beginning he resisted the supervision of the editor in chief, Bonaru, because he "was not used to black people telling me what to do," he learned so much from Bonaru that he ended up regarding him as "one of my best friends and mentors." As he developed more and more friendships with people of other races, these friendships "awakened dormant feelings of compassion, sadness, and longing." Working on the paper also opened his mind to other ways of thinking. "For a long time, I did not know there was any reality other than the one I knew," he wrote. But the wider world of the newsroom and journalism had showed him that "the world is bigger and brighter than what we sometimes see."

14 The Key Players

Leo Tolstoy's famous observation "Happy families are all alike; every unhappy family is unhappy in its own way" holds true for prison programs, too. The *San Quentin News* was a distinctly happy family when I joined them in 2012. The prisoners and the advisers were a congenial bunch. The prisoner staff in the newsroom exuded a sense of mission and pride. At that time, they all faced long sentences, and nearly all had already served more than a decade, often more. They had all made the circuit of CDCR institutions. Customarily the odyssey began in county jail, and once the prisoner was sentenced he went to a maximum-security "gladiator school." As time passed, he began to look for rehabilitation programs to work his way home. No matter how long or indefinite the sentences, each man felt he had a plan in place, and as a group they felt they were day by day getting closer to success. Most said the credit for the high morale should go to the editor in chief. Arnulfo García was a great salesman and a natural manager. He sold them on having a belief in themselves. His longtime sidekick and then-managing editor Juan Haines gave this explanation:

Figure 6. San Quentin News staff, March 2018. Photo by Eddie Herena.

By putting together a tight, team-oriented news staff, he has taken the news-paper beyond what many have thought possible. García is a talented visionary who uses his leadership skills to pave the way for expanding the newspaper to anyone interested in creating a safer public and a stronger community. Each step García takes toward this goal inspires me to develop the paper's content and relevancy in a way unlike any other news agency. . . . We also know that when the free world reads what's in the newspaper, they are astonished by the level of reform happening in California prisons. The inmate staff has one overriding mission—we believe that if we get a newspaper in the hands of every California prisoner, they will read about ways to change their lives and become better citizens when they are released from prison.[1]

García's big, impossible dream for the newspaper was gaining traction in the outside world, among officials of the CDCR, district attorneys, support groups, and mainstream media.

The staff writers and editors took their cue from him. García's journey to San Quentin was a lifelong drama of conflict, violence, and redemption. The other prison journalists did not want their life stories to end in prison.

García faced a life sentence, but he soldiered on. What they all had in common was a determination to rewrite the script for their personal struggle.

WHO ARE THESE GUYS?

Longtime adviser Steve McNamara once jokingly told me, "They did not get here for overtime parking." But a volunteer like me has no idea what the crime was that the inmate committed. That creates a lingering awkwardness.

Volunteers undergo regular mandatory "training" programs in which correctional staff customarily warn against lowering one's guard. The trainers make the point over and over that inmates often are looking for a chance to "get over" on volunteers and seek special favors. Or, we are warned, they will try and compromise you into breaking a prison rule and then use that as an extortion tool. The message is clear: you cannot trust a convict.

However, in the newsroom the barriers dissolved. One of the rules to which volunteers must adhere is that you may not ask a prisoner about his crime. Nevertheless, using the ordinary online search tools, I carried out searches on a few particularly enigmatic prisoners. This method was not always successful. On many occasions the crimes the inmates committed were so routine they never made the newspapers, no matter how horrific—even the homicides.

In my days at the police beat at the *Los Angeles Times* we referred to these deaths as "misdemeanor murders." Black-on-black crime in a city like Los Angeles would rarely rate more than a few paragraphs. Occasionally an inmate would appeal his case. A court record would then be created. After nearly three years of volunteering at San Quentin, I was in the dark about the crimes most of the *SQ News* reporters and editors had committed. In addition, I had no idea about their lives before prison, except for occasional brief mentions they made in conversation. Through great good fortune, however, I eventually penetrated the veil of mystery. Here is how it happened.

THE REALITY SHOW THAT NEVER HAPPENED

The creation of their biographies was a direct outgrowth of the increasing public interest in the *San Quentin News*. Here is how it came about. Jon Spurlock, then a Cal MBA student, received an email on April 7, 2014, from one Carlos (Los) Arias:[2]

> I am a principal in a production company in Los Angeles that is working on developing an unscripted series based on SQ News.
>
> I have had a chance to review the amazing biz plan that your team put together for the paper. I feel a major component of this potential series is the collaboration your team has had with the SQ News. I'd love to begin a dialogue with you all in order to gauge your interest in working on this project together.
>
> Really inspired by your work and would love to join forces on doing something very special.
>
> Perhaps we can arrange a conference call to discuss together.

Arias said his production company, Coyote Point Productions, was affiliated with film star and musician Ice Cube. Its credits included the 2014 movie *Ride Along*. Of course, Arias's email aroused great interest among the editors. Arias and others from his company visited the prison and met with García and the leading editors. Arias called the visit "one of the most remarkable experiences of my life."

What he had in mind was doing a reality television show about the *San Quentin News*. He called it "unscripted television." Editor in chief García went for the idea in a big way. García was convinced that having cameras in the newsroom would tell the public a different story than notoriously violent prison portrayals such as the TV program *Lockup*. Arnulfo had no idea about the production issues involved or how reality TV worked. It thrives on drama, often manufactured by the producers. Filming a pilot would have necessitated multiple cameras inside the prison. And this would have required a considerable investment of prison staff time. Not surprisingly, once the warden saw what was involved, he turned down the idea.

But before the warden pulled the plug, García and Arias did a considerable amount of preparation. To develop a story line for the show, Arias wanted to know more about the background of all the main players in the drama. García approached the writers and editors on the staff and asked them to write an autobiography. At least a dozen of them did so. These testimonials revealed some of their innermost thoughts. Many inmates freely examined their past. Until I read the biographies, I never knew what the men with whom I was working had done to earn such long sentences.

The candid biographies opened up a window, giving me a glimpse of the private thoughts of the inmates. Were these autobiographies the truth about their backgrounds? I cannot fact-check their essays, but certainly their biographies were what the inmates wanted a camera from the outside to see. Taken as a whole, the dozen essays paint a picture of a remarkably diverse *San Quentin News* staff. Mainstream news stories about the newspaper lumped them together in a blue-denim mass. Publications customarily would mention the name of an editor or reporter and summarily reference a conviction and a sentence, but they gave little in the way of context or nuance. In contrast, each essayist wanted you to know that he was more than his crime.

Society, in the form of the criminal justice system and the news media, said the prisoners were losers, failures, misfits, "convicts," but they rejected those labels. Instead, they wanted to create a new persona, no matter what the odds, and the pages of a prison newspaper allowed them to do that.

The prisoners were not trained journalists. With a few notable exceptions, most did not have education. In fact, a GED was the norm, often earned in prison. The one thing they all had in common was a common path that led them to the gates of San Quentin Prison. It was there that they met like-minded men who put the customary prison-convict games behind them.

In the chapters that follow I will present the portraits of some of the most influential men on the *San Quentin News* staff.

PART II The Characters
in the Newsroom

15 Arnulfo García

Who were the people who managed so effectively to put the issue of incarceration before the eyes of the public? The credit has to be spread around. Prisoners who paroled out were ambassadors for prison reform. They were intelligent, outspoken, and articulate. There were effective lobbying groups, empowered by internet populism, who represented the families of prisoners. There were legislators who took on this job. But they never would have gained the traction they did without a big push from the men serving life sentences inside. These were men who had tangled with the criminal justice system and lost in a big way. Yet they did not let prison defeat them.

When Arnulfo Timoteo García (aka CDC Prisoner 14022), shackled hand and foot, boarded the Corrections Department bus at Pleasant Valley State Prison in 2008 for his transfer to San Quentin, he had already been behind bars for six years and faced another fifty-four more years. García had been sentenced to sixty years to life under California's Three Strikes Law. He was introspective and occasionally angry about the harm he had done to everybody, including himself, but was undaunted because he had embraced Christianity. His last conviction was for burglarizing a home to feed a heroin addiction. Smack had proved his downfall. His brother Nicholas had been sentenced to life in prison more than twenty years earlier for the murder of a homeowner during a San Jose burglary while under the influence of drugs. When their mother, Carmen Valentine Brotherton, died in 1999, two of her five children faced life sentences in the California Department of Corrections.

Having two lifers in the same family was painful and shocking to relatives, because García's parents were hardworking farming people. Arnulfo and brother Nick eventually wound up sharing the same cell in North Block at San Quentin State Prison.

Arnulfo García's life was shaped by economic and social forces way beyond his control. To examine his path from San Jose, California, where he grew up, to San Quentin is to catch a pavement-level glimpse of postwar Mexican immigration to the US. His story also provides a glimpse into how the war on drugs played out on a personal level. García was one of thousands of young *Mexico-Americanos* swept up into the criminal justice system because of drug addiction and the California Legislature's years of "getting tough on crime." Over the previous thirty years Latinos had surpassed blacks and whites in the inmate population to become the plurality of California's imprisoned felons. What made García different from the other San Jose *vatos* (Spanish slang for homeboys) was a determination to create a positive outcome for himself, no matter how bleak his chances. A sentence of sixty years to life is a long dark tunnel with a headstone at the end.

Exploring the family history gives some insight into how the lives of the García brothers turned out the way they did. They came to be born in California because of violence in the countryside in Mexico. Arnulfo's father, Nicholas Fonseca García, was born April 23, 1924, in the small community of Moroleon in the Mexican state of Guanajuato. Nicholas Fonseca García's father, Timoteo García, had a big family, and when his wife died he married again and had many more children. A disagreement, perhaps over land, ensued between the half siblings. One day Nicholas Fonseca García's brother was killed by persons unknown. Fearing for his life, Nicholas fled Mexico for California. He arrived in Half Moon Bay, a farming community in San Mateo County, in 1940, and got a job as a ranch hand. There he met and fell in love with the daughter of the owner of the ranch. In 1950, he wed Carmen Valentine Brotherton. They had seven children, but one died in infancy.

Nicholas Fonseca García took a stern line with his children. According to both Arnulfo and Nick, their father had a violent temper. He worked hard to provide for his family, but he was authoritarian and sometimes harsh. These traits were imprinted in the memories of his sons.

Arnulfo, Nick, and their siblings grew up in wide-open spaces. The first home of the García family was a ranch in Half Moon Bay, a community fifty miles or so south of San Francisco and famous for its annual pumpkin festival. The town had barely a thousand inhabitants when they were kids. They raised chickens and tended the orchards. Later the family would move to the east side of San Jose, about twenty-five miles away.

The geographic center of the Silicon Valley, San Jose is is synonymous with the high-flying tech world—the internet, circuits, gadgets, and hard drives. But East San Jose is the *barrio*, at its leanest and meanest. Around Tully Road, King Road, Story Road, and Alum Rock Park on the east side of the Bayshore Freeway, you'd think you had been transported to 1950s East Los Angeles. This is where the García children went to school. At the time, it was the stronghold of the notorious Pachuco gang, the precursor of the Norteños, Sureños, Nuestra Familia, Mexican Mafia, et cetera. It's where Arnulfo got the crap beaten out of him in junior high school and brother Nick began to steal things and run away from home. Arnulfo wrote in a draft of his life story: "I didn't know the meaning of a Pachuco, but on my first day at Roosevelt Junior High School I began to see what they looked like, nothing like us cowboys from Half Moon Bay."[1]

The farm boy's adjustment to the city did not go well. Arnulfo developed a crush on a beautiful classmate named Dora, and she decided that this cowboy was cute. The problem was that she was breaking up with a boyfriend, David, who was a Pachuco. Confident and cocky, Arnulfo was about to get his first lesson in the law of the barrio. Arnulfo was bigger and stronger than David and decided to ignore his threats to stay away from Dora. An after-school confrontation ensued. García easily outpunched David, but he was unprepared for the beating he took from David's homies.

What happened next was entirely unexpected. Two random Anglo boys had watched the fight and decided that it was not fair. They had a gun and fired several shots in the air.

Beaten senseless, Arnulfo was fortunate that his Anglo friends gave him a ride in their '57 Chevy to a neighbor's house, where he got a T-shirt to stanch the bleeding from his face. He was afraid to go home and face his father, whose temper was legendary. Sure enough, seeing Arnulfo's injuries, Nicholas Fonseca García went ballistic. The father collected his .45-caliber pistol. He put Arnulfo in the car, and they went hunting for his assailants. Arnulfo refused to identify the Pachucos, even though he saw them from inside his father's car. Frustrated, his father drove back home. "My mother took one look at me and both of her hands went up to her face. My father said to my mother to take this stupid kid to the hospital, and walked away, the .45 still at his waist."[2]

Arnulfo's father raised roosters for cockfights that were staged regularly in the rural areas of the valley for the entertainment of the farmworkers. To pay for Arnulfo's hospital bills, the elder Nicolas had to sell a couple of his prize roosters. His dad kept him out of school for the rest of the year. When school resumed in the fall, Arnulfo saw Dora again. She had broken off with David completely. She told Arnulfo that everybody at school admired him for facing up to the Pachucos and for showing such valor in the face of the gang members.

García came of age when drug use was a phenomenon usually found in black and Latino neighborhoods in California. The term *opioid crisis* had not yet been invented. Society's answer at the time was punishment and prison.

García's loyal companion was his dope man. Most often it was a local who went by the name Coco Mo. No matter what promises García made to himself, to his wife, or to his devoted mother, he would return the phone call from the dope man and make a clandestine rendezvous. Later, while in San Quentin, García kept a detailed memoir, created, he said, to scrutinize the events of his life "to help myself, then to help others see that drugs and alcohol is a sure way to incarceration." He wrote about the excitement of getting to sample Coco Mo's product: 'When the heroin hit me, instantly all the pressure left my body: all the hate for cops, parole officers, anything in authority. I was at peace. Coco Mo said, "Ta Buena?" (Is it good?) "Yeah, it's good."[3]

Heroin use was more than a drug habit. It was a way of life for García, who would score heroin from Coco Mo, cut it, and retail it to others for money to buy more product. But that trail would eventually dry up. To get high again, the addict would turn to theft: "Then I was just like the rest of the dope fiends trying to stay on top of wherever the drugs were coming in."[4]

To feed his heroin habit, García committed burglaries and trafficked in goods stolen by other burglars. The East San Jose barrio was a ready market for all of the loot García and his friends could steal. They did not need a network of fences. They had connections from friends who would buy the goods, no questions asked.

García lived his life in a revolving door of dealing drugs, stealing, and prison. He was a known figure around the Santa Clara County Jail in San Jose and in the North County Jail in Palo Alto. During one stint in jail, his wife treated the guards regularly to homemade burritos. The cycle took a toll on those who loved him most.

"Arnulfo, every time you go to jail it's because you're drunk or on some kind of drugs."

"Everything is going to be alright, Mom."

"I hope so. I hate it when you're in jail or in prison. If you keep it up, you'll wind up spending your life in prison. They already gave your brother life in prison. Why? Because he was on damn drugs when he did that [murder]."[5]

Even in prison, García was able to access drugs and feed his habit. But when he got out in 1997, still badly hooked on heroin, he swore he would never commit another burglary, His promise lasted only as long as it took to score more drugs on the outside, and he was arrested again that year.

García 's fateful 1997 arrest meant he was eligible for a third strike and a life sentence. But thanks to a clerical error, the Santa Clara court system lifted the hold on him and let him out on $100,000 bond. García's mom, Carmen, suffered from diabetes and used a wheelchair. She put up her house to make bail. She said she did not want to die with two sons serving life terms. Little Nick was doing life for the murder committed in San Jose in 1980.

Once García was released from custody, he absconded. He paid underworld characters who specialize in smuggling people across the border. First stop was Tijuana. García was still using drugs at the time. He said the smugglers got him across the border and hid him in a shack inside a junkyard. He was all alone and badly in need of a fix. He thought he would sneak out, go into town, and score some dope. He changed his mind. His shack was surrounded by vicious junkyard dogs.

Eventually the smugglers took him to a ranch in Guerrero State, where he worked as a common *campesino*. When he first arrived there, he was physically weak and drained as a result of his heroin addiction. The *Mexicanos* derisively called him Gringo. He once asked for gloves to protect his hands. The *Mexicanos* laughed. "You only wear gloves if you work in the kitchen," they told him. He constantly reproached himself. "I wasn't used to working; I was used to sitting in a cell, figuring out how to get more heroin," he later wrote. "That had been my way of life for a long time. My body had to learn to work again, the way my father had taught me to when I was a kid."[6] But he adapted, eventually becoming a foreman and working various pieces of machinery. He met a woman there named Olivia and they formed a relationship. She bore him a child, a daughter, also named Carmen. García later wrote about cleansing himself of addiction during this period: "My mother always told me that if I have a child, I would change and appreciate the value of life. She was right, because I kicked my heroin addiction in Mexico and fathered a child who made me want to be with her every day of her life."[7]

In 1999 he was rearrested. When the FBI and the Mexican *Federales* arrived at the door of the ranch, he once again heard the familiar sound of handcuffs behind his back.

Upon his return, García learned that California law takes a dim view of absconding. He would not see the parole board for at least sixty years, meaning he would likely die in prison. (García insisted that he had actually received four life sentences because of all the enhancements. Apparently, if one charge failed to stick, another would automatically take its place to deliver the season-ending third strike.)

For three years García was in transition, first in a county jail awaiting trial and then in a "reception center" in the California prison system. Finally, in 2002, he was sent to Pleasant Valley State Prison, near Coalinga.

Though García considered himself to be cured of his addiction, his family was not so sure. He had burned a number of bridges, as addicts do. They swear they are clean, but at the first opportunity they score more drugs. They lie. They steal. And they wind up back in jail again, as his previous history had showed.

In his six years of imprisonment at Pleasant Valley García became a Christian. He also enrolled in all the self-help and rehabilitation programs he could find. But the selection was meager. Pleasant Valley, like so many of the newer penitentiaries opened in the building boom of the 1980s and 1990s, was a programming desert, miles from major population centers. And like most of the newer penitentiaries it featured only basic education programs required by state law, Bible studies led by volunteers from religious organizations, and one or two twelve-step programs to deal with substance abuse.

García requested a transfer to San Quentin from Pleasant Valley in order to be closer to his family in Northern California. He especially wanted to be near his daughter, who lived in Rancho Cordova near Sacramento. In 2008 his request was granted.

Roused out of his cell in the wee hours to begin the arduous, chaotic trip north, García began the journey that would eventually change not just his life but the lives of countless others. His sister Carmelita Vargas would later say that he came to San Quentin as a learner but would leave as a master.[8]

He felt more like a peon than a master, however, when that road trip to Marin County began. He kept a journal of the experience, titled, ironically, "The Tour," in order to describe the CDC's harsh, often unprofessional practices in transporting prisoners from one penitentiary to another. In this unpublished manuscript, García described several examples of correctional officers toying with prisoners just for the sake of humiliating them.

At about 6 a.m. the bus drivers come in, all dressed in black.

At about 6:30 a.m. a C.O. [correctional officer] comes to the tank.

He says, "All of you will be leaving. Take everything off and throw it in this cart and then move down the row."

"Now, follow these instructions all at the same time," he says. "Raise your hands, wiggle your fingers, open your mouth, stick out your tongue, and lift it up. Come on," he says, in a sing-song voice. "All together. Now lift up your nut sacks."

"Turn around. Lift up your right foot, your left foot. Now when I tell you to squat and cough, I want you to cough three times. All together: down, spread, and cough."

On the third cough, he says, "I can't hear you. Louder!"

The C.O.s standing around all laugh and tell him that we need more training. So, he makes us repeat the routine.[9]

One particularly stressful aspect of the trip was that the CDCR bus did an overnight at Wasco State Prison instead of going directly north. The officers had to assign Arnulfo to a temporary cell at Wasco, There they asked him, "Are you a Norteño, or are you a Sureño?" (the names of the two notorious, warring Mexican gangs).

He answered, "I am a Christian."[10]

That answer captures the essence of the man. He would not fit into any prefabricated prison category. He refused to live down to other people's expectations. Instead, he aspired to live up to becoming a better man.

Nevertheless, in Wasco he would wind up spending a sleepless night. Wasco had no housing unit just for Christians. Instead, they assigned him to a housing unit populated by the Norteño gang members. García relied on his personal charm and diplomacy, skills he would use to his benefit later, to explain that he meant gang members no harm and no disrespect. The gang leader decided to leave him alone, but García lay awake that night, wary of every footstep, thinking at any moment he might get stabbed, or "shanked," to use prison terms.

On that trip, however, García was heartened by what he heard about San Quentin—particularly about its rehab programs, since his experiences at Pleasant Valley had made him a believer in their efficacy. He describes a conversation on the bus:

> A white guy sitting across from my seat says he is going to San Quentin, too. . . .
>
> The black guy asks, "Do they still have a lot of programs at San Quentin?"
>
> The white guy says, "I just left there three months ago, and they have so many programs that you can't find enough time to get involved in all of them."
>
> I liked hearing this.
>
> The white guy adds, "I was there for 18 months and never went on lockdown."[11]

On his arrival at San Quentin, Arnulfo was reunited with his brother Nick. They would spend the next eight years as cellmates. Arnulfo, as the older brother, insisted on having the lower bunk, so his full cell location was 3N67L.

Five years later, as editor in chief of the *San Quentin News*, Arnulfo Timoteo García would come into his own. García used his prison sentence to launch himself into a new identity. He was no longer just another low-rider heroin addict from Santa Clara County. He would go on to make a big impact on San Quentin and corrections generally in California, but in a different way than other felons like Eldridge Cleaver, Huey Newton, and George Jackson. García was to become one of the most influential prisoners in California, but in a positive way. His dream would become a reality. He would gain the ear of district attorneys, CDCR officials, newsmen, publishers, and philanthropists. He would wield his power with a confident but delicate hand, which was much needed at San Quentin, a notorious prison going through changes of its own.

I first laid eyes on him standing on the ramp outside the educational building at San Quentin. His eyes had a friendly crinkle, as though he knew me. "I'm Arnulfo García," he said confidently, offering me his hand. "I'm editor in chief of the *San Quentin News*." He wore a dark denim jacket over a light blue shirt. He was weathered and going a bit gray at age sixty, but he had burnished, matinee-idol good looks. The moustache made me think of the Mexican film star Gilbert Roland.

I was visiting San Quentin because Nigel Hatton, a professor at UC Merced, had asked me if I would be interested in co-teaching a news-writing class for inmates with him at the prison. Hatton had been a master's degree student at UC Berkeley, and that's how we met.[12]

I had visited San Quentin only once since 1970. In 1983, I interviewed inmates about their views on the perceived schism between Martin Luther King Jr. and Malcolm X. Those interviews were part of a radio documentary I produced for NPR's *Horizons* program. I had spent just one afternoon inside, interviewing inmates enrolled in education programs.

My curiosity about California prisons revived again in the summer of 2010, when I led a graduate class at the UC Berkeley School of Journalism that explored incarceration. Financed by the Knight Foundation's News21 initiative, the class produced a multilayered website titled "California's Convict Cycle."[13] The class focused on using a wide array of multimedia tools, and the students provided excellent reporting to go along with the video, graphics, and text. The students explored how inmates segregate themselves on the yard, what happens to the remains when an inmate dies in prison, what's it's like to wear an ankle monitor GPS, and other such topics.

When Nigel Hatton asked me to join him at San Quentin two years later, I did not hesitate in accepting. As things turned out, Professor Hatton would land a grant that took him away that summer, and I wound up teaching a fifteen-week class made up of eighteen enrolled inmate students and four auditors. One of my enrolled students was a wiry, gravel-voiced black man named Juan Moreno Haines. Toward the end of the semester, Haines approached me and asked if I would consider becoming a civilian adviser to the *San Quentin News*, the inmate-produced newspaper.

The collapse of legacy journalism was well under way in 2012. Newsrooms everywhere were hit hard. Within newspapers especially, buyouts and lay-offs decimated local newsrooms. The *Los Angeles Times*, which I considered my alma mater, was a shadow of its former self. The Chandler family had put the newspaper on the block after Otis Chandler's death in 2006. Newspaper people are supposed to be hard-bitten. It's not so. They are sentimental softies. The *Times* had been my family.

A Catholic nun I once met taught a seminary class in Berkeley with a unique specialty: dealing with clergy who had lost their faith. They did not leave the church. They continued to show up. They did the liturgy. They just did not believe in God anymore. That was my own frame of mind.

And then along came this handsome Mexican guy with boundless optimism about convict journalists turning the tide of forty years of mass incarceration. And the vehicle was an eighteen-page, monthly publication produced out of a small classroom in the San Quentin educational complex. The budget cuts at the state level that had closed the San Quentin print shop meant that if the inmate-run newspaper was to continue to publish it would have to raise its own funds.

García would become a central figure in the remaking of the *San Quentin News*, the only inmate-written and edited newspaper in California and one of the driving forces transforming that prison from Johnny Cash's hellhole to California's showpiece for rehabilitation.

16 Glenn Bailey

Glenn Bailey spent more than forty years in prison for a double murder in Oakland, committed on May 13, 1972. In 2013 he emerged from nearly a lifetime behind bars a changed man. More than any other prisoner I had ever met, Bailey defined prison truth. He discovered it the hard way. Incarceration took away his youth, but amazingly it failed to break him or to make him bitter. He walked out of prison in 2013 having attained almost mythic stature, admired by prisoners and staff alike. And he brought his defiant spirit back to San Quentin, where he had earlier served twenty-one years. But he came back as a volunteer, seeking to motivate other prisoners overlooked by the system. When a prisoner attains the standing of a respected tribal elder, his inmate peers accord him the rank of an OG, short for "original gangster." Bailey was given the unprecedented sobriquet of Triple OG. After his release from prison he had business cards made. "A lifer at large. Advocate for the incarcerated. Glenn Bailey triple-ogbailey@gmail.com 510–878–8799." If you grasp the paradoxes of Glenn Bailey's life, you see the complex nature of truth refracted through the prism of penology. Surviving takes strength.

Figure 7. Glenn Bailey and Douglas Butler. Photo by William Drummond.

When I met him in 2017, Bailey was a six-foot-five, baldish man with a light complexion and a shuffling gait, and his gravelly voice spoke with the Ebonics of his West Oakland roots. Bailey and I grew up living near each other around Peralta Street in Oakland, but I had lost my ear for my native dialect years before. When we met in that February, I could barely understand what he was talking about most of the time, but eventually I got used to it, and it all came back to me. On one evening the tall old prisoner put an arm gently around my shoulder and said, "I knew your brother. Yes, sure, we used to run together." Jack Martin Drummond Jr., my older brother, used to hang out with a fast crowd in the neighborhood. I wasn't surprised that brother Jack and Glenn were running buddies.[1] My brother, however, never graduated beyond being a petty thief.

When Bailey first asked to visit San Quentin, my job was to write the request to the warden to get volunteers cleared into the *San Quentin News*. The explanation for Bailey's first visit was that Juan Haines, the associate editor, was going to interview the famous Triple OG about his friendship with Douglas Butler, an ex-Oakland cop who had arrested Bailey for the 1972 murder. This is where the story becomes complicated. Ex-officer Butler himself later served twenty years in prison for a drug-related murder. Bailey and Butler visited the prison together several Sunday evenings, and I escorted them to the newsroom. The story of their friendship was a classic tale of reconciliation and restoration.

As time passed, Glenn's clearance expired, and Haines said he needed for him to continue to visit. I renewed Bailey through May. Then the same thing happened. He had come in every Sunday, and they wanted him to keep visiting. Eventually, without objection from Sam Robinson, the PIO, Bailey was renewed to the end of 2017.

Almost from the outset, every time Bailey showed up on the yard he would be welcomed, literally, with open arms, by a number of other prisoners. Longtime correctional officers and staff members offered a knowing and respectful nod of the head. For a convicted murderer he carried uncommon gravitas.

Later, when he entered the newsroom, he would hold forth in a chair at the far end of the office with Haines, editor in chief Arnulfo García, and several other inmates not on the *SQ News* staff. They were strangers to me. Almost always these were elderly gentlemen. The one visitor I recognized was Robert Kaser, seventy-eight, who had taken my journalism class back in 2012. Kaser, a white inmate, was from Auburn, California, in the Sierra Nevada foothills and was serving a life term for homicide. He had been a mean drunk, and on one fateful occasion he had shot and killed his stepson and wounded his wife. One would never think Kaser would kill anybody. He looked like Father Christmas, pink cheeked and cherubic.

Kaser and several others became part of Bailey's welcoming committee. One typical Sunday Bailey had about eight guys in his posse. On that visit I showed them how to take a selfie photo on the iMac in the newsroom. It was as though I had invented fire. Most of these men had been jailed before the Apple Computer Co. of Cupertino, California, was even created, and they laughed and mugged for the camera.

Rarely does one see such camaraderie as I observed with Bailey and his friends.

These informal get-togethers caused me to wonder: Have I just witnessed a rehab program in the making? Rehabilitation in San Quentin was aimed at felons young enough to rejoin the workforce. But what about the elderly inmates? Really, there's nothing for them. What I had observed was that informally, under *SQ News* auspices, a support group had sprung up. A forgotten part of the rehabilitation model was the seventy-year-old cohort. Nothing was entered on the spreadsheet for them.

In July I spoke with Juan Haines about what was going on with Bailey's continuing visits. He was coming in without fail every Sunday. Haines lamented the lack of programs for the elderly. Haines talked about possible legislation easing parole for elderly prisoners (the exceptions would be for sex offenders, Three-Strikers, and cop killers). This rehabilitation community had started from the ground up. It was not imposed from the top down.

I wondered if the Bailey group would be an enduring thing, but it was interrupted later in the year when Glenn had health issues. He spent time at UC Medical Center in San Francisco getting surgery and treatment for a tumor in the left side of his face. Bailey had had several previous bouts of cancer.

HAVE YOU EVER MET A MURDERER?

In June my daughter, Tammerlin Drummond, wrote an article about Bailey and Butler that was published in the Bay Area News Group newspapers:

> Since April, the Oakland resident [Bailey] has been going into San Quentin State Prison on Sundays to share survival advice with inmates at the facility where he served 21 years. His unlikely partner on these excursions is Doug Butler, an ex-Oakland cop who arrested him back in 1972 and, in an unusual twist, ended up serving 20 years in prison himself for a drug-related murder. Bailey said he never blamed Butler for arresting him, and the two men have forged a friendship that grew from their mutual desire to help inmates serving long sentences.
>
> "I had always said that I would never go back, but when I was released, I heard that it gave so many other people motivation, and they were thinking, 'Hey, man, I can do it,'" said Bailey, 76, who was paroled from Solano State Prison in 2013.[2]

The story described how each man had seen more than his share of prison violence. And each had devised a strategy to survive to tell the tale.

At 6 feet 5 inches, Bailey is an imposing figure. He was a barber who cut the San Quentin wardens' hair. Still, there were rumors that the Black Guerrilla Family, a prison gang, had put out a contract on him. He said he sold marijuana to different prison factions, which put him on everyone's good side.

Butler, 70, who is bespectacled and professorial-looking, walked a fine line as a former cop. When prison officials segregated him for his personal safety, he asked to be allowed into the general population, a courageous move for a police officer, one of the most hated inmates. While working in the law library, Butler said he helped a member of the Mexican Mafia with his legal case, and they in turn put out the word to leave him be.[3]

Once out of prison both men found that they wanted to devote their lives to helping other men stay out of prison. Butler, the ex-policeman, had served twenty years. He was fifty-seven when released. A friend on the police force gave him $2,000 to get him on his feet again. He got employment right away. Later he worked for Cypress Mandela Training Center, which gives a sixteen-week boot camp for men seeking jobs. Bailey's life after prison had been sketchier. He had been incarcerated practically his entire life. Before serving his time for the 1972 double murder he had been jailed as a juvenile as well as an adult. All told, he had served fifty-two years behind bars when he walked out of Solano State Prison a free man. He had nothing more than the $200 in street money the CDCR gives paroled inmates. His sister took him in. Later he got shared housing near his old neighborhood in West Oakland. His wife had moved to Nevada, and she shared some of her Social Security check with him. He did not sit at home feeling sorry for himself. "I'm now beginning to see the good in all the wrong I did. I'm just going back and sharing with people because everyone can't do what I did. Everyone can't survive," Bailey said.[4]

THE ARTIST'S PORTRAIT

Bailey remained to me an enigmatic person. The more I learned about him, however, the more I realized that his life was much more nuanced than I had ever realized. Juan Haines of the *San Quentin News* wrote this about him:

In 1972, he killed two people connected to the powerful, Black Guerilla Family (BGF). The BGF is a legendarily black organization with ties inside and outside of prison. Many of their exploits were criminal. "They kidnapped me and were going to kill me," Bailey said. "I was never regretful for killing them." Shortly after the murders, Oakland police officers, Victor Grant and Doug Butler, arrested him. He was convicted and sentenced to life in prison. "I never looked at Doug or the police in a negative way because they arrested me," Bailey said. "I was in the wrong, and they did their jobs."[5]

Dr. Ayodele Nzinga, a Bay Area poet and playwright as well as executive director of the Lower Bottom Playaz, discovered the depth and complexity of Bailey's character. Nzinga wrote a play, *The Lifer*, based on Bailey's experiences. It ran in Oakland in early 2018 to good reviews, and the playwright had plans for taking it on the road, possibly for staging inside prisons. Dr. Nzinga told an interviewer, "One of the things that fascinates me about incarceration is it gives people time. And that's not just metaphorical. I mean literally, time. People, especially poor people, operate on a survival mentality. In prison, you're given a lot of time you have to fill some kind of way. And so for the first time ever some people get a chance to expose themselves to other philosophies, to sit with themselves to actually get in touch with themselves."[6]

The play revealed that Bailey's extraordinarily long sentence was the result of opposition by the Alameda County District Attorney's Office. The DA wanted Bailey to cooperate in prosecuting another defendant. Here is an excerpt from the play.

> DA: Bailey, we got him, all you got to do is cooperate and all will be right with the world.
>
> BAILEY: All is right with the world; it's some of us who could use a little dusting off.
>
> DA: Just give me a name Bailey.
>
> BAILEY: I can't do that.
>
> DA: You willing to lose your date for this?
>
> BAILEY: I can't help you.[7]

His refusal brought him a seventeen-year enhancement to his sentence.

The Alameda County DA's office opposed his release all the way up to his departure from prison in 2013. Nevertheless, he let bygones be bygones. He even befriended the district attorney Nancy O'Malley and actively supported her in her tough 2016 reelection campaign. O'Malley attended a performance of *The Lifer* and took pictures with Bailey. He remained stoic, stubborn, principled. and brave. The *Mercury-News* writer described Bailey as having attained "equanimity." Sam Hurwitt wrote, "That equanimity extended also to the people who put him in jail. Bailey introduced Nzinga to the district attorney (Nancy O'Malley) who prosecuted him."[8]

Bailey's was an uncommon and vivid story of a convict's journey to enlightenment. Prisoners often aren't able to tell their stories in their own words, and Nzinga, an artist, appreciated that fact. She took his rambling reminiscences and fashioned them into powerful statements, expressing them succinctly and authentically in the way many West Oaklanders talk and fellow prisoners understand.

Another factor that kept Bailey in prison longer than the customary time his crime warranted was his adamant refusal to express the scripted "remorse" statement that the parole board required. Here is the scene from the play, when Bailey was asked if he regretted the murders:

BAILEY: I thought I addressed that. I thought I been addressing that all along. I can't take it back. All I can do is try to be who I want to be, who I should have been trying to be—a better person, not to advocate any kind of violence, to help people. But I can't take that back.

COMMISSIONER 1: How do you feel about it?

BAILEY: If you asking me if I have nightmares about it. No. I don't have nightmares about it because I know them two people I killed. I would rather generalize and say that to take a life is not a good thing. It's a terrible thing.

COMMISSIONER 1: Ok so you regret taking a life. But you don't regret killing the two people you murdered?

BAILEY: I knew them people. They had pistol whipped me and I thought they was going to kill me. So, I ain't gonna sit here and tell you that I feel for them, not people like that, no I can't tell you that. I don't feel no whole lot of regrets about that; but I regret taking a life.[9]

As a result, the parole board denied him release on multiple occasions. Those rejections never broke him. "I want just a little bit of what I done earned. I have done everything that I was supposed to. I programmed . . . I don't feel like I need to be on no parole. So, with all the respect that thought deserves, tell them I said, they can stick that parole up they ass," he says in his most defiant speech from the play.[10]

PEACEMAKER

Bailey lived through the violent racial struggles in the California prisons beginning in the 1970s and lasting through to the present. During that time, he was responsible on several occasions for defusing racial tensions in the prisons where he was housed. Juan Haines wrote about one incident from the 1980s:

> A corrections officer passed Glenn Bailey's San Quentin cell and saw Bailey in the 4-x-10-foot cell with two other inmates. "What the hell's going on in there?" he growled.
> Bailey, towering over him at 6'5", stepped out from his cell.
> "Do you know what we're doing?" Bailey asked the officer, making him shrug his shoulders. Before the officer could utter a word, Bailey continued, "Me, that Mexican dude and White dude, are talking about how to keep the peace on the yard during these holidays coming up."
> Embarrassed, the officer left them alone.[11]

Similarly, the Glenn Bailey character in *The Lifer* worked toward keeping the peace, even behind bars:

> I try to make the point, we a community in here. It's all about communication. There's a lot in communicating. I tell 'em to keep two or three books and read. I break it down to them about consequences, and how paying attention to consequences can teach you. The hole full right now with people that was on the yard three months ago. Two men fighting, and everybody get locked up. I tell 'em find some other form of entertainment. If you can't handle the consequences of something maybe you should rethink trying to do it. I tell my story. I tell them it can save them a lot of time.[12]

THE TRIPLE OG RETURNS

After a long stay in the hospital Bailey returned to his weekly visits to San Quentin in 2018 and was greeted warmly. He had lost weight. The surgery had left one side of his face partially paralyzed, and he wore sunglasses all the time because his left eye occasionally drained. But he made the two-tenths-of-a-mile hike from the visitors' parking lot to the SQ Media Center. Doug Butler chauffeured him to the prison because Bailey was unable to drive.

Glenn Bailey, the man, stands out because he made use of his extraordinarily long prison to become a better man himself and to share his experience with others. After leaving prison he found a way to bring his wisdom to bear in counseling other inmates, and the *San Quentin News* was there and made it happen. His message matched the pragmatic, balanced view of prison and incarceration that the newspaper's editors promoted. His message onstage was one of hope.

> If you go through the system like I did and everybody tells you what a terrible guy you are—I don't worry about that. I don't let that bother me. What I know is—that it wasn't a wasted experience. My life isn't a waste because I learned something and in learning something I can't find anything negative about that. Some people go prison and take classes. . . . The prison was my class. My option was to make it until tomorrow. To make it till tomorrow; you got to survive. There are things I never lost. My family and friends stood by me. I was never here, not in my mind. It's been over 40 years—I know things have changed, some of the places I remember might be gone, but the streets are there, and I got all the rest of it in my mind. . . . You got to be a person of your word or you ain't nothing. I been true. I can say that and can't nobody ever tell you nothing different. I will get out. I'mma get out cause that's the plan—so you look for me—A lifer at large.[13]

I assigned *The Lifer* to my UC Berkeley students. The students all got the point that you don't define somebody by the crime he or she committed.

In November 2018, Bailey, Dr. Nzinga, and I were on a panel at UC Berkeley sponsored by the Department of Drama, Dance, and Performance. "Incarceration, Art, Social Justice and Policy" was the topic. Glenn Bailey and I had grown up on the same block in West Oakland. I was a professor of journalism at UC, and he had spent almost his whole life in prison. And I thought to myself (not for the first time), "There but for the grace of God go I." But in learning about the integrity Bailey had shown during his incarceration, I had to admit that he had shown strength, leadership, and courage in his life, even though he spent most of it behind bars.

17 Juan Haines

On November 9, 2017, on the eleventh floor of the City Club in San Francisco, the hard core of the Bay Area's working journalists gathered for an awards banquet. Here the Bay Area chapter of the Society of Professional Journalists bestowed the Silver Heart Award on longtime *San Quentin News* editor Juan Moreno Haines. The citation read as follows: "Haines has encouraged first time journalists to use their time in prison to report on the courts, the prisons and the conditions of incarceration. With Haines' encouragement and mentorship, their work has contributed to deeper understanding of the prison system by those both inside and outside the prison walls. Haines's writing has also appeared in the Hastings Poverty and Law Journal and Above the Law."[1]

Haines, the diminutive, gravelly-voiced prison writer, would have loved to have been there. But he was sitting in his drafty North Block cell in San Quentin State Prison ten miles away. He had served twenty years of a life sentence for robbing banks in San Diego. On December 7, 2018, Haines described himself and his life in a candid interview with *Pacific Standard:* "I'm 61, kind of short, skinny, balding, missing tooth in the front. Energetic. I'm a Navy brat. I grew up mostly in San Diego County. I did two stints in the Army; both ended not so well. Then I started getting into trouble, had drug and alcohol problems."

Haines was born in a naval hospital in Charleston, South Carolina. His father was a chief petty officer in the US Navy. His father died while Juan was in prison. He had no other relatives. He was junior class president at Samuel F. B. Morse High School, where he graduated a year early. Later he served four years in the US Army.

He first went to prison in 1983. After his 1996 bank robbery conviction he arrived at San Quentin in 2005. Before joining the newspaper, he worked as a maintenance technician in the Prison Industry Authority.

Haines looked at the world through the eyes of a man five-feet-seven inches tall and was nicknamed "Shorty." His height was an incentive for him to compensate. Many times, when I walked across the yard, I saw Shorty sweating profusely on the basketball court and competing against opponents a foot taller, twenty years younger, and forty pounds heavier.

Haines held several roles at the *SQ News* in his approximately ten years on the staff. He was managing editor when I arrived in 2012, but his feisty, outspoken style got him demoted. Editor in chief García encouraged him to join self-help groups to help him cope with his anger. He emerged a changed man. He mended his ways, toned down his act, and worked his way back to the title of "associate editor."[2]

If anybody was essential to the newspaper, it was Haines. I have not counted bylines, but I would be willing to bet that Haines has written more stories for the paper in the past ten years than any other person. In addition, he has generated more ideas (and more paperwork!) than anybody else. He was constantly juggling meetings, projects and, dare I say it, schemes. He was the perfect idea man when Arnulfo García was editor in chief. He thrived on his dozens of contacts with journalists and activists in the free world, and, as someone with a way of turning a phrase, is probably the *SQ News* writer most often quoted in the outside world of media.

Haines was a student in the first prison journalism course I taught back in 2012, and it was he who invited me to become an adviser to the *San Quentin News*. Many others can also say that Haines was their first point of contact.

Emile DeWeaver was a staff writer for the *SQ News* who could claim that Haines gave him a boost in his morale:

That first time I stepped into the *San Quentin News,* I sat with managing editor Juan Haines. He helped me accomplish some things, things that go on every day in the rehabilitative atmosphere at San Quentin but things that astonished me. What they were are secondary. I thanked Juan profusely for his help. He tilted his head to look through his glasses, amusement playing on his face.

"We have to help each other," he said. "If we don't help each other, who will?"

We.[3]

Haines consumed books and wrote reviews for the newspaper. He was a fixture meanwhile in the prison creative writing project Brothers in Pen, managed by Zoe Mullery. As a reporter, he wasn't concise and often handed in copy that was just as he had written it down in his notebook, but he was competent and tireless and loved reporting.

Tommy Winfrey, a white inmate, met Haines shortly after Juan became managing editor: "Juan is the kind of guy some people find abrasive, but I appreciate his perspective. It is never argued, whatever else is said about Juan, that he is a great editor. He is tough and drives people a little bit crazy sometimes, but he knows his business. I have felt supported by him as a writer and as a friend many times over the years. We don't always agree on issues, but at least we can have a conversation about those issues in a grown-up way."[4]

When the Society of Professional Journalists presented the award, two of Haines's longtime friends, San Quentin volunteer Lizzie Buchen and former *SQ News* columnist Watani Stiner, accepted it on his behalf and read his acceptance speech. The audience, steeped in the internet-diluted, pivot-to-video journalism of today's industry, listened to a sermon about old-school, shoe-leather reporting:

As a young, black American I felt unheard and unseen. Since I couldn't find myself in mainstream media, what I did see seemed fake. I know more now. Since then I have taken a close look at the state of journalism, worldwide, and I've learned that I was mistaken. What I had been witnessing, was not fake news, it was lazy news. It was single sourced, narrow in focus and missing professional objectivity. All this was done in the name of expedience over quality. The priority for news agencies was being first with a story with little concern over outcome.

Committing journalism is a hard and sometimes deadly job. All of us in this room are committed to supporting our fellow human beings in ways that attempt to respect that Navy brat who is looking for him or herself. To do that reporters have to be committed to talking to people, many people, and in depth. It is our job to give voice to the voiceless and to make the invisible, visible. Journalists play a critical role in a democracy—we are tasked with giving voice to people, not corporations, not government entities. We represent the weak and the disenfranchised because in a democracy, you can only be counted if you *are* counted.[5]

Such reporting may now be as dated in its methods as the dingy walls of San Quentin Prison, yet the role it plays is more critical than ever.

18 Rahsaan Thomas

Rahsaan Thomas was serving a life sentence for homicide and other charges when he was named sports editor of the *San Quentin News* in 2014. He was thrilled: getting that job fulfilled a lifelong dream. "The experience is especially remarkable because it wasn't supposed to happen for so many reasons. I am not even supposed to be alive," he wrote in his Coyote Point Productions biography.[1]

Born and raised in the rough, tough, and dangerous Brownsville section of Brooklyn, Thomas wore his nickname "New York" as a badge of honor. He cut an imposing figure in the newsroom. Tall (size 12 shoe), light-skinned, and athletic, he was a commanding presence in newsroom conversations with his powerful voice. He was probably the most gregarious member of the staff and also one of the most productive. He had a way of finding stories everywhere, and many went way beyond the scope of sports. He had a breathless, colorful writing style and a naturally observant nature. His talent was discovered by the Marshall Project, which gave him a regular publishing outlet in the free world. His photograph appeared regularly in mainstream publications because he was often standing near iconic sports figures when they visited the prison. He occasionally appeared in mainstream TV programs because he was intense and expressive. Producers liked him because his dark eyes would get big and his hand gestures stabbed the air when he pressed home a point.

On May 1, 2016, CNN aired a program featuring Bay Area comedian Kamau Bell's San Quentin visit, which included a meeting with Thomas on the yard.[2] Bell's *United Shades of America* series won a number of journalism awards, and he owes Thomas a vote of thanks. Rahsaan was the most engaging part of the show. Thomas gave the comedian a rundown of the advantages of being in a level 2 (low-security) environment:

> BELL: OK. And can I ask how long you're in for and what's your sentence?
>
> THOMAS: I'm a lifer with—I (was) convicted (of) second degree murder, attempted manslaughter. I have a 55 to life sentence. I'll probably never go home.
>
> BELL: Fifty-five to life?
>
> THOMAS: Fifty-five to life, so level two is a blessing.
>
> BELL: So you consider this a blessing?
>
> THOMAS: This is. I mean they've got free college here at San Quentin. I'm meeting you. This would not—level four, this wouldn't happen.
>
> BELL: Level four, they don't bring in unknown comedians to talk to you?

The Rahsaan Thomas of his Coyote Point Productions autobiography was matter-of-fact about his often-violent struggle for survival in New York.

> My 14-year-old brother being shot in front of me was the biggest catalyst to my becoming a convicted killer. I was 17. A short thug with a gun was robbing us. Bullets flew and I ran, leaving my little brother to fend for himself. He was shot in both legs.
>
> Someone murdered my father when I was 12. We weren't close. He had just started coming to pick me up on weekends right before he died. They found him in the back of a bar with his wallet missing and throat slit.
>
> Those incidents changed the way I thought. I vowed I would never be helpless again. After that day, I always carried a weapon.[3]

Thomas admitted he was not one of Brownsville's leading citizens when he departed New York for the sunny climate of Southern California, where his fortunes improved. His lifestyle changed. He drove a Benz. He was eating well. He acquired a female friend in the record business, and "Our future looked bright."

One night, said Thomas, some "friends" of his tried to rob his lady friend. "They showed up late to meet us in a mall parking lot with bad intentions. After following them to a deserted spot in the corner, we parked our vehicles side-by-side. Their red Ford backed into the spot right by my Black Mercedes SUV. One guy waved me out of the truck. I trusted him and thought the business would be friendly," he wrote.[4]

His lady friend was carrying a duffle bag. Had she been willing to give it up, Rahsaan Thomas's life would likely have turned out different. Instead his Brownsville instincts kicked in.

> In the heat of the moment, I never thought to tell her, "Just let them take your bag." My mind flashed back to when my brother was shot and the Warrior mentality kicked in. I fired where I saw his firearm. His partner reached for something in his waistband and I shot him where his gun was also. I fired 12 shots. One died at the hospital, the other guy survived but needed months to get back the use of his arm.
>
> The case was portrayed as a drug deal gone bad, when what really went bad was their robbery attempt.[5]

What went even worse for Thomas was that his lady friend turned her back on him and pled the Fifth Amendment in court. But peering out from the depths of his life sentence, the man called New York saw reporting for the newspaper as part of his ticket to redemption after arriving at San Quentin. "Someone said to talk to 'Shorty.' They took me to meet him just outside of *San Quentin News'* office door. Shorty is Juan Haines, the managing editor of the inmate-run newspaper. The little dark-skin brother was friendly and eager to help. He advised me to join the Journalism Guild and a Creative Writing class. I got the schedule for each and showed up ready to join and learn."[6]

Thomas recognized that he had a lot of work to do if he ever wanted to get out of prison. He was willing to work toward gaining that elusive "insight into your crime," the magic words the parole authorities want to hear. Writing for the newspaper was just a beginning, he realized.

> The atmosphere in the (newspaper) office is relaxed, but professional. We joke, laugh, eat all day, and even argue, but we don't play. Every month we do our part to put out a professional newspaper on time. It is especially special because our group of talented cons provides a unique perspective. . . .

We also practice what we preach. Most of us are in self-help groups. I have taken Anger Management, Making Good, a victim-awareness group; an Islamic version of Narcotics Anonymous; and Restorative Justice, a group that seeks to change the justice system from one focused on punishment to one focused on healing the victim and offender.

From taking Restorative Justice, I found out I need healing and have started that process. It is hard to take responsibility for things that I didn't even do. However, whether details make the shooting legal or illegal, the results are morally wrong and stupid all the same. I killed a man over a bag that wasn't even mine, with an unregistered gun, in the middle of a business transaction in which I had no business being involved, in broad daylight, in a parking lot where innocent bystanders could have been injured.[7]

19 Richard (Bonaru) Richardson

These were Richard Richardson's rules for surviving in prison. He learned them early:

1. Believe none of what you hear and only half of what you see.
2. Know how to make a knife and how to use it.
3. Don't share anything, hang out with, or eat with or smoke with "whites" and "Sureños."
4. Don't borrow anything.
5. Don't accept anything for free.
6. Don't read any "kites" (handwritten notes) slid under your door.
7. Don't join any prison gangs.
8. Respect those that respect you.
9. Don't have sex with men, period![1]

Bonaru Richardson wears tightly plaited braids, which he winds closely around his skull. The hairdo makes his scalp itch. Regularly he gently taps his pate. He never scratches it. His hair is his most distinguishing feature, along with his nickname, Bonaru. He has always been the guy with the braids. His usual expression is a scowl of concentration, but it easily breaks into an infectious smile and self-deprecating laughter. A *Los Angeles Times* writer once described Richardson as looking like Snoop Dog.[2] Yes, they are both tall and rangy black men, and they have braids, but that's where the resemblance ends. Snoop is a successful businessman who turned simple lyrics, weed, and having fun into a music/media empire. Bonaru maintains the smiles and easygoing manner, despite having never gotten an even break.

Richardson took over the reins as editor in chief of the newspaper after Arnulfo García stepped down in 2017 to become chairman of the editorial board. Richardson was one of the 2008 print shop veterans who, along with Aly Tamboura, restarted the newspaper after the twenty-year hiatus. He mainly worked on layout and design. He kept the news operation on an even keel after García moved to another role.

Born in East Los Angeles in 1973, Richardson had a chaotic home life. His mother drove him and his sisters and brothers three hundred miles to escape his brutal father. Richardson spent most of his early life in and out of state institutions. He started out at the juvenile level and worked his way up.

> When I turned 12, I bought a chrome deuce-five caliber with a white and brown pearl handle that I took apart and put together every day. Surprisingly, I was not arrested with the gun, but I did get arrested for receiving stolen property, trespassing, petty thief and fighting. . . . When I turned fifteen I dropped out of school and started back selling drugs, which placed me right back in juvenile hall for seventy days. I was arrested for car theft and joyriding. I was unable to walk when I got booked into juvenile hall because I had multiple K-9 bites. The police thought it would teach me a lesson to have his dog chew on me after I was apprehended and handcuffed because I had run from him. My hatred towards police officers grew and I lost all respect towards them.[3]

He never killed anybody, but eventually his forty-seven-year minimum sentence was longer than that given for most homicides. In 1991 Richardson was hanging out with his buddies when a member of his group fired shots at a Modesto policeman and missed. Though Richardson says he did not fire the gun, at age nineteen he ended up pleading guilty to assault with a firearm on a peace officer and was sentenced to six years in prison.

I did not take any vocational classes or further my education while I was incarcerated. I had already earned my halftime off my sentence for doing nothing, so I didn't have to go to school, get a trade or attend any programs. All I had to do was stay out of trouble, sit around and look stupid. When I paroled, I was well on my way to recidivate. I began selling drugs a couple years after my release because my Jack-in-the-Box checks only covered my child support obligations. I was arrested again on December 12, 1997, for robbing the home and person of Ms. and Mr. Hodges and sentenced to 47 years in prison.[4]

Bonaru had run afoul of California's two-strike minimum sentence, a product of the tough-on-crime era. During his tenure with the newspaper, at least half a dozen staffers with murder convictions paroled out, but Richardson would not be eligible to go before the parole board before the expiration of his normal life expectancy.

When I first pulled up to San Quentin in 2007, I saw West Block and my heart dropped. Seeing San Quentin up close enhanced my reality of what a prison really looks like. Despite all the rumors and stories about the murders and deaths that surrounded this prison, when I got off the bus I signed up for every program that was available. With the help of an incredible lady named Jody Lewen, the director of the Prison University Project at San Quentin, Jorge [Heredia] and I signed up for college courses and graduated the same year with an Associates of Arts degree. With Jody's guidance I learned how to accept responsibility for my actions and change my way of life.[5]

He was assigned to the print shop, and it was there that he made another important friendship. "A prisoner named Arnulfo Timoteo García came to the shop as a clerk. Every day he cooked himself and others a feast for lunch. I didn't know him but the food he cooked smelled great," Richardson wrote. He added:

One day Arnulfo came into the room where Aly [Tamboura] and I were sitting at, eating a big bowl of something that sucked the saliva right out of my throat. He asked me, as he did every day, "Do you want something to eat?" Like always I would say, "I'm good." This went on every day until one day Harry O (Michael Harris) overheard Arnulfo offer me some food and I told him, "I'm cool." Harry O spun around from his desk with a mouth full of food, swallowed and said, "What's wrong with you, you're not supposed to turn down food that's offered to you. That's a sign of disrespect." Arnulfo just stood there smiling shaking his head as if he agrees. That's not what I was taught but from that day forward I inhaled everything Arnulfo cooked.[6]

García, who would go on to become editor in chief, was a great visionary, but he was not a detail-oriented person. Richardson had a sharp eye for organizational detail. This talent extended beyond laying out the newspaper. He gave advice on how things should be run and kept an eye on who was doing what. In his self-deprecating way, he became the most valuable player in the organization. He was like an executive officer.

In late 2013 Bonaru Richardson was awakened in the wee hours in his San Quentin cell and without warning was put on a bus for transfer to a private prison in the Central Valley. The CDCR was at this time engaged in a peekaboo game with the federal courts about reducing its inmate population, which was substantially above its capacity and judged to be "cruel and unusual punishment" under the landmark Supreme Court *Brown v. Plata* decision. One of the methods the CDCR used to appear to be in compliance was to move prisoners off the CDCR books and place them instead in private prisons. Bonaru was a prime candidate for such a transfer. He was not a lifer, and his record was clean of any negative disciplinary points. Richardson told me the CDCR intended to send him to Mississippi, but there was no room. Instead, his destination was the private prison in California City, owned by the Correctional Corporation of America and located in Kern County.

The Sacramento CDCR officials neglected one important fact. Richardson was the only person in San Quentin who knew how to operate the vintage printing press located in the Prison Industries Authority workshop. That printing press was used once a year to produce the popular eighteen-inch-by-twenty-two-inch San Quentin calendars, which decorate many offices throughout the state. That was Richardson's assignment when he was whisked away. Without Bonaru Richardson, no 2014 calendars.

His transfer was immediately rescinded and the warden sent a special automobile to collect him. Richardson never made it to the California City Correctional Facility. He returned to San Quentin the following day.

On December 23, 2018, a Sunday, Sam Robinson, the public information officer, called Bonaru to the Captain's Porch (the administrative offices just inside the entry to the castle area of the prison) and told him his forty-seven-year-minimum sentence had been commuted. Richardson had served twenty-one years. After getting the welcome news, Bonaru said he expected to go free later in 2019. He was planning to parole to Modesto, where his wife Lakeesha Butler lived. Unfortunately, his request for parole was denied. Richardson was the last remaining prisoner from the handful who had resurrected the paper from oblivion in 2008. All the others had walked out of San Quentin. His crime? A robbery. Nobody was harmed. But it was a "second strike," carrying a minimum forty-seven-year sentence. Richardson has spent his adult life in seven different California prisons.

20 Watani Stiner

LARRY JOSEPH STINER, AKA WATANI

Watani Stiner had the earliest conviction date of anybody on the newspaper when I joined in 2012. His criminal offense occurred in 1969 in Los Angeles, and that crime was one of the biggest stories I ever wrote (with the legendary reporter Kenneth Reich) for the *Los Angeles Times*.

It was a chilly fifty-five degrees in Los Angeles on January 17, 1969. I was taking some economics courses at UCLA, and after class I rode my Suzuki 250 motorcycle from Westwood to the *L.A. Times* office downtown to begin the night shift. When I entered the office and stowed my jacket and helmet in the cupboard near my desk, the city editor put me straight to work. I learned that a shooting had just taken place at UCLA, where I had spent the morning! It must have happened just as I left.

Ken Reich, who normally wrote about politics, had been sent to the scene. Over the next few hours, Reich called in several times. I took down notes and wrote the story in plenty of time to make the 8:00 p.m. regular edition. The published story carried a joint byline, mine and Reich's, and was placed on page 1.

Figure 8. Watani Stiner attending an event at San Quentin after his release on parole. Photo by Eddie Herena.

The facts were simple. Two members of the Black Panther Party, Alprentice "Bunchy" Carter and John Huggins, lay dead in UCLA's Campbell Hall. They had been killed by gunfire, and police suspected a rival black group, called US, of carrying out an assassination. The headline read, "Two Black Panthers Slain in UCLA Hall."

The lede of my story read: "Two members of the Black Panther Party were shot to death in a UCLA hall at the conclusion of a meeting concerning a proposed black studies program, police reported."

Larry Stiner, as he was then known, was a member of US, along with his brother, George. Writer Jessica Pishko, who interviewed the former Larry Stiner in 2014, gives this account of what happened:

> Larry Stiner and his brother George, two members of US, were both at the event. Larry (who would later change his name to Watani) was there working security detail but says he was unarmed. He was just twenty years old and majoring in political science through UCLA's "High Potential Program," which was intended to facilitate a greater number of minorities at UCLA, where, even today, less than four percent of undergraduate students are African-American.
>
> In the days following the shooting, Larry Stiner, wounded in the shoulder by a bullet from Huggins' gun, discovered that he and his brother, as well as

a man named Claude "Chuchessa" Hubert, were wanted by the police under the theory that they, as members of US, had planned the attack with the intention of killing members of the Black Panthers. The Stiner brothers turned themselves in; since they hadn't shot anyone, they thought they would quickly be released. Hubert was never arrested and never heard from again.[1]

Larry Joseph Stiner and his older brother George Phillip Stiner were tried and convicted of conspiracy to commit murder and sentenced to life terms. But that was not the end of the story. On March 30, 1974, the brothers Stiner escaped from San Quentin. They vanished for two decades. In February of 1994, Watani Stiner, then forty-four, gave himself up to US authorities in the South American nation of Suriname and was returned to prison. Brother George, forty-six, was still at large.

When I was teaching my Introduction to Journalism class at San Quentin in 2012, I had a student named Ronald E. Taylor. He was an older inmate who walked with a cane. He was serving a life sentence for his part in a robbery-homicide in Southern California. Most of his written assignments carried the familiar imprint of '60s black nationalist rhetoric. One day Taylor approached me after class and said, "You know, there's an inmate here that says he knows you." I did not make much of it. But a few days later as I was leaving the education building, Taylor, who was standing near the basketball court, called me over. He was standing with a tall, wiry black man with horn-rim glasses who towered over me. The man introduced himself as Watani Stiner and added, "But I was Larry Stiner back then." The Campbell Hall homicides suddenly rushed into my memory. Of course, how could I forget? It was one of the biggest stories I had written in my young career, made even more memorable because the legendary Ken Reich approached me afterward and said I had done a good job as the rewrite man. Stiner had remembered my name from the story's byline.

At the time Watani and I shook hands on the basketball court, he had been in prison for eighteen years after a twenty-year odyssey on the run that ended with his return in handcuffs from the South America.

Watani Stiner wrote a column for the newspaper titled "An OG's Perspective." In prison slang *OG* means "original gangster." It refers to a man who has served a lot of time and has gained a lot of wisdom. Stiner's column gave fatherly advice to younger inmates, urging them to cool it and make a plan for their lives. Jessica Pishko described Stiner's role this way:

> "An OG's Perspective" highlights Stiner's role as an older African-American man, giving advice to younger men entering the prison system—a role that isn't invented just for the paper. He rules the yard with a quiet authority, very different from the behavior outsiders might expect from an inmate. Many of the men he mentors grew up without fathers; Stiner's eldest son also grew up without his father. This is something Stiner feels keenly, the regret at placing his family second to his revolutionary ideals.
>
> As he once wrote: "In San Quentin, I'm now looked up to by the younger generation as an 'OG'—original gangster. Every day I see the lost souls of our troubled youth—the holes in their spirits and the yearnings for the broken fathers who have abandoned them. I pray they aren't mirrors of what my own children will become."[2]

Writing about himself in the third person, this is how Stiner explained himself to Coyote Point Productions:

> Born in Houston, Texas but raised in South Central Los Angeles, Watani's revolutionary journey was spearheaded by the Watts revolt in August of 1965. Seeking direction for his intense desire to resist and change an unjust society, he joined Kwanzaa creator Dr. Maulana Karenga's cultural national-ist organization "Us" and quickly rose in rank. His dedication to the Organization and to the Black Power movement led to a life sentence for conspiracy to commit murder in the wake of a highly publicized shootout that left him wounded and two Black Panther Party leaders, Alprentice "Bunchy" Carter and John Huggins, dead on the U.C.L.A. campus in January 1969. Watani and his brother (co-defendants who never fired a shot), would serve five years of that life sentence before escaping from San Quentin State Prison and fleeing the country in 1974.[3]

As part of the deal to return to prison in the US, said Stiner, his Surinamese family members were to be allowed to come to America. But that did not happen. One day a Dutch film crew was shooting a documen-tary on the Lower Yard at San Quentin when they were approached by a tall black inmate who began talking to them in Dutch, the language Stiner had learned during his twenty years living in the former Netherlands colony in South America. Dumbfounded by their good fortune, the documentarians included Stiner's story in their film, which was shown on TV in Holland. Shortly after the Holland broadcast, Stiner's family was allowed to come to the United States. Stiner wrote:

> After eleven years of being shuttled from one foster care home to another while lacking the proper food, healthcare and education, Watani's six Surinamese born children finally received Visas that would allow them to come to the United States. With his wife's blessing, Larry Jr. [the child Stiner left behind after fleeing America] agreed to take on the huge responsibility of raising the Dutch-speaking teenaged siblings he had never met. Watani was overjoyed and relieved that his long-suffering younger children would soon be in America with family.
>
> With his children now all grown and fairly well adjusted, Watani has focused heavily on his writing and is receiving a high level of outside interest in his personal story as well as in the column he writes for the newspaper of San Quentin Prison. He has reached out to and developed a good relationship with Ericka Huggins, a former Black Panther leader and the widow of one of the men killed forty-five years ago in the U.C.L.A. shootout. Having recently spearheaded the biggest restorative justice event in the history of San Quentin, the two of them plan to continue working together to promote productive dialogue and to serve as positive examples to current and future generations.[4]

Watani Stiner was found suitable for parole and departed San Quentin in early 2015. He continued to write and publish his memoirs. He reconciled with Ericka Huggins, widow of the slain Black Panther John Huggins, as part of a program to promote the restorative justice movement.

Pendarvis Harshaw, a Howard University graduate and a student in the UC Berkeley Journalism School, volunteered for the editing class at San Quentin and worked with Stiner on his column. After graduation Harshaw wrote a blog of his own titled *The OG Told Me*. It eventually was self-published as a book.[5] Harshaw wrote this account of his meetings with a wise old man from the prison yard:

> Stiner, a self described "COINTELPRO Survivor," has a tale that makes him the Forrest Gump of the Civil Rights era. He was there for the Watts uprisings. He joined a Black militant organization. . . . During Stiner's second stint at San Quentin, he began to write. Letters, poetry and even articles. One piece of

his prose landed in the hands of Ericka Huggins, the widow of one of the men he was initially charged with murdering. Huggins and Stiner met, developed a friendship, and stay in contact to this day. Even though Stiner has now been released due to his age and the overcrowding of prisons in California, he and Huggins have yet to meet again in person (due to legal reasons).

But I've seen Huggins, and she speaks fondly of Stiner and his growth as a person and a writer. And I've seen Stiner, he speaks candidly about his urge to continue to reconcile any differences between Huggins and himself.

He's open about everything, his crime, Civil Rights, his family and even how he escaped prison. When asked how he did it, he always replies "really fast," followed by that same laugh he had when he was in San Quentin.

As people matriculate out of the system, it's an honor to see them flourish as writers and civilians. People such as Stiner, or Troy Williams, who is now the editor at the Bay View Newspaper in SF, make me proud for the time I served in San Quentin's newsroom.

Stiner not only continued to write but toured the country and talked to student groups and gatherings of the formerly incarcerated. He was a living museum piece representing the Black Power movement, as well as a prison survivor. He cut a dashing figure. The walking stick and fedora distinguished him as a tribal elder.

21 Kevin Sawyer

A full generation separates Watani Stiner from Kevin Sawyer, both of whom stand out among the newspaper crew because of their strong political beliefs. Sawyer was born in San Francisco two years before the Watts Riot. He earned a college degree from Cal State Hayward (now Cal State East Bay). He was exceptionally well read, especially about FBI misfeasance and black political movements. He was an intellectual, a musician, and one of the few black inmates in California who had a white cellmate. Before coming to prison, he had a long career in the telecommunications industry. He had a sharp eye for detail, kept meticulous records, and was a perfect fit as the newspaper's business manager. His ambition was to produce a PBS-type documentary on the history of the *San Quentin News*.

Sawyer was the liaison with the librarians at the University of California, Berkeley, to make sure all the editions of the reborn *San Quentin News* made it into the Doe Library collection. Sawyer was a student in my 2012 Introduction to Journalism class at the prison. He wrote clear, grammatical prose, a practice that set him apart from most of his classmates. Later, I edited several of the pieces he wrote for the *San Quentin News*. He was a challenge to edit. His pieces were thoroughly, even exhaustively researched. But occasionally he would slide a politically tendentious comment or two

Figure 9. San Quentin News writer Kevin Sawyer receiving the Aronson Award given by Hunter College. Photo by Eddie Herena.

into his copy. "Who is saying this?" I would ask. He would flash a smile, and we'd look for an attributable source.

Sawyer's political philosophy, though passionately stated, resonated very little with the other newsroom inmates, even though most of the writers and editors were black. García especially used to kid Sawyer about being a black militant. Sawyer himself shrugged this off, perhaps sensing that he was among the last of those carrying the torch for the days of "fighting the man by any means necessary." When I began researching this book, it was Sawyer who recommended Eric Cummins's remarkable study *The Rise and Fall of California's Radical Prison Movement*.[1] Cummins places the end of the radical prison moment in 1980.

The *San Quentin New* sports editor, Rahsaan Thomas, made this observation about his colleague Sawyer: "We call Kevin a revolutionary because he knows an awful lot about black history, black leaders, and the equal rights struggle. The brown-skin brother talks in proper English and has an air of an aristocrat about him. He keeps intelligent conversations going, with his recall of facts from all the books he has read."[2]

Sawyer was soft-spoken, erudite, and congenial. He related especially well with the Cal student volunteers I brought to the prison. It would be easy to see him as a helpful graduate student teaching assistant. He was a mentor to a number of UC Berkeley students. Sawyer made a big impression on Allen Marshall, a UC Berkeley undergraduate, who wrote that working with Sawyer revealed to him that prisoners were not that different from anybody else.

> An inmate that helped me realize this was Kevin [Sawyer]. While editing, I worked with him and we talked about his life. He told me about how he used to work with electronics and televisions, driving all around the Bay Area. "I used to drive by San Quentin all the time. I never imagined I'd end up here," Kevin said as he shook his head in disbelief. In this moment of vulnerability, Kevin revealed to me a startling and now obvious truth, that all inmates were at one point just normal people.
>
> On reflection, the fact that this truth startled me or needed to be shown to me at all is shocking in itself.[3]

Marshall was a junior majoring in English, a transfer student from Santa Rosa Community College who supported himself working at the Trader Joe's on University Avenue in Berkeley. He had completed the Sonoma County Law Enforcement Chaplaincy program before coming to Berkeley and was a regular member of a Christian church in his hometown. He had also participated as a volunteer in relief efforts in Nicaragua, Zambia, and South Africa. Marshall's easy rapport with Sawyer was an outgrowth of Marshall's chaplaincy training to keep an open mind and an open heart.

Reading Sawyer's Coyote Point Productions autobiography was the first chance I got to see how he came to be a San Quentin inmate. Sawyer prefaced that story by writing

> I suppose mine is a who-do-you-believe story. The authorities in power tell one story, and I tell another. The fact is, though, I do not care what anyone believes. It is not my goal to convince anyone about anything concerning me. All that ended long before I ever went on trial for a crime. Through the many subtle forms of social engineering, people only believe what they are told to believe.
>
> Read on and form your own opinion, if you are not predisposed to lean on your biases, prejudices, and preconceived ideas about prisoners. Where

crime and punishment fall, both parties in opposition, prosecution and defense, have an equal incentive to misrepresent facts or to tell fantastic stories. The truth rest[s] somewhere in the middle. With that being said, you be the judge.

"Black men born in the U.S. and fortunate enough to live to the age of eighteen are conditioned to accept the inevitability of prison. For many of us it looms as the next phase in a sequence of humiliations. . . . I was prepared for prison. It required only minor psychic adjustments."

I was not in prison the first time I read those words. However, over the last two decades I have learned to recite the unabridged paragraph from that piece in George Jackson's book, Soledad Brother.

For those of you who would ask me why? I answer: If you have to ask, then you'll never understand my reasons, irrespective of what answer I provide. Then too, in another 50 years any questions, and my retort to them, will probably not matter, except perhaps to posterity.

This is why I write: for them, not for those in the present. The next generation will one day stand on my shoulders, long after my corpse has succumbed to some natural or unnatural cause and is vanquished through the ravages of time. Hopefully, they will want to know then what is happening right now.[4]

Through his twenties Sawyer had made a start on a settled middle-class existence. He was hired at MCI, one of the early telecommunications companies, and moved up the ranks. He finished his bachelor's degree in communications at Cal State Hayward, and he and his girlfriend had bought a house in Pittsburg, California, a suburb in the Sacramento Delta. That's when Sawyer entered the criminal justice system.

The last vignette is a sojourn that began in November 1996. Seven months earlier, at age 32, I was arrested for the first time in my life. The original charge was prowling, trespassing, or "walking while black." A subsequent illegal search of my parked vehicle turned up my Colt .380 semi-automatic handgun. That, however, is not what the police report says. Moving right along.

I accepted a plea bargain for three years of summary probation, a fine, community service and moved on about my business, with a plan to have my record expunged at the conclusion of my court probation. I had too much going for myself than to risk going to jail. . . .

Several months following my arrest, after learning I was on probation, a homicide detective came to my home to "discuss it" with me after receiving information about my arrest. Unbeknownst to me, information concerning my arrest was now being circulated to other police agencies.

Now that I was officially in the system. I had a target on my back. I was that guy: young, educated, moderately successful, and black. By virtue of all these facts, I was a threat to someone's society.

Still, never have I been apprehended for doing anything dangerous. I asked the detective what he was investigating. He said, "I'm not at liberty to say." At that, I stopped talking to him. He was fishing, and any innocuous information I provided could implicate me in whatever he wanted. I was a "person of interest" so I remained silent. Law enforcement calls this "refusing to cooperate," irrespective of the First Amendment, the Fifth Amendment and Arizona v. Miranda.[5]

The district attorney accused the bookish, thoughtful soft-spoken Sawyer of carrying out a crime wave from 1994 to 1996. Sawyer listed his alleged offenses as car theft, stolen credit cards, burglaries, sexual assault, attempted assaults, robbery, attempted kidnapping, assault with a deadly weapon, and assorted other crimes. He remarked, "My bail went from $750,000 to 'no bail,' to $1.5 million. It seemed to me then, as it does now, that black people are not given a bail amount. Instead, we are held for ransom." He added, "After 35 years of living, I was now a convicted felon, bound for state prison. By this time, I had exhausted the services of three attorneys, went through 650 jurors, and stood before seven judges."[6]

Sawyer had read lots of books. He said he had read more than 350 since his imprisonment. He was a self-taught litigant. He maintained a stream of litigation against the Department of Corrections and Rehabilitation. He kept the California Attorney General's Office on its toes. Acting as his own lawyer, Sawyer filed a number of complaints against prison officials. He maintains that prison officials mistakenly pegged him as a member of the Black Guerrilla Family prison gang and subjected him to illegal searches. When he was transferred from Solano State Prison to San Quentin in 2011, his writings were confiscated, and most were later returned. Sawyer said nineteen items in his collection were never given back.

In addition, Sawyer was convinced that prison officials had copied his writings. He had taken the precaution of labeling every page of his writings with a copyright warning. The CDCR found itself defending a suit alleging copyright infringement. "In one of my boxes I found a receipt that read 'Black August material referencing George Jackson and other revolutionary documents indicative of the Black Guerilla Family Prison gang,'" Sawyer wrote in the Coyote Point Productions biography.[7]

By that time, he had served nearly twenty years of a forty-year sentence. When he went to prison, his family was in shock. "When I received a letter from my mother, she wrote: 'Kevin, I finally cried.'"[8]

In journalism Sawyer found a way of establishing a new identity, that of a crusading journalist, in the mode of Mumia Abu Jamal, the Death Row inmate in Pennsylvania. "Working for *San Quentin News* I hope to do the same in some capacity by delivering relevant content to all readers who will one day, I hope, change the way American penal colonies are run, while making sweeping reforms to the criminal justice system. That will be my testament to posterity where I was impacted by a system that is broken and did something to fix it."[9]

Sawyer was a prolific writer, publishing stories not just in the *San Quentin News* but also in a variety of prison-reform publications. In 2016 Hunter College in New York named him the winner of the Aronson Award for Community Journalism. He found a producer from Hunter College willing to help him to make his long-planned documentary on the history of the newspaper.

California governor Jerry Brown had proved to be generous in issuing pardons and commutations during his eight years in office. Sawyer asked me to write him a support letter. I did, but I suspected that the odds were long. Here is part of my letter:

> Sawyer is a prolific writer, publishing stories not just in *San Quentin News* but also in a variety of prison-reform publications. In 2016 Hunter College in New York named him the winner of the Aronson Award for Community Journalism. He found a producer from Hunter College willing to help him to make his long-planned documentary on the history of the newspaper.
>
> Mr. Sawyer is a proud man. He does his job and does it well. He's soft-spoken and intelligent and a force for harmony in the newsroom. He enjoys the respect of his fellow inmates, the volunteers and the UC students I've introduced him to. I respect him for the principled stands he has taken on social issues, and I ask that you recognize that he is a man of character. He has spent 20 years in prison, facing the set-piece demands of incarceration, and he has emerged a better man. I want him to be able to use his talents for the good outside of prison.

Please give Mr. Sawyer the second chance he deserves. He has many years of productive life ahead of him. He has already served more than 20 years behind bars. The $75,000 per year keeping him in prison could be better spent elsewhere.

Sawyer's suit against the CDCR for withholding his property was dismissed at the US District Court level.[10] He appealed to the Ninth Circuit Court of Appeals, which found enough merit to agree to review the case and in 2019 ruled in Sawyer's favor. The case was returned to the US District Court.

Everything comes with a cost. Sawyer was convinced that the CDCR was holding back his commutation effort because of his litigation. He said he was the only *San Quentin News* staff member who was never interviewed about his commutation request.

22 Asians in the Newsroom

One day on my way to the Media Center, I saw four Asian inmates hanging out talking. "Is this the Asian caucus?" I asked facetiously. They laughed. David Le, the design editor at the newspaper, responded, "You're welcome to join!"

Unlike blacks and Latinos, Asians are underrepresented in prison. And when the news media mention Asians in prison, the public is nonplussed. How can members of the "model minority" be felons? Asians represent around 15 percent of the California total population. But in prison they are barely 2 percent, or a bit more than a rounding error. You never hear stories of their incarceration. Ironically Asians were overrepresented on the staff of the newspaper, given their small numbers inside the prison.

The Asian convicts who worked on the *San Quentin News* usually found themselves in jobs that involved technical skills, such as using complex software or keeping records. They worked quietly and reliably and seldom engaged in the newsroom banter. They were guarded with their emotions and rarely expressed an opinion. Occidentals have often used the term *inscrutable* in describing Asians. It's a stereotype, but in prison they did present a stoic, reserved front, compared to the more demonstrative blacks and Latinos in the room. They were keenly aware of their small

Figure 10. Jonathan Chiu, running a marathon at San Quentin. Courtesy of Christine Yoo.

numbers and their vulnerability and isolation in prison, where race is a constant undertow.

Cambodian-born Phoeun You was a student in my 2012 Prison University Project journalism course. His family had come to the US to escape the Khmer Rouge genocide. "I have very few memories of Cambodia from childhood. What I do remember are the thunderous sounds of bombs and gunfire."[1] He had grown up in Southern California.

> Long Beach was where I was exposed to new ethnic groups, such as Blacks and Mexicans. At least here, I saw other Asian kids; and for that brief moment this brought me a little comfort. The environment was different from the slow pace to which I had become accustomed. I went from a small town, Ogden, Utah, with all white people, to the hustle and bustle of city life. In Long Beach, I was surrounded by unfamiliar territory. There were gangs (Crips and Sureños) on every corner of the block. Coming home from school, I would often hear shootings near or around my house. At first, I was scared but managed to adjust to the new city and my surroundings. Today, I am still easily startled by the sound of loud noise.

He wound up in prison because he sought to protect his nephew, who had been beaten up by some Mexican juveniles. Armed with a shotgun, Phoeun and the nephew drove through the neighborhoods for two days looking for the youths who had carried out the beating. And on March 23, 1995, he found them:

> We drove until we spotted a group of what appeared to be Mexican gang members. I told my nephew to slow down as we passed by. Just as we got close, I leaned out the passenger side window and fired multiple shots into the crowd. As I fired, I could see bodies diving on the ground. For a few seconds after the shooting, I felt good. Shooting them felt like I was in a fight and I had counter-punched my opponent and landed some power punches. Unsure of the outcome, we headed home. Later that night, I felt numbed. The numbness quickly turned into fear and paranoia. The feeling of uneasiness I felt eventually led me to flee out of state.[2]

The shotgun blasts killed one Mexican youth and wounded four others. Phoeun You, at age forty-two, had been in prison ever since. In prison Phoeun You became an active participant and group leader in rehabilitation programs, besides his work on the newspaper. "The programs taught me how to question what I thought. They also showed me how to connect with my emotions," Phoeun You said. "I started understanding who I am and what happened in my life. In the programs, I had the chance to listen to survivors of crime tell their stories. That took me to another level of understanding of my impact on the people I harmed. After doing this work and then listening to survivors speak about their hurt, their hurt became mine."[3]

Phoeun You gained some international attention. He was featured in a *Los Angeles Times* video about prison inmates who write their own obituaries,[4] and soon afterward a story on the subject was posted on the London *Daily Mail* website.[5] One of the UC Berkeley students worked with Phoeun You, and she discussed his crime with him. Jesse Lau, a Cal undergraduate born in Hong Kong, found it hard to reconcile the man she was talking to with what he had done those decades ago.

> I'm constantly struck by the degree to which inmates at *San Quentin News* reflect on their crimes, even after so many years of being incarcerated. One afternoon, I was editing an article on Utah bringing back the firing squad as

an option for people on death row, and Phoeun You and I had an interesting discussion about whether firing squad could be considered "more humane" than lethal injection. He told me that he used to be on death row, and that he wouldn't pick firing squad because his experience with guns as part of a gang left him traumatized (he still has dreams about gunfire, and thinking about it makes him anxious). He also showed me a creative essay he wrote recounting his crime from the perspective of his victim. The essay describes a child coming home from school when a man pulls up in a car and shoots him. It ends with a scene in the hospital showing the victim lying on a bed, realizing he was going to die. It was the first time we really had a substantial conversation with each other, and I remember thinking: how could Phoeun possibly have committed this crime? The narrative he told about his incarceration simply didn't match up with my impression of him, and this contrast really concretized my belief that people can change, despite their past.

Later Phoeun You was accepted into a training program that taught him to write computer code, and he was preparing for a date with the parole board. Like dozens of other Southeast Asians who came to the US as refugees from the Vietnam War, Phoeun You faced immediate deportation once he left San Quentin.

The same fate awaited Borey (Peejay) Ai, thirty-four. Born in a Thai refugee camp after his family fled Cambodia, Peejay was brought to the Central Valley as a child. There he encountered hostile black and Latino gangs, and they clashed. He said coming to America was a culture shock for his family. Ai was serving a life sentence for his part in a robbery and murder committed when he was fourteen years old. The DA offered him a plea bargain, which he accepted: life in prison. He told me that he had been in prison a year before he understood what he had pled guilty to. Ai was an enrolled student in my first prison Introduction to Journalism class in 2012.

To look at Peejay, one would assume he was Native American. He looked like every Navajo I'd ever met. He braided his hair Indian-style. The resemblance was not accidental; he pointed to his attendance at Native American sweat lodges for helping him turn his life around. "In 2004, I was invited to the sweat lodge community through a friend of mine, and it changed my life," said Ai. "After a while, I began to step away from my gang, and stopped drinking, and joined the Red Road program. There, I learned about victim impact, and it solidified my commitment to change. . . . In San Quentin, I used those skills to flourish."[6]

When Peejay was granted parole from San Quentin in 2017, US immigration agents were waiting for him. He was taken to a detention center in Southern California. The US government intended to deport him.

The same fate awaited Phoeun You, who was preparing for his parole hearing in 2018. ICE would likely be awaiting him too.

The backstories of the other Asian journalists were all over the map. Adnan Khan, thirty-two, a South Asian and a producer in the video department of the newsroom, had also gotten off to a rough start in life. "Khan spoke of his father leaving him nothing but a set of hats. When a teenager teased him about one 'ugly' hat, Khan responded in violence and ended up in continuation school. Then his mother moved away, leaving Khan with relatives who asked him to leave because he was acting out. The homeless teenager eventually landed in prison for taking part in a robbery where his co-defendant stabbed and killed the victim."[7] The victim was a marijuana dealer.

Khan's bittersweet first visit with his mother after having been in prison for ten years was featured on the *Ear Hustle* podcast on March 12, 2018. He had gone so long without a hug that he spent time in his cell practicing how he would embrace his mother when she came to the prison.

Chung C. Kao, fifty-four, looks the part of a Chinese underworld character, much more so than San Francisco's notorious real gangster Shrimp Boy Chow. Kao, muscular, with close-cropped hair, wiry, and covered with intricately drawn tattoos, had been born and raised in Taiwan. He was a prolific and careful writer. He left the *San Quentin News* when an opening presented itself in the Last Mile rehabilitation program for training in writing computer code. He told me that he had two sisters, both of whom were lawyers. He was the family's black sheep. He was serving a life sentence for second-degree murder. "Dad loved me so much that I wish I could go back in time to make up for the decade he stood heartbroken for me."

While in prison, Kao sought peace of mind using some mindfulness practices he had learned in China. "My culture helped shine light on a non-violent path in prison," Chung Kao said while performing tai chi movements. "I was lost swimming in an ocean of inner conflict. Only focus, tenacity and faith have returned me to center, time and again."[8]

Kao was an inventor besides being a writer and tai chi exponent. While a prisoner, having served twenty-three years, he created a voice-coded trigger lock for a firearm. It could be traced by police if the gun were to be stolen. He developed the mechanism while working with Last Mile. "There's nothing like it on the market," he said.[9]

Born in Hong Kong, Jonathan Ming Chiu, thirty-five, holds three pass-ports, one from the United Kingdom, one from the US, and one from Hong Kong. Sentenced to fifty years to life in prison for a murder he com-mitted in August 2004, the mild-mannered Chiu shot to death country-and-western musician Travis Parker, thirty, in a Los Angeles parking lot behind a music store where the victim gave violin lessons. Chiu, twenty-one at the time, was romantically involved with Parker's ex-girlfriend, Meredith DelFosse. Parker and DelFosse were fighting it out in court over his visitation rights with their daughter, Tricia, then age three.[10]

> I intended to marry Ms. DelFosse and intended to acquire custody of Tricia. I went to confront Mr. Parker on that day and I carried a handgun legally registered to me. After a short confrontation, I was so angry, I pulled out my gun and as Mr. Parker and I struggled with the gun, I shot him twice—one on his side and one in the back, which resulted in his death. I was arrested the day after and admitted to the crime and went to a jury trial where I was found guilty of First Degree Murder and the use of a firearm resulting in death enhancement.[11]

The jury deliberated for just an hour.

In March 2018, Chiu, the design and layout editor for the *San Quentin News* since 2015, received a visit from his mother for the first time in twelve years. The last time she had seen him he was being held in the Los Angeles County Jail shortly after the murder. In the interim Chiu's mother decided to return to live permanently in Hong Kong. He said she had friends and family there and had never really fit into Southern California. She had never learned English. Chiu said he had trouble communicating with his mother. He had forgotten much of his Cantonese. The few Chinese prisoners in prison spoke Mandarin. In 2015 I introduced Chiu to Jesse Lau, the UC Berkeley student, also from Hong Kong. Later Lau told me it was an awkward conversation because Jonathan could not express himself well in Cantonese.

Chiu's older brother also came for the March visit. Jonathan had a nephew he had never seen. He learned that his brother had named the child "Quentin."

Jonathan Chiu was the systems administrator for the *San Quentin News*. Later he was promoted to managing editor. In addition, he created the paper's monthly crossword puzzle, a job he relished. He joked that he sometimes received "hate mail" because of the puzzle.

At age thirty-five Chiu had become a long-distance runner, having completed three marathons while in prison.

His hopes for freedom lay with Governor Brown, whom Chiu petitioned in 2018 to commute his fifty-year sentence.

> I committed the wors[t] crime any person can commit, which is murder. I personally believe that if someone committed the same atrocity to any of my family members, I would want that person to be imprisoned just as me. However, this is in conflict with another belief I know and have seen in person, a belief in second chances and that a person can truly change their ways. I have seen many people I trust found suitable by the state and are home now with their loved ones. I know I do not deserve to go home. All I want to do is show the community that I am not the same person who made the wrong choices 13 and half years ago. Whether this commutation is granted or denied, I am content in serving the rest of my life in prison for my actions because every day I spend is a day that Mr. Parker misses, and his love[d] ones live without him.[12]

The Chiu sentence of fifty years to life bears the indelible imprint of racial bias in criminal justice. He committed an unpardonable crime, a cross-racial homicide, and the victim was white. The other offenders "found suitable," to whom Chiu referred in his letter, were all perpetrators of same-race homicides, and these were prosecuted as second-degree murders. Nevertheless, Chiu never mentioned the race factor. Instead, in humility, he asked for mercy.

Even though the odds of commutation were heavily against him, he never gave up. Running those marathons was a metaphor for doing his time in prison: "Being in prison is already pain enough, you might think. Do I really need to run to find pain? When the judge first sentenced me to life in prison, I thought many times about ending my own life. But after staring at my situation over the years, I realized that my life is a privilege that my victim doesn't have anymore."[13]

Jonathan Chiu was sentenced to a term of fifty years to life for a murder he had committed when he was twenty-one. His first visit to the parole board was originally scheduled for 2048. On the day before Thanksgiving 2018, he learned that Governor Brown had commuted his sentence to a term of seventeen years. He has already served fifteen. Chiu, thirty-six, was by then the managing editor of the *San Quentin News*. He told me that on the fateful Wednesday that he received the news he was running errands and was not in the Media Center during the morning. When he got back in the afternoon, he was told he had to report to the Captain's Porch, a suite of offices near the entrance to the prison. When he arrived, he said he went to the office of the associate warden.

Awaiting Chiu was a phone call from the governor's commutations lawyer, who told Chiu his application for commutation of his sentence had been granted. He was shocked, saying he had not expected it. I had written a letter supporting his application, and even I thought it was a long shot for the governor to grant it. But there it was.

Chiu told me he might get to visit the parole board in July of 2019, and he might get a release date and walk free before the end of 2019. He said he wanted to remain in the Bay Area, and he might look up his marathon training buddy Eddie Herena, who had been released on parole a few weeks before. But the question remained: Who would do the crossword puzzles for the *San Quentin News?*

23 Aly Tamboura

Aly Tamboura, one of the charter members of the revival of the *San Quentin News*, would qualify as the poster child for prison newspaper rehabilitation. He went from prison obscurity to high-tech stardom, all within a year.

In San Quentin Aly was classified as just another black American prisoner, but his father came from the African nation of Mali, and from the outset one could tell that he defied any preset category. His English was faultless. His prescription lenses gave him an intense, owlishly serious expression. But that alternated with a big cheerful smile. He was self-confident, was often outspoken, and had uncommon technical smarts. Before coming to prison he had worked on engineering projects that took him around the world. "Tamboura's prior experience includes 20 years working in the underground utility industry, including 12 years as the founder and CEO of a geotechnical company. He managed and completed large and complex underground utility analytics for government and private entities."[1] The foregoing passage from Tamboura's CV indicates he was unusual among inmates. It continues, "In his spare time, Tamboura is

175

Figure 11. Aly Tamboura and Mark Zuckerberg. Photo by Chandler West of CZI.

a scuba diver, spear-fisherman with a passion for underwater photography and video."

Given his background, Tamboura naturally was chosen to be a member of the first wave of prisoners accepted into the Last Mile project that trained inmates in writing computer code. He made the most of that opportunity.

When I first arrived in the newsroom in 2012, Aly was just emerging from a trip to the Hole. The prison management had searched his newsroom computer and discovered a photograph of a female correctional officer. The picture was in no way salacious, but it was a security breach nevertheless. The incident was an early indication that Tamboura sometimes flew close to the flame.

He once told me a revealing story about taking risks in prison. An inmate, who shall remain nameless, had his family burn DVDs of recent motion pictures, including "some pornography," in Tamboura's words, onto a flash drive, which would be smuggled into the prison. (Flash drives were officially considered contraband.)

The smuggled movies would be shown secretly to the whole inmate population in the middle of the night each weekend on San Quentin TV, the in-house, closed-circuit television system that is wired into the cells. The contraband movie would be placed on a special secret channel setting just for these clandestine events. Once the movie was completed, San Quentin TV would automatically be restored to its normal, innocuous channel slot. All the information about the rogue channel was spread throughout the inmate population via word of mouth, even to prisoners on Death Row.

(Inmates may purchase special TV sets for their cells. The sets must be made of transparent plastic so that no contraband may be hidden inside.)

The rogue TV channel stayed in business for "a couple of years," according to Tamboura. Its undoing came about when San Quentin experienced a power failure. The timing mechanism for screening the smuggled movies thus went off line for several hours. When the timer resumed, it was out of sync. It was the middle of the workday, and suddenly San Quentin TV screens began showing porn.

An investigation ensued, and one inmate faced disciplinary action, meaning the Hole, but he never revealed who his confederates were.

Tamboura knew an inordinate amount of detail about the rogue television caper!

Why would anybody do such a thing in prison? Nobody charged money for viewing the movies. The whole purpose was to hack the system.

Editor in chief García was an excellent judge of character. "When I first met Aly [Tamboura], I thought he was too smart. I didn't think I was going to be able to establish a good conversation with him. But over time, working with him in the print shop, I found that his knowledge was useful, not only to me but to other men around him."[2]

Tamboura, at age fifty, walked out of San Quentin in late 2016, having received parole after serving nearly fourteen years following his conviction for making a death threat. The victim was his ex-wife. He told me the dispute had involved his ex-spouse looting his business. He said his defense lawyer offered him a plea bargain that would have given him a three-year prison sentence. Tamboura had a clean record and was confident he'd win at trial. Instead, he was convicted on two counts and was given a sixteen-year sentence. In a 2009 documentary on the *San Quentin*

News, Tamboura explained the offense this way: "I told my wife at the time, now my ex-wife, that I was going to kill her because of the infidelity and I was convicted of making a death threat. Under the penal code they called it terroristic threats so I was convicted of a terroristic threat and a 10-year gun enhancement."[3]

Once released, Tamboura prospered. He landed a job, and his employer sent him to a tech academy in San Francisco to build on his code-writing skills. He said the academy took him to the "next level." I met Tamboura in the Agave Restaurant on Franklin Street in Oakland on December 6, 2017. I needed to deliver him a baseball cap bearing the *San Quentin News* logo. He had remained active in the newspaper's affairs. Having rebuilt its website, he was continuing to put recent issues up on the internet. He thought of himself as part of the team. In return for the baseball cap, he'd promised to give me a custom-made T-shirt emblazoned with "Free Bonaru," a reference to the newly installed editor in chief, Richard Richardson, serving a forty-seven-year sentence.

Tamboura gave me a thumbnail sketch of how his career had taken off. He was in high demand. Priscilla Chan, wife of the Facebook founder, was recruiting him for a position with her philanthropic organization Chan Zuckerberg Initiative (CZI). His was a success story that boggled the mind. In one year he had gone from making a dollar a day to making hundreds of thousands of dollars per annum.

In early 2018, Tamboura visited San Quentin again as part of a group tour offered to Facebook employees. During the tour, other inmates and a few correctional officers came up to greet him, some giving him a big hug. His coworkers were puzzled. They thought he was joking when he said he had done nearly fourteen years as a prisoner.

24 Little Nick's Story

It was a Sunday in 2017 when I drove to Napa through heavy Memorial Day traffic, arriving at the apartment of Nicholas Balentine García and his wife across the street from the Walmart and parking in a remote corner of the lot. The ground floor apartment was spick-and-span. Nick, sixty-four, and Monica, fifty-one, sat together on the couch like teens. She touched him. They held hands.

Nick, the younger brother of editor in chief Arnulfo García, played a supporting role in the *San Quentin News*. He would help out in loading and unloading the freshly printed newspapers. Nevertheless, the story of Nick and Monica gives vivid insight into prison truth, the kind of story that leaves you shaking your head because it's all about family and tenacity. Even Arnulfo García said the story of his sister-in-law's devotion was one for the books. California's criminal justice system often breaks people, but then along comes a Monica García.

Nick's wife was religious, deeply so. Her email address was "christianheart." Three handwritten devotional statements were taped to a mirror over the sink in the bathroom. But she didn't mention God even once when she talked about her relationship with her husband. She talked about "mind over matter." She had heard Nick tell his stories before.

She nudged him to tell more, or to redirect him, or to have him finish some part.

I don't think I asked more than five questions in ninety minutes with the couple. Nick had a great sense of oral history, like his brother, Arnulfo, the longtime editor in chief of the *San Quentin News*. Nick relied on gesticulations and paused for effect. He leaned forward and squinted for emphasis. Monica sat quietly, listening intently. Nick's hair was brownish blond, unlike that of his brother Arnulfo, who was a total *moreno*. Nick had been even blonder when he was younger. He was a hand shorter than Arnulfo too. Nick had just returned to the free world after serving forty years in prison for murder.

But it's Monica's story that I'm really after. So far in this book I've told the stories of the inmates who showed determination, resourcefulness, and ingenuity during their incarceration. I've not mentioned the women on the outside who supported them, women like Monica, whose story is unique in the annals of prison relationships and deserving of special mention.

Here's the gist of it. Monica was married for more than twenty-eight years to Nick. All that time, he was serving a life term. She bore him four children, all conceived and delivered while he was incarcerated. California allows conjugal visits (which are officially called "family visits," lest taxpayers get the idea that the CDCR condones sex).[1] Monica put all the children through college, including a daughter who graduated from UC Berkeley. Their costs were paid by scholarships. Her marriage proved more durable than 90 percent of those in the free world. Nick said proudly that she came to visit him every weekend for twenty-eight years. She even brought the newborns into the prison visiting areas. Whenever the CDCR would transfer Nick to another prison up and down the state, Monica and the kids would follow.

To the casual observer, a woman falling for a lifer is a formula for disaster. It's the missing lyric to the Eagles hit song "Looking for Love in All the Wrong Places." But women fall for lifers with regularity all over the country.[2] At least three members of the *San Quentin News* staff with whom I have worked have married women while serving life sentences. In at least one case, the inmate married a volunteer whom he met in a prison rehabilitation program. Every prison has a strict rule forbidding "over-familiarity" between volunteers and inmates. If a correctional officer observes it going on, the inmate goes to the Hole and the volunteer has her entry privileges revoked. In one notorious case, a newspaper staffer, already married, was observed to be overly familiar with a female volunteer, and he was promptly whisked away to the Hole and thence to another prison.

Sexual attraction happens in prison. Even distinguished journalists (!) are not immune. Lynn Bartels, then with the *Albuquerque Tribune,* once fell under the spell of a sweet-talking convict inmate. Bartels wrote: "My relationship with the [New Mexico] corrections department was still a little shaky. I had shattered all credibility after a disastrous relationship with a maximum-security inmate I met while covering the infamous Independence Day Breakout in 1987. Only years later can I joke about my relationship with the prisoner, who was paroled several months after the breakout."[3]

In California, the CDCR mandates that handshakes be the only form of touching allowed between volunteers and inmates. The rules are more relaxed for families in the visiting room, where embraces are allowed.

Explaining the operation of the *San Quentin News* would be incomplete without a discussion of the relationships and the attachments that the men form with the two dozen civilians who visit them regularly.

Naturally, after months of working with the inmates, volunteers become friendly with the inmate writers and editors. The no-touch policy makes for occasional awkward and artificial situations. Nevertheless, the young women whom I escort in from UC Berkeley abide by the rules. They know the third rail when they see it. On one occasion, however, I saw a female student drape her arm around the shoulder of an inmate outside the education annex building, and I had to read her the riot act.

The confines of newsrooms in the free world are notorious for spawning office romances. Perhaps that's because news people work together intensively on challenging projects. Of course, romantic attachments would be off limits in the *San Quentin News* office. What I have observed, though, is that women civilian volunteers often encounter men who give them their undivided attention. The inmate is genuinely delighted to spend time with the female journalist. His attentiveness is a form of flattery. These work relationships become friendships and may lead to genuine fondness. It's a prison setting, but they are human beings. The students, who usually visit for only a semester or two, graduate and go on to take up their professional lives, while the men remain behind bars.

The more long-term senior-level volunteers must undergo regular training, which some refer to as "brainwashing," during which prison officials stress over and over that the inmates are manipulative, possibly predatory, and that visitors need to be constantly on their guard. No sharing of personal contact information is to be allowed. A strict dress code is enforced:

A. No transparent clothing.

B. No tank tops/sling shot tops.

C. No strapless, halter, spaghetti straps and/or bare midriff clothing.

D. Tights are an acceptable alternative to hosiery for wear under dresses or skirts.

E. Skirts will be no more than 2 inches above the knee. Slits in the garment shall not expose more than mid-thigh.

F. No dress or sport shirts/blouses unbuttoned past the second button from the top of the shirt/blouse.

The default dress for veteran female volunteers is all black. Many times, I've had to lend apparel to UC students, male and female, who were stopped at the East Gate because correctional officers objected to clothing. Either the color was unacceptable or, in the case of women, the clothing was deemed to be too tight. I keep a pair of chartreuse corduroy pants in the trunk of my car for just such occasions (the "pants of shame"). I began carrying the spare pants after one incident when I had to drive a student to the nearby Target to buy her a pair of suitable trousers.

Family members are subject to more invasive scrutiny, even occasional strip searches, because the authorities suspect contraband smuggling during visits with family.

For a nominal fee, inmates can have photographs taken with their families in the visiting room. Some of the men have not seen relatives for years. The photos become treasures. They smile together, while behind them are murals depicting escapist outdoor scenes. The palm trees or waterfalls in the background make the settings look far from normal. Nevertheless, the pictures often decorate their workstations in the media center.

Sometimes the men share their joys as well as their sorrows with fellow staff members, or even with advisers. Once a staff member opened up to me about his fears that his stepdaughter was hanging around with the wrong crowd. The irony was that the complainant had himself been a gang member and was serving a life sentence for a murder committed in a dispute over drugs. The bad companions he complained about were his own biological daughters!

The prisoners experience occasional despair or a sense of helplessness when it comes to managing any kind of crisis while they are in prison. That's the lesson Nick García learned early on in the forty years he was in prison.

Nick was sentenced to life in prison for a murder he had committed in the course of a bungled burglary in San Jose while he was high on PCP. After his imprisonment his then-wife, Veronica, divorced him, and he lost touch with his two children.

When I met Nick and Monica in their living room, Nick had been free on parole for fewer than six months. He was still living in a halfway house in Hayward and came to Napa on visits. During the last eight years of his imprisonment, Nick shared a cell in San Quentin's North Block with his older brother Arnulfo. It was Arnulfo who first told me the story of the star-crossed romance of his younger brother and Monica. Arnulfo was as baffled as I was that such a thing could have happened.

Monica was fourteen when she first met Nick, who was then serving his life sentence at the California Men's Colony in San Luis Obispo. She met him on her birthday in August 1980, two years after the murder for which Nick was sentenced. Monica's father was also an inmate there. He was Nick's coworker in the huge prison plant that manufactures license plate tags for the DMV. Monica's dad, Chuck, was serving a four-year sentence for involuntary manslaughter. Chuck had caused the death of his girlfriend, Dottie, who died of a head injury he inflicted in a drunken fight.

Monica first saw Nick when she and her stepmother came to visit her father. They were sitting together at a picnic table on the prison grounds. She remembers Nick asking, "Hey, Chuck, is this your family?"

"Yeah, this is the guy I work with at the tag plant," her father replied.

It was love at first sight. Chuck, an inmate himself, tried his best to discourage his daughter. "Right man. Wrong place," he told her.

Nevertheless, Monica decided that Nick was the man for her, and they became pen pals. Nick said he was ambivalent. He thought they would just be friends. After all, he was thirteen years older and facing the long, dark tunnel of a life sentence.

Nick recalled that Monica's father once told him, "I would like you to write to my daughter. She doesn't have any male friends. If she writes you and asks you a question, answer it fully. She's really particular about the answers to her questions." Monica would write letters that were fifteen to twenty pages long, Nick said. "Sometimes I don't write back, or just write three quarters of a page, and cut it short. It was just friendship. All along she had a different agenda. She was very young." Their correspondence went on for more than eight years.

During this time, Nick appealed his case, and he was returned for a time to Santa Clara County Jail. Monica hitched rides from Sacramento with her cousins to San Jose to see him. Later when he was returned to prison, she would catch the Greyhound bus for the overnight trip down the highway to visit him in San Luis Obispo.

Once Monica was eighteen, she could make her own decisions. At age twenty-two, she and Nick were married.

Nick's life was in turmoil long before he ever went to prison. He had run away from home the first time when he was four years old. He had a juvenile record and an addiction to drugs and alcohol. He and brother Arnulfo would sometimes team up to carry out residential burglaries. In one case, said Nick, he and Arnulfo were in the midst of taking a victim's belongings from her apartment when she returned home. Caught red-handed, the two burglars apologized. "We took everything out of the truck and put it back in. She never called the cops," said Nick.

Unlike brother Arnulfo, who was determined to turn his life around once he was sentenced to life, Nick was not a model prisoner. He collected a disciplinary record for drug and alcohol use. But he said twelve years of "one-on-one therapy" while in prison helped him come to terms with his character flaws and made him a better man. When I met him in 2012, he had settled down. He had a plum job. He was the clerk in the prison's package delivery office. Inmates are allowed quarterly care packages from home. They line up dutifully in the afternoons to collect their goods. Nick was also a fixture in the *San Quentin News*. He was not a writer. He would lend a hand in clerking chores and odd jobs. For example, he would help distribute the bales of printed copies of the paper when they arrived from the printer.

Meanwhile, his wife Monica was struggling to raise a family on her own.

California at that time allowed prisoners serving life sentences the privilege of "conjugal visits," in which the husband and wife would have sleepovers inside special accommodations in the prison, referred to on occasion as the "Boom Boom Room." In the years that followed her marriage, Monica gave birth to four children.

"My mom said I have mind over matter," Monica told me that day at her apartment in Napa. "I believe I can make things happen. My father was an alcoholic, and I was not going to have that life." She bore Monica (the oldest child) and Adam. Nick wanted just one more child. Monica delivered twins.

How could she possibly manage raising four children on her own with a husband serving life in prison?

For the first five years of marriage and motherhood, Monica's brood had no stability, as she followed Nick up and down the state from one prison to another before he finally landed at San Quentin in 1995. She and the children were living in Sacramento at the time. She was standing in line awaiting her visit at San Quentin when she asked other women in the line where they lived. She learned that many of them lived in Napa. They all said the same thing: it was affordable, it was close to San Quentin, and it did not have the terrible street violence of other small towns in the area. So Monica and her kids moved to Napa. That was the turning point. "It was a huge blessing," she said. "It was a good place, quiet, no violence or bad behavior." But then she was evicted from the first apartment building because the landlord said the children were too noisy.

She and the children were rescued by her boss, a physician, whom she helped care for his elderly patients. The same doctor owned an apartment building. Monica and the kids moved into his building, where she and the children lived for the next eighteen years. They gained much-needed stability. She moved in when the twins were four. Because of the safe and affordable apartment, the children were able to attend the same schools and keep the same friends during their growing-up years.

"I had help from county, food stamps, general assistance, housing. And then I went and got a job," Monica said. "I've been a caregiver for eighteen and a half years for the same company."

Monica joined a Christian prison ministry in Napa for support, and the children went to weekly Bible classes. She also enrolled her kids in a support program for children of incarcerated parents.

Project Avary of San Rafael was founded in 1999 by Danny Rifkin, comanager of the Grateful Dead, and Earl Smith, a San Quentin chaplain. This nonprofit offers a summer camp as well as year-round programs for youngsters who have parents in prison. The García children attended Avary camp from a young age. Daughters Monica and Sabrina later took paying jobs with Project Avary. The *San Quentin News* later reported their story:

> Sabrina was conceived during a family visit in prison and had to build a relationship with her father through prison visiting rooms, where a lot of Nick's friends and other prison families watched her grow up.
>
> She entered Project Avary at age eight, and now mentors the next generation of kids coming through the program. She credits Avary for providing a safe place to connect to other kids in the same situation.[4]

Nick and Monica's daughter Sabrina also found the love of her life in prison. She married an Avary co-worker.

"I'm proud to have her as a part of our family," said John Atkins, Sabrina's father-in-law and Avary board member.

Sitting on the couch that day in Napa, with Nick's prison sentence finally behind them, Nick and Monica behaved like honeymooners. In twenty-eight years of marriage, this was the longest sustained time they had ever spent together. "It was mind over matter, stability and Christianity here in Napa," Monica said. "Weird, but that's how we did prison life."

25 He Came to Me in a Dream

PRELUDE

The headline of the March 1, 2016, editorial in the *San Quentin News* read, "Editor-in-Chief Steps Aside to Pursue Other Dreams."[1] It was Arnulfo García's swan song:

> In 2011 I was asked to step into the shoes of Editor-in-Chief; a job that I knew was going to be difficult, but former Editor-in-Chief Michael Harris had confidence that I could do the job. Until then, I had run from all my problems, afraid to face the unknown.
>
> People always saw something in me that I couldn't see in myself. Michael believed in me and told me with confidence that I was given the opportunity to be a voice for those that were not able to speak for themselves.
>
> I've been at San Quentin for almost eight years and working for the *San Quentin News* for over six years and Editor-in-Chief for almost five years. I have to say it's been challenging, but very successful.
>
> Perhaps the proudest moment during my tenure came when the Society of Professional Journalists awarded the *San Quentin News* the James Madison Freedom of Information Award. The citation praised the newspaper for producing a high-quality publication under extremely difficult circumstances. We set out to get the San Quentin newspaper into every

prison, and I am proud to say we have accomplished that goal. The time has now come for some changes to pave the way for a new era for *San Quentin News*. I will be stepping aside as Editor-in-Chief.

ACT I

In late May 2017 Arnulfo García had been talking for months about his court case. He had asked me to write a support letter for him, and I did. He also introduced me to his lawyer, Dan Barton, who had represented him for the sixteen years he was in prison. García tried on several occasions to describe the legal labyrinth he was navigating. He was serving a sentence of sixty years to life as a Three-Striker for small-time burglaries to feed his heroin addiction and then, following a bureaucratic mixup where he was let out on bail, an escape to Mexico. What this meant was that he would have to serve a minimum of sixty years before he would have a date with the parole board. He would be more than a hundred years old.

García told me in May of 2017 that he had a habeas corpus hearing set. I did not think much of it. He had had hearings and big court dates before. But this one, he said, was make-or-break.

Around this time, he was absorbed more and more with his case. The court date in San Jose was set for June 29. García did not know the time or the department. I got the information from Barton.

I researched a bit and discovered that García's judge was the Hon. Deborah Ryan, a Schwarzenegger appointee. I shared her bio with García. He was unsure when and how he'd be transported to San Jose. I went in one Sunday in early June and visited the newsroom. He was busily cleaning out his workspace by his computer. He had a small cabinet filled with personal effects, including many spices he added to the burritos for the afternoon feasts in the newsroom. (The meals served in the SQ newsroom would be well worth a whole separate chapter. A UC student once pitched an idea to *Gourmet Magazine* to do a feature on high-class prison cuisine. She never heard back.)

When I went in on Wednesday, June 28, 2017, he was gone. They had collected him at 3:00 a.m. All his personal property in his cell had been boxed and sent to R&R (reception and release). Arnulfo García was cooling his heels in the Santa Clara County Jail, gone from San Quentin, never to return.

García's hearing was set for the following day. I arose at 7:00 a.m. The courtroom opened at 9:00 a.m. I had no idea when his case would be called. Driving to San Jose in the commute traffic from Oakland is no small undertaking. Without breakfast, I set off at 8:05 a.m., taking a roundabout way to avoid the horrors of 880 or 101. I went via 680 toward Dublin and crossed from east to west through Southern Alameda County to Milpitas, finally arriving at the spartanly gray San Jose Civic Center complex.

Not one but two deputies did independent searches of my belongings at the courthouse entrance. Eventually I made my way to Department 27. It was 9:40. I hoped I was not too late. This courtroom has a small entry door that looked like a private office. The courtroom was the size of an ordinary UC Berkeley classroom for fifty students. The audience sat in four rows of fourteen seats each. Aly Tamboura, the longtime *San Quentin News* writer and one of García's oldest friends, greeted me at the door. I sat down next to him. Next to me was the woman who managed the halfway house in Hayward where Arnulfo's brother Nick had been living since his parole a few months before.

Several members of García's family were there. I did not know any of them. I recognized Barton, the lawyer, sitting inside a railing with all the other lawyers.

When I arrived, a feeble Latino in green county jail togs was sitting with his lawyer at the defense table. A tall blonde woman stood beside him doing simultaneous translation.

I saw Arnulfo García sitting alone in the rear row of the spectator section on the far side of the courtroom. His hands were cuffed in front of him. He wore faded orange jail clothing. He flashed a subdued, confident smile when he saw me.

We waited patiently for the earlier case to conclude. The old man in green sat in silence as the judge droned on. The defendant was a career drug dealer and user. Judge Ryan was spelling out to him how he would be spending his future: fourteen years, starting in county jail. She had it broken down into days. She included a bunch of other possible monetary penalties.

Once this prisoner left the courtroom, it was 9:55 a.m.

At 9:59, a burly, baldish white bailiff took off García's handcuffs. With a big smile the bailiff gave him a "thumbs up," guiding García from his place in the spectator section to the defense table where he sat with his attorney.

Judge Ryan asked the defense and prosecution in García's case to approach the bench. Two attorneys from the defense team and two prosecutors stood before her and had a muffled conversation. The tension mounted, and the general public watched anxiously as criminal justice did what it does, secretly but in plain sight.

Shortly before the conference at the bench, the Santa Clara County DA, Jeff Rosen, a participant in more than one *San Quentin News* forum, entered the courtroom. Rosen had met García at the prison just a few months before and apparently took a personal interest in this case. The right pants cuff of the DA's trousers was tucked in the top of his socks. I wondered if he had pedaled over on a bicycle. He sat on the spectator side of the rail, like any other member of the general public. Tamboura and I glanced at each other, each of us raising an eyebrow, knowing that an appearance by the DA is not an everyday occurrence.

Barton's request for a writ was based on a "Romero" motion, under which a judge may remove a strike, or both strikes, from being used in a defendant's sentence if circumstances warrant it and it is in the "furtherance of justice." The defendant is then resentenced to a term based on the single, latest offense. In García's case, that would be a simple residential burglary. He had already served sixteen years, way more than burglars customarily serve. Granting the Romero petition would mean that García would be eligible to be resentenced and most likely would be released from county jail and allowed to enter transitional housing in the free world.

His fate rested in the hands of Hon. Judge Ryan. Her blue eyes seemed seldom to blink. On occasion, sitting high up on the bench, she would clasp her hands in front of her, seeming to signal, "I've heard enough. Let's wind it up."

She appeared regal because a four-foot-diameter circular "Eureka" Seal of the State of California, gold on dark blue, graced the wall behind her. The off-the-record conference between judge, prosecutors, and the defense dragged on.

Sam Robinson, the PIO back at San Quentin, sent a text to Aly Tamboura's iPhone, "What's going on?"

Judge Ryan occasionally smiled approvingly. At 10:03, she called for "The People versus Arnulfo T. García."

The judge said she was impressed with García's achievements during his incarceration. She noted his thick folio of letters and endorsements. She said she had seen a copy of the *San Quentin News* and thought it was a worthwhile publication. Tamboura and I exchanged smiles. She also took note of the support García enjoyed, looking out in the audience to where DA Rosen sat.

She agreed to schedule the Romero habeas corpus hearing. She set a date for July 10, about two weeks later. Meanwhile, she said, she would ask pretrial services to interview García and determine a level of appropriate supervision for him at the "transitional housing" arrangement in Hayward. The woman from that house was sitting next to me, and she was evidently pleased. The judge said these preparations were to be completed by July 10.

ACT II

Then came the Big Wait. Each day I expected García would be released to the halfway house. It did not happen. It turned out that he was still on San Quentin's books. The Santa Clara County sheriff was not releasing him until San Quentin lifted its hold. On July 7 Tamboura sent me a message, "Arnulfo is still in Santa Clara County Jail. His lawyer says 'soon. very soon' on his release. Jail wanted him to process out at SQ."

It dragged on. July 10 came and went. A week later, I messaged a group of Arnulfo's friends who wanted to know what was going on:

> This just in. Arnulfo called a few minutes ago. He is still in Santa Clara County Jail. Sheriff refuses to release him. His lawyers are working with Judge Deborah A. Ryan who ordered his release "notwithstanding any CDC retentions." A certified copy of her order has been sent to Sacramento. Meanwhile, Arnulfo says he is being patient. His lawyers say the Sheriff is holding him illegally. Go figure.

I got a friend-me request last night from Arnulfo García on Facebook. At first, I thought Arnulfo had been sprung. It was from Arnulfo's nephew, a student at Butte College, who has the same name.

On July 19 I sent out another update:

Tomorrow (Wednesday) a drama will be played out in the case of the State versus Arnulfo T. García. In Dept. 24 of the Santa Clara County Superior Court the judge is expected to vacate the life sentence of the long-time editor of *San Quentin News*. The Hon. Judge Deborah A. Ryan last week had ordered García released "not withstanding any CDCR retentions," but the Sheriff balked and wanted to return him to San Quentin for "processing out." Tomorrow's expected court order would clear the way for García to be released to a halfway house, ending more than 16 years in prison.

I had to send out another update after the hearing:

This info comes from two sources. Aly Tamboura, who was at the hearing, and Carmelita Vargas, Arnulfo's sister.

1. As expected, the Santa Clara County Judge signed the order vacating Arnulfo's 60-to-life sentence.

2. Carmelita went to a person whom she describes as "main jail officer in charge." That person informed her "they still need a drop hold from SQ."

3. Carmelita sent me a copy of the Superior Court order. In big bold, handwritten letters it says, "DO NOT TRANSPORT BACK TO CDC."

4. Carmelita's assessment, "same o same."

Three main players are involved here: The Santa Clara County Sheriff, the CDCR and the Superior Court. Hard to figure where the hangup lies.

García called me several times from jail. He did it through the maddening pay-as-you-go phone system. You have to give them your credit card number. He would usually ask for an update on how the newspaper was doing, and he would ask about any gossip. Sometimes he would ask me for phone numbers of other people, and I would supply them if I had them.

He mentioned that he was being moved around within county jail. Having come in as a lifer from San Quentin, he was given a more strict level of custody. Using his customary charm, he managed get himself moved into a less supervised living situation.

On July 21, 2017, Tamboura emailed me a photo. It showed Arnulfo García sitting in the front seat of a red convertible parked in front of 150

Figure 12. Arnulfo García when he was freed from Santa
Clara County Jail. Photo by Aly Tamboura.

West Hedding Street, the main jail in San Jose. He was in profile talking
on a mobile phone. Free at last. His sister Carmelita Vargas sent me a text,
"He's out!!!!"

ACT III

Off he went to live at the Hayward halfway house, where Nick had stayed.
Arnulfo had a mobile phone and an email address.

He would call regularly and give me an update on all the things he was doing. Foremost in his conversation was the reentry project he planned. For more than a year he had talked about building a retreat, some place in rural California, where recently released convicts could work on a farm, the way he had done when he was on the lam in Mexico. He would get together with reentry experts like Daniel (Nane) Alejandrez, of the prisoner-support group Barrios Unidos in Santa Cruz, and Doug Butler and other people familiar with these programs. García was insistent that the reentry program be in a rural area, away from the temptations of the inner city. He figured, rightly, that paroling a felon back to his old haunts would send him back among the bad companions that got him in trouble in the first place. He talked about setting up a foundation and applying for grants.

I had long ago learned not to underestimate García's big plans. Over the years everything he said he wanted to do eventually came to pass. The newspaper circulation had grown from five thousand to thirty-six thousand by late 2017. He had wanted to bring public officials and educators into San Quentin for face-to-face dialogue with prisoners, something that had never been done before. He had laid the groundwork for production of an in-house magazine to be titled *Wall City*. He had set up a partnership with the Haas School of Business. He had managed to raise $250,000 from the Logan Family Foundation, despite longtime adviser Steve McNamara's opposition to the grant application.

Even though García was free, his colleagues back in the newsroom were never far from his thoughts. I was tasked one Sunday with the job of sending Arnulfo a list of the shoe sizes of all twelve of the *SQ News* staff members. He had promised them all a pair of new sneakers.

Several times García mentioned that he was working for his brother in construction. I could not help but wonder how he was paying for things. I received a steady supply of updated pictures of García at family gatherings with his daughter and his sister Yolanda. He still did not have a driver's license.

He phoned me in early August. We talked about getting together. I had not seen him since the hearing in June. No urgency. We'd do it when he had settled down. He told me a long story about getting a new suit at Jos. A. Banks in San Mateo. He said he had been open with the salesman and told him he was on his way to a job interview. The salesman was impressed when García told him he had been in prison for sixteen years. He picked out a beautiful blue suit. He was proud of it. Later he sent me pictures of himself wearing it. "Ankle bracelet off. Interviewing for a job," said his text message. It was the suit in which they buried him.

ACT IV

> His goals are real, his impact is real. Lately, he's entered my
> dreams (in one, he grabbed me by the shoulders and told me
> "calm down").
>
> Bo Kovitz, *Wall City* magazine, Spring 2018

It was September 23, 2017, a lazy Saturday, and I was lying on my couch in the afternoon. I had dozed off. The phone rang. It was Aly Tamboura, "Are you sitting down now? I have some news. Arnulfo and his sister were killed. It was a car wreck in Hollister."

"Oh, shit. No, no, no."

I sent an email to all the *San Quentin News* volunteers and to Sam Robinson, the PIO.

> Just got word. Arnulfo T. García, SQ News former executive editor, died in
> an automobile accident near Hollister.
>   Aly Tamboura was informed by Arnulfo's daughter.
>   Also killed was Arnulfo's sister, Yolanda Hernandez.
>   That's all I know.
>   I plan to visit SQ News tomorrow.

Bo Kovitz, a UC Berkeley student, responded first: "What?"

Robinson: "No!!!!"

I knew Robinson would let the prisoners know.

The next day, Sunday, I visited the prison. Sonia Shah, another volunteer, had come in earlier on Sunday and done a circle gathering. These talking circles or peace circles are a therapy approach for handling emotional crises and draw on Native American, folk, and aboriginal traditions. They are often used in prison, and it seemed to have settled the men emotionally by the time I arrived.

The men were in shock. These hardened criminals, in the eyes of the press and the public, struggled with their loss. They were devastated. Richard (Bonaru) Richardson was so overcome that he was absent from the newsroom.

Me? I had that icy, soul-less, numb feeling of suppressed emotion, grief denied. It goes back to the deaths I've known, of my parents when I was a child, and later of my wife when she died of breast cancer complications. But I had to be strong for the men. I needed to reassure them that we would hold together and move forward. When I walked in, I saw the newsroom lacked the customary bustle and vitality. A week or so before and without warning or explanation, the San Quentin Prison management had seized the computer CPUs. New CPUs were brought in some weeks later. But during this interim, the newsroom operation was on pause. Men were sitting around talking to each other in subdued tones.

One computer was left in the newsroom, an iMac, and layout editor Jonathan Chiu was working to pull together the next edition of the paper. The correctional officers had seized all the CPUs, but they had left behind the monitors. They had assumed, erroneously, that the iMac was merely a monitor because it was unattached to any box.

The loss of the computers and Arnulfo's death brought the *San Quentin News* to an emotional low point. Without the tools to do the stories and the layout, the men saw no reason to come to the newsroom. They were not abandoning ship. They were hanging out together on the yard or in their cells. They were grieving in their own way. But it was hard to justify bringing in student volunteers if there was no work to be done and there were no computers on which to do it. Nevertheless, the students wanted to come in so they could be of some comfort to the men.

On September 25, I messaged the UC Berkeley volunteers:

Trigger alert. Because of the untimely death of Arnulfo García, the newsroom atmosphere will likely be more emotional than usual. I went in yesterday. The men are fine. Sonia Shah had come in earlier and done a prayer circle. I was not there, but it was heavy. [Marcus] Henderson [aka Wali] confessed to crying, and he was not the only one. Krissi [Khokhobashvili] came in all the way from Sacto and was a great, warm presence. So, when I got there at 5:30 the men were coming back from dinner and had gathered themselves.

I gave Henderson and Juan my pitch that they had to get a grip and move forward in realizing Arnulfo's goals for the paper.

Thence, things settled in and the place began to hum with more energy than it has had since before they confiscated the computers.

Sonia is returning today for a reprise of the prayer circle.

In general, the prisoners are handling things better than the volunteers. They have each other. Volunteers usually have nobody who understands what the SQ thing is about, much less what the special quality was that Arnulfo had.

Please be patient. Many saw Arnulfo as a brother.

To the outside media, Arnulfo García was much bigger in death than he had ever been in life. What attracted the interest of the media was the irony of his enjoying freedom only a few months before he died. What they could not grasp was what he had accomplished in the six years that he was editor in chief of the prison newspaper.[2]

Arnulfo García's funeral took place on October 5, 2017, in a Protestant church in Santa Clara. The Church of the Valley is just down the street from the Lima Family Funeral Home and a couple blocks from two major cemeteries. Death is a part of the everyday retailing in that neighborhood. I passed a shop that advertised "Affordable Caskets."

The service for García and his sister Yolanda Hernandez was held in a church with a tall A-frame roof and a spacious sanctuary. García and Yolanda had no connection with this church, which has a youngish, progressive, white congregation but was a suitable classy venue for the funeral.

A GoFundMe campaign, launched by Tamboura, had netted more than $30,000, enough to cover the funeral expenses and purchases García had made on Tamboura's credit card.

The majority of the audience was Mexican American—friends and family of the deceased—lots of kids and a couple of babies. Next was a substantial representation of ex-convicts—not just from San Quentin but from other prisons where he had stayed. They were joined by CDCR officials and García's friends among the volunteers from the *San Quentin News*.

I arrived late, so all the printed programs were gone. The only handout left was the Twenty-Third Psalm, which I had memorized when I was eleven. The sanctuary was full, probably two hundred souls, with about twenty people standing in the back. A woman pastor presided. The closed coffins of García and his sister Yolanda were displayed in the front of the church. Three floral sprays stood in front. A trap drum set was positioned on the altar, but the drums were not used. Instead, a small-framed man named James Edward (Jaime) Marquez from Barrios Unidos in Santa Cruz, a prisoner support group, played a musical interlude on a traditional Central American wooden flute.

After the pastor gave a eulogy she called upon groups of friends or family to talk about the deceased. Because it was a double funeral, most of the program consisted of remembrances told from the heart with great emotion.

The high point came when Rev. Deborah Johnson of New Thought Church in Soquel spoke about knowing García before he came to San Quentin. He had been confined at Pleasant Valley State Prison for four years before coming to San Quentin, and that's where his effort to redeem himself had begun. Rev. Johnson lit the place up with her refrain, "You haven't heard the last of Arnulfo García!" and the applause rose up as if on cue.

A mariachi serenaded the mourners at the gravesite. I sought out Nick García and pressed in his hands three flash drives of data, text, and pictures that Arnulfo had entrusted to me. The outside temperature was around eighty-five degrees. A couple of people fainted and EMTs rolled in just as I departed.

I thought I knew García pretty well, but the speakers brought out sides of him that I had not known about. The funeral convinced me that he was a most remarkable man, and his death illuminated his life. He went from sixty years to life, to two months of freedom, to an early death.

Bo Kovitz was not alone in having the former editor appear in a dream. It happened to me too. Since his death, I've worn a rubber wristband inscribed with the words "I am Arnulfo García." (Jacques Verduin's GRIP program had dozens of them made to memorialize the late editor. Everybody in the newsroom wore one.)

My dream was vivid. I was in a large auditorium. It was filled with young people. They might have been students. Someone asked me about the wristband. I said, "I am Arnulfo García!" They cheered. I then cried out, "Viva Arnulfo García!" And at that moment somebody asked, "He was your comrade?" I felt tearful pride welling up inside me. Even after I had awakened, I felt proud.

"You haven't heard the last of Arnulfo García," Rev. Johnson had said at the funeral. I hoped not.

PART III

How It All Came Together

26 The Press in Prison

This study has examined the evolution of *San Quentin News* inside San Quentin Prison since Warden Robert Ayers Jr. gave the green light for the presses in the print shop to roll again in 2008 following a twenty-year hiatus. Nobody had ever heard of *Orange Is the New Black*, the highly successful Netflix series that allowed us to see Piper Chapman's stay inside federal prison through her eyes. Facebook was still in its infancy. Twitter was a little more than a year old but hardly a household word. Mobile phones were widely used, but they were hardly "smart."

Now I want to examine what happened when the brave new world of internet connectivity overtook mass incarceration. The CDCR's view of San Quentin's prison newspaper changed 180 degrees. Instead of regarding it as a nuisance, the CDCR came to see it as an asset.

The prison system was facing an unprecedented overcrowding crisis when the *San Quentin News* resumed publication, but it would be another three years before the Supreme Court of the United States in *Brown v. Plata* would rule that California's prison system was guilty of inflicting "cruel and unusual" punishment on inmates because of overcrowding.

The *New York Times* reported in 2011, "Justice Anthony M. Kennedy, writing for the majority in a 5-to-4 decision that broke along ideological lines, described a prison system that failed to deliver minimal care to prisoners with serious medical and mental health problems and produced 'needless suffering and death.'"[1] The ruling was a breakthrough. It set an actual numerical limit to how far California prisons could go over their design capacity.

How bad was the overcrowding? Robert Sillen, appointed by the federal court as the receiver-in-charge of the CDCR health system (or "czar," as the newspapers called him), did a tour of San Quentin in 2006.

> To reach one of San Quentin's medical clinics, you must walk past a row of 20 maximum-security cells with inmates confined behind fine crosshatched wire, barely visible. The floor is strewn with trash, puddles of water and worse from the runoff of inmate showers from the tiers above. Soap and hair drip off the guardrails of the walkways, leaving a slippery mess to dance around as you approach the clinic, which is shoehorned into a converted cell. A mildewed shower curtain hangs in front of the clinic's entrance to keep water from spraying directly into the medical area. I have run hospitals, clinics and public health facilities for the past 40 years, and medical care in California prisons is unlike anything I have ever seen. Inhumane is the nice term for the conditions. . . . The resulting patient health outcomes tell a gruesome story.[2]

OUT OF SIGHT, OUT OF MIND

The appalling conditions caused by overcrowding in California's prisons did not come to public attention through diligent reporting by the mainstream media. This prison crisis occurred at the time the state's newspapers were watching their business model slowly collapse, as Craigslist took away classified advertising and retailing went to the internet. Add to that the decision by most newspapers to foolishly distribute their content free on the internet. Paid subscriptions shrank.

The federal courts, namely US District Judge Thelton Henderson in San Francisco, took the lead in exposing the appalling prison conditions.[3] Even then the public prints failed to demand access to the prisons to see what was going on. Newsrooms were shrinking. Veteran journalists were taking buyouts. The *L.A. Times* no longer employed a dedicated reporter on prison conditions such as I had been in 1970–71. Even a big paper could not afford such a luxury. (Curiously, in 2018 the *L.A. Times* did have a dedicated reporter covering the marijuana beat!)

But almost as soon as the *San Quentin News* began to publish again, its writers zeroed in on the health care and overcrowding issues. In the November 2008 issue, the headline read, "California Officials Openly Defy Federal Judge."[4]

> California officials face fines of up to $2 million per day for refusing a federal judge's order to turn over $250 million in state funds needed to jump-start construction on over $8 billion in improvements ordered to bring the medical facilities in its state prisons up to constitutional standards.
>
> The state's long-running battle with U.S. District Judge Thelton Henderson heated up Monday when lawyers for Gov. Arnold Schwarzenegger and State Controller John Chiang questioned the judge's authority to force the state to hand over the funds, or even to order the changes in the California Department of Corrections and Rehabilitation's medical facilities.
>
> Henderson, who in 2006 appointed a federal overseer to manage the state's beleaguered prison health system, responded to the attack on his authority at the hearing with an order that the funds be transferred by Nov. 5. Failure to comply with his directive, says Henderson, will result in both Schwarzenegger and Chiang facing a hearing for contempt the following week, and the potential for as much as $2 million per day in fines.

Keep in mind that at that point the *San Quentin News* printed just five thousand copies, most of them circulating inside the prison. It did not have a website. Even in primitive nonsearchable form, a website would not arrive until 2010. However much the paper covered the overcrowding/health care crisis, the message had limited circulation, particularly outside the prison.

CHANGING MEDIA LANDSCAPE

Internet media gave a great deal of power to interest groups that were focused on mass incarceration. These activist groups arose around the same time the prison newspaper reappeared. The digital world allowed even small voices to be heard far and wide.

We used to teach "mass communication" in colleges. Practically all those academic programs have been renamed and are now referred to by the more amorphous title "media studies." The reality of today is that effective media no longer address "mass audiences." Effective media reach niche audiences. That's why mass media such as broadcast television, radio, and cable TV have continued to shed audience. In the early days of the mobile phone we talked a lot about "citizen journalism," but we did not know what that would look like. At first, the idea was that private citizens would send mobile phone video to TV stations or YouTube, and that would be a big breakthrough. Yes, a cottage industry sprang up using such video. But the bigger effect of citizen journalism lay elsewhere. As we were later to learn, online affinity groups with a political agenda became a powerful citizens' editorial page. It's called internet populism.

Niche audiences relied at first on Yahoo groups, but then came Facebook, which allowed people with common interests to find each other and stay in touch. In the past the families of prisoners had found themselves alone, isolated, and powerless. A family member would be sent to prison, often far from home. His or her relations would be left behind scrounging for information on such topics as visitation regulations, conjugal visits, how to send money, and how to make phone calls. Obtaining that information from CDCR was a challenge. The inmate population in California reached 160,000-plus at the height of the crowding crisis. Each one of those inmates had a family on the outside. Every inmate in a cell represented the loss of a son or daughter, father or brother, mother or sister. Imprisonment touched families deeply in the outside world. It's counterintuitive, but jail often brings families closer. By definition, family is where you go, and they have to take you in.

How big an audience was there for niched information about inmates in California prisons?

That potential audience is much larger than one might have expected. Some recently released research indicates that, within families, incarceration is much closer than six degrees of separation. In December 2018, *USA Today* published this report:

> Among the findings, obtained first by USA TODAY, were that half of adults in the USA have an immediate family member who has been incarcerated.

That's about 113 million people who have a close family member who has spent time behind bars.

The study by FWD.us, an organization critical of U.S. immigration and criminal justice policy, was done in partnership with Cornell University. The conclusions were drawn from a survey of more than 4,000 people, a sample size representative of the U.S. population.[5]

In 2019, according to the correction department's Facebook page, the CDCR had approximately 45,000 parolees and 114,000 inmates in thirty-five prisons, plus 3,500 inmates in conservation camps, 4,200 inmates who had been shipped to out-of-state private prisons, 670 inmates placed in exclusively juvenile facilities, and 6,100 inmates placed in other contract facilities.[6] That is a considerable audience by itself. Each prisoner would likely have an average of three family members. But the FWD.us study would indicate that the number of affected families in California is much larger. The FWD.us study give no estimates as to the degree of a family's involvement with the person in prison.

The pervasiveness of ex-prisoners in California came home to San Quentin warden Ronald Davis, a veteran of more than twenty years in the CDCR, through an incident that affected him personally He told the story to US Rep. Jackie Speier (D-San Mateo) when Speier visited the prison on June 19, 2015 (I was allowed to sit in on their meeting). After moving into a middle-class Northern California neighborhood, Davis discovered that one of his neighbors had at one time been incarcerated. His friendship with the neighbor had given him important new insights about how prisons work, from the inmate's point of view.[7]

When mass incarceration struck, Yahoo groups were the first resort of families, as well as ex-convicts and activists, to protest the crackdown. The Yahoo groups later migrated to Facebook. California Prison Info and Support had more than three thousand members in 2018. As lobbying groups go, the numbers were modest, but the followers of this group were exceptionally engaged and motivated. They reported on the well-being of incarcerated family members, sought information about what to do in medical emergencies, asked about arcane CDCR policies, and waged political campaigns in support of changes in the laws. They stayed abreast of policies that might affect their family members. They campaigned actively for ballot propositions seeking to roll back mass incarceration. They made their wishes known to legislators in Sacramento. The group's goal was prison reform. They proclaimed that "as a Group we are concerned about Prisoner Abuse, Prisoners' Rights, Health care, Rehabilitation, Recidivism, Public Safety, The Death Penalty, Parole Issues, Sentencing Laws, Three Strikes, Wrongful Conviction, Mandatory Minimums, The Drug War and more."[8]

MESSAGE TO THE GRASSROOTS

A larger prison reform group, Prison Reform Movement (PRM), was created on Facebook by a Tennessee woman, Carole Leonard, who wrote about why she took this step:

> In 2003, I joined some Yahoo groups that were focused on prison reform. I met Wanda Valdes in one of the groups and she shared with me what Florida Department of Corrections did to her husband, Frank Valdes. Valdes was murdered by 8 Florida Correctional Officers—literally stomped to death. I was repulsed. In the California prison groups, the stories of medical neglect and abuse were just as horrifying; It was hard to believe the level of depravity in the prisons—each story I heard was so heart wrenching, and horrifying. I just couldn't sit back and do nothing. These families needed help, the prisoners needed help—so I started a group called "Inmate Activists."[9]

The name changed to PRM in 2005. The numbers in 2018 were still modest, twelve thousand members and more than thirty thousand Twitter followers. Leonard worked as a home health aide in Tennessee while studying for her BS in criminal justice. She estimated that she spent around six hours a day working on PRM and other prison issues. She had the help of four co-moderators. Nobody was paid. This could not have happened in 2008 because they would not have had an efficient means to stay in touch. "My outreach has brought families together in their prison journey, they now know they are not alone and have support from others experiencing the same things. . . . The one thing I am most proud of is that I have created places where people can share, support each other, and become more aware of our nation's criminal justice system and actually become involved."[10]

PRISONER STORIES AS ENTERTAINMENT

Meanwhile, popular culture took a remarkable turn. *Orange Is the New Black* was the most notable departure from the usual media tropes about prison. The public's tastes changed in a short time. Maria Reynolds discovered the change firsthand. Before *OITNB* came to television, Reynolds tested the market for a prison memoir, as she wrote on *Huffington Post:* "I wrote a memoir that, like *Orange Is the New Black,* not only tells my story, but shares the lives of the women I served time with. I got out of the system. Most of them did not. I tried to publish my award-winning manuscript but was told over and over, 'It's an amazing read but no one cares about the life of an unknown junkie.'"[11]

Later, once *OITNB* became a big hit for multiple seasons, Reynolds wrote, "The series continues to humanize the women, sharing their stories, their challenges, and how even when there are moments of hope and light, the reality of the downward spiral comes back to haunt them. You can call them evil for the crimes they committed, but there is a subtle message that should be louder. . . . Incarceration takes away the very things that might enable women to rebuild their lives."[12]

OITNB soft-soaped prison life. It took a clean-cut, young white woman, not the usual offender, and trapped her in the criminal justice web. Piper lets a romantic relationship get her in trouble, and the next thing we know, she finds herself trying to survive in a federal prison.

It is fiction, and *OITNB* author Piper Kerman readily admits that. The TV series does not try to depict real prison life. It would be too grim. Nevertheless, *OITNB* opened the imaginations of millions of viewers to the emotional toll of incarceration.

To glimpse real-life prison life, we would have to go to reality TV. The program *Lockup,* which stressed violence, disorder, threats, and conflict, has been a staple on cable.

The problem with *Lockup* is that all the episodes have a monotonous sameness. All the prisons look alike, and so do the inmates with their ill-fitting clothing and their garish tattoos. Inmates and staff are awkwardly conscious of the cameras. Prisoners rarely speak more than fifteen seconds. As a viewer, I know I am intruding on a scene that will go back to normal once the video crew is gone. And what the prisoners say we all heard many times before. We see the squalor, the menace, the fear; we hear the superficial bravado. It's all the producers can do to come up with manufactured story lines to make one episode look different from another. Each jail or prison is portrayed as the worst of the worst. We are participating in a shallow video drive-by, lacking even the spontaneity of a *Cops* episode. The viewer is quickly numbed and bored.

Lockup has no larger message, no lesson, no discovery. The prisoners remain opaque and inaccessible on an emotional level.

THE *EAR HUSTLE* PHENOMENON

By contrast, nothing illustrates the changing landscape in public tastes quite like the spectacular success of the podcast *Ear Hustle,* produced inside San Quentin, featuring hosts Earlonne Woods and Nigel Poor with production help from Antwan Williams. When it premiered on June 4, 2017, Woods and Williams were inmates, while Poor was an arts professor at Sacramento State University (Woods has since been released). In its first month the podcast logged 1.5 million downloads. Funded by the John S. and James L. Knight Foundation, through an initiative called Podquest, *Ear Hustle* was selected from among 1,537 entries from fifty-three countries. At the end of its first year *Ear Hustle* recorded more than six million downloads. As I write, it has been downloaded more than fifteen million times. It went on to win a 2018 Webby award as best documentary. The award recognizes excellence on the internet and is presented by the International Academy of Digital Arts and Sciences.

Poor told a journalism website that the formula was basic storytelling. "*Ear Hustle* is, to my understanding, the first podcast to ever be completely produced inside a prison. . . . We are not a crime podcast. We concentrate on the everyday stories of life inside prison from the perspective of those who live it. We really concentrate on the small details that help give life meaning and really explore how you make a life once you become incarcerated."[13]

Ear Hustle was not the first radio program to originate from San Quentin. Veteran Bay Area journalist Nancy Mullane worked with inmates to produce a public radio program called *Life of the Law.* Its archive lists more than one hundred programs. They explore the big policy issues in criminal justice. *Ear Hustle* avoids confronting these issues head-on. Nevertheless, in telling simple stories of a prisoner's day-to-day existence, the *Ear Hustle* subjects illuminate a wide spectrum of problems that most people have wondered about but had no one to ask. This is what *Rolling Stone* said about the podcast:

> "Racism, violence, compassion. I think we're getting at the stuff, maybe in a quieter way," Poor explains. In humanizing prisoners, their project should go a long way towards changing minds about how and why we imprison people for decades.
>
> "You can't get people interested in changing laws without getting the public to care about these people," Poor says. "I hope when people realize that Earlonne is serving 31-to-life for attempted robbery, it makes them say, 'What the fuck? Our justice system is so messed up.'"
>
> When asked about getting out, Woods responds enthusiastically. "HELL YEAH!" he writes. "It's sad that I've been here all of these years based on politics [politics being the three strikes law]. But yes, I think about getting out every day, as well as every two years—that's when they have elections in California. I'm only a ballot measure away from getting out."
>
> "The one thing every prisoner in the world share[s] is the thought of getting out," Williams writes. "This podcast is teaching us a great skill set that we want to apply to our lives once we leave here. We want to help change a world we will ultimately be returning to."[14]

The podcast has won praise from practically all of the critics.[15] But some African Americans were more guarded. How come you have a white woman as a cohost, they asked? The question is a valid one and deserves a serious answer. Nigel Poor was essential to the program's success because she gave the average listener access to the conversation. Woods, Williams, and the other inmates gave the program authenticity through their voices. The mixture was just right.

I worked for years at then-National Public Radio (now NPR) beginning in 1979, during the time that Susan Stamberg was the host of the award-winning program *All Things Considered*. *ATC* went through a number of male hosts, all of whom were competent and talented, but what made *ATC* special was Stamberg. Her secret was that she was guileless. She would ask the questions that the average listener, not the specialist, wanted to know about. The questions were basic ones. "How does this work? Please explain it to me." Stamberg made issues accessible by expressing curiosity and genuine interest. On *Ear Hustle,* Woods in his worldly way and Poor in her unaffected questions were a perfect match. Woods would not be as effective without Poor to play it straight. She fed lines to Woods, giving him a natural entrée into explaining a prison's byzantine rules. She might have been the best "straight man" in the radio business since Bud Abbott.[16]

EARLONNE: You're now tuned into San Quentin's 'Ear Hustle' from PRX's Radiotopia.

NIGEL: Hey, E, tell everyone how you heard about this story. You really ear hustled this one.

EARLONNE: I think it was back like in January. I was in the chow hall, and I'm waiting in line for dinner and there was a couple of dudes behind me and one was telling the other guy about this 115 he got.

NIGEL: A 115 is a rule violation.

EARLONNE: Right. Except, this wasn't about contraband or a fight. This was about an actual escape. So, you know it got a little interesting. Right? I'm, I'm, I'm hustling this one.

NIGEL: I'm sure you are.

EARLONNE: So, I did one of those, "I'm not listening to what you're saying" things, and turned around just so I can really identify the guy, and later, I saw him on the yard, and he was in front of the area where the white guys kick it.

NIGEL: Mmhmm.

EARLONNE: And, he's an older guy, but he was busting down, doing burpees, getting his money. Right?

NIGEL: Yeah. Nice.

EARLONNE: So, I waited for him to finish his set, and then I walked over to him, and I'm like, "Excuse me, sir. My name is Earlonne. Can I holler at you for a second?" And, we started talking and I told him about the podcast, and I was like, "Look, man, I was in line the other day, and it was you and another guy, and you was telling him about a 115 you had, and it was a very interesting story, and I would hope that you can come down to the studio so we can talk about it." And, he was like, "No." [intro music] I'm Earlonne Woods, a prisoner at San Quentin State Prison in California.

NIGEL: I'm Nigel Poor, a visual artist who works with incarcerated men at San Quentin.

EARLONNE: And, together, we're gonna take you inside. [catchy beat] What's up, listeners?[17]

The mixture of voices and accents puts the listener at ease. Woods has a naturally avuncular presence. He was funny, intelligent, and linguistically from the street. Poor was unmistakably a white woman with a classroom-like sensibility, interested, encouraging, but not pushy.

Ear Hustle is a conversation that would never take place in real life. It could happen only in the dystopic space of a prison. Nevertheless, both hosts were welcoming, as though everything was perfectly normal. They relaxed you before you heard some genuinely upsetting stories.

STEVE: I've been denied 3 times. This is my fourth parole hearing coming up now.

EARLONNE: Steve Wilson has been in prison, on and off, for about 30 years.

NIGEL: He didn't want to talk to us at first because he had that parole hearing coming up. He didn't want to say something that might be used against him.

EARLONNE: Which is smart, because if your parole hearing is successful, you get a date. It's what everyone wants: a date to get out of prison. And that's what we're talking about on this episode: what it takes to get out of prison. [bumping melody]

NIGEL: So, Earlonne, Steve Wilson didn't want to talk to us.

EARLONNE: Uh-uh.

NIGEL: This was way back, before we even did our first episode, so maybe he didn't know what we were talking about, and, honestly, we didn't even know what we were doing. [both laugh]

EARLONNE: Maybe. I mean, I explained it to him. You know, I'm like, "Hey, man. Uh, we'll hold this story off until after your parole hearing." And, after talking to him like that, he agreed to holler at us.

STEVE: I thought I had a good chance at parole the last time. I had a low risk of recidivism. I had over 20 years of clean time with no write-ups. I had no violence in my, my history except my commitment offense in 1979. [dropping beat]

NIGEL: Commitment offense. That's the crime that put him in prison in the first place.

EARLONNE: In 1979, Steve Wilson murdered his father-in-law on a ranch in California. It was a complicated domestic dispute that we're not gonna get into here. But, basically, Steve's wife left him and he went to her father's ranch to get her back. But, his father-in-law wouldn't allow him on the ranch. So, long story short, Steve kidnapped his father-in-law and ended up killing him, shooting him twice, I believe.

NIGEL: It's been almost 40 years since that murder and Steve's now 73 years old. But, it's not just his crime that's keeping him in prison.

STEVE: Every time I go to the board, uh, there's always just one rule violation, a 115 that I got about, um, 30 years ago. And, um, every time I go to the board, they bring it up.[18]

The other technique that helped *Ear Hustle* succeed is that its subjects talked at length, not in a fifteen-second sound bite. As I've mentioned before, most prisoners are great conversationalists and excellent storytellers.

Postscript: Earlonne Woods left San Quentin in December 2018. Gov. Jerry Brown commuted his thirty-one-year-to-life sentence to time served. His departure was joyful for him, but it was an occasion for *Ear Hustle* to regroup. Another cohost would have to be chosen, and Woods would be a hard act to follow.

Because of the popularity of *Ear Hustle,* Woods's release made the A-Wire of the Associated Press:

Woods, 47, was recently released from San Quentin State Prison after California Gov. Jerry Brown commuted his 31-years-to-life sentence for attempted armed robbery. Brown cited Woods' leadership in helping other inmates and his work at "Ear Hustle," a podcast he co-hosts and co-produces that documents everyday life inside the prison.

Woods has since been hired as a full-time producer for the often funny and at times heart-wrenching podcast, which has been a smashing success since its launch in 2017. The show's roughly 30 episodes have been downloaded 20 million times by fans all over the world.[19]

TEDX TALKS

The online profile of San Quentin took a giant step forward with the onset of TED Talk events inside the prison January 22, 2016. Organized by longtime *San Quentin News* volunteer Delia Cohen, TEDx San Quentin is an independently organized TED Talk event, and more than twenty-four speakers have been added to the TEDx platform.[20] The signature moment was the appearance of former US Treasury secretary Robert Rubin on a program with Curtis (Wall Street) Carroll, a self-taught expert on the stock market.[21] These events brought the prison and the inmates to the attention of a much larger and influential audience.

The TEDx event tied SQ inmates into a bigger mainstream intellectual conversation. And it had major fallout. Almost immediately it brought in distinguished journalists such as Quentin Hardy, then of the *New York Times* and later Google, Josh Quittner of Flipboard, and eventually magazine designer Sarah Horowitz, all of whom volunteered to work in the San Quentin newsroom. It also brought interest from Neil Barsky, founder of the Marshall Project, which began publishing written pieces from *San Quentin News* writers, including Rahsaan Thomas. The ever-expanding network of relationships was an insurance policy against any future attempts at banishment.[22]

Ron Davis, the San Quentin warden, spoke at the first January 2016 TEDx Talk: "Everybody has ideas about prison, but two things echo from today: opportunity and responsibility. Hearing these guys talk about accepting responsibility and then having them take advantage of the opportunities that we've provided will help them become successful members of our society." Davis was giving voice to the newest CDCR philosophy. And he was speaking to an audience beyond the walls of the prison.

PRISON PUBLIC INFORMATION GOT SMART

The California Department of Corrections and Rehabilitation customarily played defense in dealing with the media. Through the years, it hunkered down and grudgingly reacted to press inquiries, which were often looking into something unflattering. The department maintained a cadre of public information officers arrayed around the state, one at each of its thirty-five institutions. It also had a headquarters press office with about twenty-five employees in Sacramento. The day-to-day work was feeding the press information on disturbances, deaths, lockdowns, contraband arrests, escapes, and routine conflicts that are the ebb and flow of incarceration.

When the overcrowding issue got to the courts, the public relations arm came under immense pressure because the federal courts, specifically Judge Henderson, had the CDCR back on its heels for months.

The public relations arm emerged from that crisis substantially changed. Here's what happened. In 2011 a Scotsman named Jeffrey Callison joined CDCR with the title of press secretary. In May 2016 he took on the title of assistant secretary for communications.

Before joining CDCR, Callison, educated at the University of Edinburgh in the UK, had worked in public radio, first in Santa Cruz and later in Sacramento. He was a classical music host but later covered news. His background reflected experiences in public institutions committed to openness in information.

More importantly his UK upbringing gave him a different idea of how prisons run. Prison terms in the UK are not nearly as long or as harsh as in the US. The British also reportedly have a greater commitment to basic decency than do American prisons. Such amenities as private toilets are taken for granted in UK lockups.[23] San Quentin's open-air latrines are a notorious fixture of the landscape, just like the iconic gun towers. Everyone pretends not to notice. It's an indignity we take for granted.

Callison's appointment signaled a departure in the way the CDCR had been dealing with the public. Callison encouraged information to flow from California's vast prison enterprise, but it had to be massaged through Sacramento's public relations goal of putting a happier face on imprisonment. Almost lifting a page from the playbook of former San Quentin warden Robert Ayers Jr., Callison's office emphasized success stories, training, rehabilitation, graduations, and surprisingly, human interest stories.

The CDCR has two websites. The site www.cdcr.ca is the official page, featuring rules, regulations, announcements, and reports. It logged around 962,000 unique page views per month in early 2018. The other, the site for the *Inside CDCR* newsletter, which carries human interest stories about staff and inmate programs, has come alive with new, generally upbeat content. In 2018 it featured stories about the music group Los Tigres del Norte visiting Folsom Prison, an inmate basketball team in Riverside County competing in a basketball tournament, and inmate artwork at the California Medical Facility in Vacaville. Per month in early 2018 the site logged more than 167,000 unique page views.[24]

Callison's influence was felt following the forty-five-day suspension of the *San Quentin News* in 2014. The newspaper had published the so-called yoga picture mentioned in chapter 11. Warden Kevin Chappelle's decision to punish the newspaper created a storm of negative publicity for San Quentin and the CDCR. It was Callison's intervention that resulted in the mutually beneficial deal assigning a public information officer in Sacramento to edit and fact-check the paper.

Callison and his press office decided to enter the social media game in earnest. In 2017 they did a Facebook video live from Avenal State Prison in Fresno. It was streamed on the department's website. In 2018 live video was done with the staff of the *San Quentin N*ews and later with the producers of *Ear Hustle*. As of 2018, the department's Twitter feed had more than eleven thousand followers, and the department's Facebook page had forty thousand "likes."[25]

A VICTIM OF ITS OWN SUCCESS

The *San Quentin News* had a major role in the trend toward making the prison more transparent. Thus it had a beneficial effect on the prisoners. Many had a better chance at rehabilitation, release, and reentry into society because the paper was able to bring authentic information about prison issues to a motivated outside public.

At the same time another trend was under way. The state's political leaders came to accept that the costs of mass incarceration were unbearable. The 2018 estimate of more than $70,000 per inmate per year was staggering. In addition, the federal courts were breathing down Sacramento's neck. The 2011 realignment policy undertaken by Governor Brown was intended to take the heat off the state by sending more inmates back to the counties, either to serve out their sentences in county jail or to be supervised on parole. Other inmates were shifted to private prisons, some out of state. Critics saw this as something of a shell game. Nevertheless, an exodus from state prison had begun: "'Realignment effectively reduced the state's prison population by more than 27,000 in the first year of implementation,' the PPIC [Public Policy Institute of California] report said. 'As expected, jail populations increased, and, in many counties, jails reached or exceeded capacity.' The overall jail population increased by less than 9,000 inmates. 'As a result, Realignment led to a reduction in both the prison population and overall incarceration levels.'"[26]

PPIC concluded that despite the exodus recidivism rates were only modestly affected. No crime wave ensued. The report took note that realignment had been described as "one of the most far-reaching criminal justice reforms in recent U.S. history," and "the most significant correctional reform in decades."

The state really had no choice. The federal courts said either build more prisons or let more inmates go to bring the numbers back down toward the design capacity.

Every issue of the *San Quentin News* publishes in the masthead the latest figures on the local inmate population. In 2018 that number floated around four thousand.

But the change of fortune did not hit me until I noticed that some of the newsroom stalwarts began to leave on parole. The first wave included Gary (Malachi) Scott, Richard Lindsey, and Watani Stiner in 2013–14. All three were important contributors. Scott was sports editor. Lindsey handled design and layout. Stiner wrote his OG column.

Aly Tamboura was the next to leave on parole. The trend hit home in earnest when I heard about Governor Brown's list of inmates granted commutations for Christmas in 2017. Two names that I recognized were Emile DeWeaver and Charles David Henry.

Henry had been convicted of attempted murder of his ex-girlfriend in Los Angeles in 2004. At San Quentin, Henry did yeoman work as a writer. Having worked in politics before coming to prison, he also helped in the philanthropy work. I read about his commutation on the internet. When I visited the prison a few days later, he was gone. I never had a chance to say good-bye.

DeWeaver, serving a life sentence for murder, received a commutation but was not released outright. He was given an earlier date with the parole board than he otherwise would have had. In late 2018, DeWeaver was freed on parole. But his brother and crime partner remained at San Quentin.

Eddie Herena, the photographer, announced that he had also been found suitable for parole, and he walked free in late 2018. On his first day outside prison Herena and his family visited the beach.

What had been "a bridge too far" when I first arrived in the newsroom in 2002 was increasingly seen as a Yellow Brick Road, leading to an enchanted world beyond in the newsroom.

Three inmates approached me to write support letters for them. I gladly consented. But I did so with concerns about how they would be replaced. It made me think back on the letter I had written May 8, 2014, for Arnulfo T. García, shortly before he was to return to court to wipe out his sixty-year-to-life sentence.

> My biggest concern is not whether Mr. García will succeed when he leaves San Quentin, but how will the newspaper survive without his vision and his leadership?
>
> My fondest hope is that on the outside he might become an even stronger advocate for the newspaper. He will bring this success story to the attention of many more people, and Mr. García's good works will find an even larger audience. He has the key element, which is a simple vision, that bringing human stories to people's attention will make things better, even in prison.

27 Philanthropy

Accolades and recognition would not have been sufficient to keep the *San Quentin News* in business, as the printing costs alone were more than $6,000 a month. As described in chapter 10, the prison's print shop closed in 2010, and from then on the *San Quentin News* was on its own. Initially, Steve McNamara, one of the civilian advisers, stepped in and set the paper up as a nonprofit, and he helped secure funding from foundations. When I showed up in 2012, the paper was paying for the printing and distribution costs with funds from several local foundations, including the Marin Foundation, Annenberg, and the Columbia Foundation. The paper had around a $60,000 cushion, according to managing editor Juan Haines.

The inmates could not legally pay any outside vendor. Instead, the newspaper worked through what is known as a "fiscal sponsor," which behaved like a comptroller in managing financial accounts. It issued checks against invoices, all outside the prison. Media Alliance was the fiscal sponsor for the *San Quentin News*. Founded in the 1970s as a progressive, social justice media organization, Media Alliance makes itself available as a fiscal sponsor to hold funds for smaller nonprofits and pay their bills. McNamara held the checkbook for the Media Alliance funds. He was, in effect, the business manager and treasurer of the *San Quentin News*.

In June of 2015, Jody Lewen, executive director of the Prison University Project (PUP), told me she wanted to incorporate a course on investigative journalism into the PUP curriculum for San Quentin prisoners. At that time PUP offered only an introductory journalism course, which I had two taught two terms of during two separate semesters. She asked my advice. Her proposal, though never adopted, ended up changing the way the *San Quentin News* was funded and managed.

I put Lewin in touch with Robert Rosenthal, then-director of the award-winning Center for Investigative Reporting in Emeryville, California. Lewen, who holds a PhD in rhetoric from UC Berkeley, had an ambitious plan:

> The project would in fact be creating an introduction to investigative journalism class for students in the college program at SQ. The idea would be, if possible, to partner with students from the (UC Berkeley) J-school, who might work with them as collaborators on specific investigative projects. In this case, they would not just be supplying content—they would be learning the craft of journalism as would any other students in a similar class.
>
> Another possibility would be creating a system whereby students in the class at SQ were paired with research assistants on the outside who would assist them in accessing the materials they needed to do their work. In either case, there would surely be lots of details and logistics to work out.[1]

Rosenthal was all in favor of the idea. He and Lewen scheduled a brainstorming meeting. Rosenthal was no stranger to San Quentin. He was a frequent guest speaker at a highly regarded rehabilitation program called GRIP, run by longtime volunteer Jacques Verduin. The program, Guiding Rage into Power, is described as "a best-practices, comprehensive offender accountability program" with a twenty-year track record.

When Rosenthal visited PUP, he also got a tour of the *San Quentin News* office, where he met the editors. He liked what he saw. Editor in chief García talked about his big vision for expanding the paper, the value of the Haas Plan, and the need for foundation funding to stay afloat. Rosenthal came away impressed. He and Lewen talked about another meeting that would include Jonathan Logan and Alden Feldon of the Jonathan Logan Family Foundation. The foundation says its mission is "promoting world-changing work in investigative journalism, the arts, the environment, education, equity and inclusion, and documentary film."[2] Feldon held the title of director of programs.

Rosenthal couldn't make the big meeting with Logan and Feldon, but Lewen was there to greet them. The meeting was productive. The participants committed $50,000 to the *San Quentin News* cause. This was just the start. "The rest is history," Lewen said of the meeting.[3] Asked how much funding they needed, one of the editors said $25,000. "I interrupted and said, actually they need $250,000," said Lewen. Logan and Feldon did not bat an eye. The Jonathan Logan Family Foundation kicked in the $50,000 in late 2015, with a pledge for an additional $200,000.

Ironically, Lewen never was able to get the investigative journalism class off the ground. Nevertheless, the Logan Foundation grant was a critical step forward. It allowed the newspaper to proceed with the planned expansion in circulation. The staff was also able to hire an outside development director to search for continuing foundation support. And the grant occasioned a significant change in the power relationships between the inmates and the civilian advisers. McNamara had used the power of the purse strings to influence policies on the newspaper, according to Arnulfo García, the editor-in-chief. McNamara took exception to the partnership with the Haas School of Business. The original deal between García and Professor Nora Silver, the business school professor, was that the Haas team would do seven hundred hours of consultation and create the business plan, and the paper would pay the $10,000 consultation fee.

That payment was never made.

In a July 2014 letter to Professor Silver, written on the letterhead of the Prison Media Project, McNamara described himself as the paper's "de-facto publisher/business manager. I am responsible for the paper's revenue and expenses through the non-profit I established, the Prison Media Project."

McNamara went on to play down the value of the Haas Plan and claim that the agreement for the $10,000 payment was invalid. "I wish to express my deep concern about the aim of the Haas Business School to extract $10,000 from the San Quentin inmates who staff the newspaper. I understand that a former student, Jon Spurlock, has said the school made an agreement with two inmates to have $10,000 paid for the work of six students who spent five months on a business plan that was a class project."[4]

Pointing out that no actual contract had been signed, McNamara said,

> I handle the newspaper's finances but was never contacted about this expec-
> tation. Belatedly there was an approach that circumvented me to use news-
> paper printing and distribution funds to pay the business school. The prin-
> cipal donor of our funds (a member of the Haas family) was aghast to learn
> of the school's push for payment. She strongly forbid such a diversion of
> funds and wondered why the school did not view its work as a charitable
> contribution. Seeking to be paid $10,000—or paid anything—for five
> months work by six students undermines the very foundation of this historic
> and exceptionally successful volunteer program.

The McNamara letter brought to the surface the long-standing tension between the inmate editors and the original advisers about who was actually running the show. When the newspaper had resumed operations in 2008, the reporting and editorial staff had no journalism training whatsoever. García himself admitted that he did not know how to turn a computer on. The result was that the original advisers, McNamara, Lisetor, and Eagan, were the staff. They made decisions not just on layout and headlines but on story selection, in addition to reading the copy that the inmate writers brought in.

One day when the civilian advisors came into the newsroom, they found that the inmates were making those choices and decisions themselves. The prisoners had taken off the training wheels. The advisers, in effect, became guides on the side. Yet as long as McNamara was writing the checks, he had a great deal of influence, and his veto on paying the $10,000 was final.

Not long after McNamara made his decision, García and I went for another walk in the Lower Yard and watched the Canada geese patrol the baseball field. He was apologetic. "Hey, it's nothing we can really do. He [McNamara] is the guy who signs the checks." García thought that I had lost face because I had brought Professor Silver into the picture and she was going to hold me in some way responsible. In practical terms the $10,000 was a bygone. The Haas School of Business could easily absorb the loss. And it had derived a great deal of free publicity nationwide because of the unique partnership with the *San Quentin News*. García and

I both shrugged and listened to the occasional rustle and squawking of the geese.

Jon Spurlock, one of the Haas MBA students, wrote a polite response to McNamara on July 21, 2014:

> There was no attempt to "extract" the fee from SQN. Nora [Silver] was in an information vacuum after the end of the project, and she volunteered of her own accord to negotiate the fee if SQN was in hardship. I simply expressed to Juan and Arnulfo that she deserved a timely response on status. Because they are men of high character and men of their word, I sympathize that Juan and Arnulfo wanted to repay the debt, even in the face of financial distress.
>
> After I was informed about concern over the fee jeopardizing the paper's near-term finances, I talked to Nora and she expressed that she'd like to completely forgive the debt and move on. I conveyed this to SQN and Sam about the same time as (and independent of) your letter.[5]

Spurlock ended his letter with a plea for cooperation.

> Steve, I understand that you don't agree with or support what my Haas team was asked to do, but I hope that we can move forward productively, collaboratively, and amicably in their best interest and in accordance with their wishes. I'll reiterate that I really appreciate all you do for the *San Quentin News*, and I look forward to working with you more in the future.

The squabble over the $10,000 was a turning point in the evolution of the newspaper. García and the editors made a decision to place the Logan Family Foundation grant with a new fiscal sponsor, outside of Steve McNamara's control. The new fiscal sponsor was the Social Good Fund, and the inmates formed the Friends of San Quentin News as its fundraising arm. Longtime adviser and former *Pacific Sun* publisher Steve McNamara remained active but played a more circumscribed policy role once he was no longer the sole party who could disburse funds. He was instrumental in arranging the San Quentin forums and in upgrading the *San Quentin News* website (discussed in a later chapter).

Once he was on a firm financial footing, García began to unveil his other big plans.

28 The Forums

Marisa Rodriguez, a lawyer in the San Francisco district attorney's office, and a group of her fellow prosecutors visited the *San Quentin News* in 2012. The event launched an educational initiative that eventually influenced hundreds of attorneys in the state and around the country. Rodriguez had a connection to the newspaper through her adoptive father, Steve McNamara, one of the influential original civilian advisers to the newspaper and former publisher of the *Pacific Sun* newspaper. The prosecutors met with San Quentin prisoners, chosen by editor in chief Arnulfo García. The prisoners sat around in a big circle facing the lawyers and talked about what had led them into a life of crime. They talked about their time in prison. They talked about their feelings about their victims. They talked about getting out.

What made the encounter remarkable was that for most of the prosecutors that meeting was the first time they had heard prisoners talk about what happened to them after the courts found a defendant guilty and the judge pronounced sentence. When the trial was over, prosecutors collected their papers, put them in briefcases and left the courtroom. What happened next to the convicted defendant became somebody else's problem. During the decades-long mass incarceration policy, prosecutorial

225

indifference toward how the CDCR operated was a factor in the prison excesses that the Supreme Court in *Brown v. Plata* later found to constitute "cruel and inhuman" punishment.[1] It took an initiative by prisoners to put the justice system's provincialism on display.

On March 1 of the next year Rodriguez returned to the prison with her boss, George Gascón, the San Francisco district attorney. Thus the *San Quentin News* forums, one of García's most inspired ideas, were born. García created the forums after US District Court Judge Thelton Henderson suggested that the public come inside San Quentin to observe the vast number of programs inmates take to advance their rehabilitative efforts.

García's own long experience as a felon had taught him how "criminal justice provincialism" works, or, more properly, does not work. The various agencies of law enforcement are too busy doing their own things to worry about the impact they have on other departments. District attorneys think they have done their job when they obtain a guilty verdict. After that, it's somebody else's problem. Always the pragmatist, García wanted them to know it was their problem too. He wanted to get people to sit down together and frankly discuss their experiences. He had great faith in people sitting down and reasoning together.

Using McNamara's good offices, García was able to arrange the visit by the prosecutors from San Francisco. For more than two hours, twenty-five prisoners talked about how the rehabilitation programs worked and did not work at San Quentin. They hardly spoke with one voice, but not a single one claimed to be innocent. In this case, there were twenty-five different stories. The content of their accounts was not as important as the fact that the conversation was taking place at all. García justified the forums this way:

> The only way to begin fruitful and honest conversations is to take honest, fact-driven storytelling across prison walls. . . . The importance of the news forums is to give public safety officials and concerned citizens the opportunity to talk to and interact with inmates who have decades of experience behind bars and have taken full responsibility for their past crimes. The topic is always centered on incarceration, rehabilitation and re-entry. When we report on forums we bring readers into a world that has honest conversations between the inmates and prosecutors, teachers, judges and other concerned citizens.[2]

It took a Three-Striker serving a sixty-year sentence to figure this out and to make a dialogue happen. The forums proved to be popular and effective. The give-and-take with inmates, García hoped, would influence prosecutors when they reviewed a case. Whenever a convict comes up for parole, the DA from the sentencing county may weigh in. Almost always the DA will oppose parole. It's routine. If the prisoner commits a crime after parole, the DA's hands are clean.

The forums were a way of attacking that strategy, and it worked. Santa Clara County District Attorney Jeff Rosen paid multiple visits to the *San Quentin News*, along with members of his staff. Rosen had 192 prosecutors in his office. He said he wanted them all to visit San Quentin. On his first visit in April 2014, Rosen had these thoughts:

> "It's not very often that I'm in a room with a lot of guys who've committed serious crimes," Rosen said to the room full of convicted murderers, robbers, and three-strikers.
>
> "I agree that a lot of people don't know what happens in prison, and I'm one of them," Rosen said. "I didn't give much thought to what happens to defendants after they are convicted."[3]

He returned again in 2018 for another forum. In the meantime, Rosen had visited Germany and had an inside look at prisons there. He compared what he saw with what he knew about California. He expected the German prisons to be harsh because of the reputation Germany gained during the Third Reich.

> "I'm Jewish, and a lot of my family has survived the Holocaust," Rosen said. "When my parents learned that I was going to a German prison, they didn't take it very well."
>
> ... His expectations were that the German prisons were going to be much like the American ones.
>
> "When I got there, I found out German prisons were a lot like the ones in Norway and Sweden," Rosen said. "Their prisons are a lot different than the ones in the U.S. Inmates cook their own food with butcher knives, forks, pots, and pans. There's a regular kitchen. Each person has his or her own room, which is very important regarding space. Their system doesn't have maximum or minimum-security prisons. The amount of time you're serving determines what prison you're at—like a prison for 5 years or less. The staffing is much different—for every inmate there's a staffer. They have lenient

visiting rules. Prisoners can earn passes to go see their families. Very few violate the rules and don't come back after getting a pass.

District Attorney Rosen returned from Germany sounding like a prison reformer: "I think it's very valuable for me to come to San Quentin, and then go to other [California] prisons to see what they are like—to see the bleakness. Most of the prisons I've been to are disgusting. There is little rehabilitation."[4]

What forum participants like Rosen heard from prisoners—black, white, and Latino—were testimonials that rehabilitation at San Quentin was real. The common thread was remorse and hopes for a second chance.

For example, Azral Ford, then forty-three, looked as if he had been sent over from Central Casting. He said he had once been a prison enforcer for the Aryan Nation. He cut an imposing figure, heavily tattooed, muscular, and missing some teeth. His nickname was Big Az. Nobody kidded him about it. He had been in prison for seventeen years. His prison experience began when he was fourteen. "Incarceration has been a nightmare and a blessing because it has allowed me to grow," he said, adding:

> I've been a perpetrator of violence. It happens everywhere. It happens here too. Where that comes from is this place of fear. We're in a world where there are a lot of unknowns. The easiest way to build a sanctuary is to build a fort. The violence within your own circle is more harsh. We do that because of a lot of shame. So, I want to build these rules to take away the shame. It's a twisted world we live in. The only way it's going to stop is to look at it like a sickness.[5]

Another white inmate said his imprisonment had helped overcome his racial hatred.

> "These programs teach us that we can and should take responsibility," said David Basile, who has recently been found suitable for parole after serving more than 30 years behind bars for murder. "I was a racist. I only realized the magnitude of my faulty belief system after taking American Government offered by Patten University. During that class, I noticed how I had limited myself through buying into lies and misrepresentations about my fellow man. It was then when I began to develop tremendous empathy for the black man's plight and the shame I had to deal with for my previous actions and behavior toward the black man.[6]

Prosecutors customarily see an accused person only from one perspective: sitting with defense counsel at a table in front of the judge. Prosecutor and defendant don't face each other. But in the prison forums, the participants sit in a circle. The arrangement of the chairs seems to make a difference in how the discussions unfold. "The circle process forces us to look at ourselves," inmate Lynn Beyett said. "When we're sitting in the circle, listening to each other's stories, all you have to do is close your eyes and you'll hear your own story."[7]

> "It's not about locking a kid up. It's about understanding the root causes behind criminal thinking, like anger and rejection. It's about listening to what is happening in the kid's life," said Philip Melendez, convicted of two first-degree murders.
>
> "When the strategy is to lock the kid up, all they learn is how to become a better criminal," added Melendez, 37, who has been incarcerated for 18 years.[8]

Adnan Khan, thirty-two, was serving a life sentence for a murder and robbery conviction he received at age seventeen. He stated in a forum, "We live in a punitive society, and we are seeing its results. The community and society should take responsibility as well as the individual for what went wrong."[9]

By the end of 2017 the newspaper had hosted fourteen forums. District attorneys from San Mateo and Marin Counties attended. The most ambitious forum for prosecutors took place January 26, 2017, when San Francisco District Attorney Gascón joined more than two dozen prosecutors from around the country, from as far away as Baltimore. They met with thirty inmates. The gathering was so large it had to be moved to the Protestant Chapel because it would not fit in the newsroom.[10]

> The Portland, Oregon, district attorney Rodney Dale Underhill wanted suggestions on how he could make better-informed decisions when he knows he has a conviction and must advise on a prison sentence.
>
> "Be able to talk to us," [inmate] Anthony Ammons said.
>
> Vaughn Miles [another inmate] added, "Trust your judgment about what you've witnessed today."

Reporter Juan Haines duly recounted these events for the inmate readers of the *San Quentin News,* and the word went out to the felons. But the more important outcome would be what happened in court during future sentencing and whether DAs would oppose parole for felons "found suitable" to return to the streets.

"Holding people accountable is needed for re-entry," San Francisco DA Gascón said to the *San Quentin News* staff.[11] "What you are doing here is of incredible value. I think any of you, with the right support, could make a big difference outside of prison." He added: "It's great if we do this in San Francisco, but greater if it spreads. We incarcerate more people in the United States than any other country in the world. Even though there will always be a place for custody, at the rate we are doing it, it's socially irresponsible and financially unsustainable."

The forums were not confined to prosecutors. Other visitors included US Rep. Jackie Speier (D-San Mateo) and J. Anthony Kline, the presiding justice of the First District, Second Division of the California Court of Appeal.

Speier had been a victim of violence herself. She had taken a shotgun blast to the body and had been left for dead on the tarmac in Jonestown, Guyana, when her boss, Congressman Leo Ryan, was killed in November of 1978. At one point Speier asked a group of fifteen prisoners ranging in age from twenty-nine to sixty-two if drugs were available in prison. One of the older inmates interjected, "Tell me what you want. I'll be back in five minutes."[12] The congresswoman laughed.

"I think that what you've done here is remarkable," Speier said to the prisoners at the forum. "The ability to go from hyper-masculine to hyper-empathetic, that's a skill set needed in the community. I am hopeful about the transition that society is making about the prison population. The movement is getting away from Three Strikes and the death penalty because it is very costly. There has to be a better way to atone for offenses."[13]

J. Anthony Kline, presiding judge of the State Circuit Court of Appeal, came to San Quentin with a remarkable background. He had been Gov. Edmund G. Brown Jr.'s roommate at Yale. In Kline's early years of practicing law he had been a prison reform advocate and had worked to form a prisoners' union within the CDC. Later, he became Jerry Brown's chief of staff and was eventually appointed to the bench. Kline said he was impressed with the sincerity and the level of introspection the inmates displayed in the forum. Judge Kline suggested that "people on the outside" needed to hear the inmates articulate how and where their lives had gone bad, along with their suggestions on how to prevent others from making the same mistakes.

Kline acknowledged that the definition of insight is difficult for the courts to determine. "I'm shocked at the level of insight needed to get out of prison, and nobody knows exactly what it is. . . . It is talking about reasons for the commitment offense. Most people cannot do this. I don't think judges and lawyers can do this. However, I'm impressed about the level of insight in this room."[14]

Kline's parting advice was simple: "You need to send the *San Quentin News* to all judges. Judges are major players in reform."

29 A New Narrative

Danny Murillo from Norwalk, California, spent six of his fourteen years behind bars in the infamous SHU (Security Housing Unit) at Pelican Bay State Prison. At age eighteen he entered prison after accepting a plea bargain to two counts of robbery. Murillo served his time at Pelican Bay when that prison had the reputation as the harshest and most severe in the CDCR. He later told an interviewer, "Solitary confinement is designed to fucking break you. Not just emotionally—spiritually. In spite of that, I was able to build up a type of resilience. I didn't let that place take ahold of me."[1] Once released, he went on to graduate with honors from the University of California at Berkeley in 2015 and began a career as a distinguished legal researcher.

In October 2017, Oprah Winfrey visited Pelican Bay State Prison, which she described as "the most notorious state prison in America," for a segment on CBS's *60 Minutes*. While there, she ventured into the SHU, where inmates like Murillo had remained in solitary confinement sometimes for decades at a time. The Winfrey program illustrated the abrupt change that overtook California's prison system in a few short years.

Winfrey toured the cellblock and engaged in conversation with inmates inside their cells. Winfrey held the microphone and talked to the inmate through the food slot in the door. Normally, all visitors to Pelican Bay wear bulky antistabbing vests. Not Winfrey. She was given an exception to the rule, perhaps because the prison officials wanted CBS viewers to think Pelican Bay was not as violent as it has been portrayed in the past.

The visit provided an update to the landmark 1993 CBS *60 Minutes* broadcast that looked into the same prison. Renowned investigative journalist Lowell Bergman produced the segment shortly after the "supermax" Pelican Bay lockup opened for business as a part of California's incarceration expansion. Bergman's broadcast announced to the world that penology in California was taking a draconian turn and that Pelican Bay was the showpiece. As Mike Wallace described the institution, "The State of California that runs it proudly proclaims it's the wave of the future, designed to isolate prisoners who, they insist, are out of control, too violent, too unpredictable to be housed with the run-of-the-mill murderers and rapists."[2]

Solitary confinement was "the wave of the future," according to *60 Minutes* in 1993. But by the time Winfrey visited more than twenty years later, California authorities were singing a different tune. Scott Kernan, the then-director of the Department of Corrections and Rehabilitation, accompanied Winfrey during her visit:

SCOTT KERNAN: That was a policy [solitary confinement] that was intended to save lives and make prisons safer across the system. It *was* a mistake, in retrospect, as we look back—

OPRAH WINFREY: But you said earlier it worked?

SCOTT KERNAN: It did work.

OPRAH WINFREY: It worked in reducing crime in the general prison population?

KERNAN: Yes.

OPRAH WINFREY: Why did it not work?

SECRETARY SCOTT KERNAN: It didn't work because of the impact on the offenders.

OPRAH WINFREY: I'm sure you've heard that statement from Justice Anthony Kennedy, who says, "Solitary confinement drives men mad." Does it?

SCOTT KERNAN: I think it does.[3]

Kernan's public admission on *60 Minutes* represented revisionism at the highest levels. His comments reflected several important changes in policies and laws in California in the twenty-first century that departed from the tough-on-crime stances of the 1970s through 1990s.

These changes resulted in dramatic declines in the incarcerated population. After reaching a peak of some 256,000 inmates in 2006, the number of incarcerated people in California state prisons and county jails dropped by around 55,000 by 2016, according to a report by the nonpartisan Public Policy Institute of California. The rate of incarceration fell in that time period from 702 per 100,000 residents to 515—"a level not seen since the early 1990s," the report said.[4]

Winfrey followed up her *60 Minutes* scoop with a thirty-five-minute conversation with black ex-convict Shaka Senghor. Taken together, the two stories were remarkable departures in the long and unhappy history of media narratives about prisoners.

The show was featured on the OWN cable network, which, despite not having the clout of her former network, still reached deep into America. It was especially trusted among older women, with whom Oprah had great credibility.

The OWN website promo for the interview declared: "When he was just 17 years old, Shaka Senghor was convicted of second-degree murder, and he went on to spend 19 years in prison. Shaka arrived in prison seething with anger and resentment, refusing to take responsibility for his actions."[5]

Wearing shoulder-length dreadlocks and buffed, Senghor looked fresh off the prison yard. But he was hardly angry or resentful. Instead, he spoke to Winfrey about not just regret but remorse.

"I was waiting on mail call and when you're in solitary confinement, that's the most important part of the day, outside of eating, because you're just hoping that somebody thought about you," said Senghor, describing the moment he decided to turn his life around. He had received a letter from his oldest son, age eleven:

I opened the letter and [forgot about] all the street savviness and the prison toughness, and I just crumbled to the ground. For the first time I was seeing myself through the eyes of a child I helped bring into this world. And I read the letter, he said, "Dear Dad, mother told me you was in prison for murder.

Dear Dad, don't murder anymore. Jesus watches what you do. Pray to him and he will forgive you for your sins." That part was what just shattered everything. If I never get out of prison, I refuse for that to be the legacy for my child. I couldn't go through life with that being the final way that he sees me. . . . It was the first time I could see myself as this monster in my child's eyes.[6]

Senghor's revelations about coming to terms with his criminal past marked a turning point for Winfrey, who in the recent past had been severe with criminal offenders in her interviews. She was not just sympathetic with Senghor. She was empathetic too, sometimes finishing his sentences for him.

As part of an assignment, I convened a group of UC Berkeley students enrolled in my *San Quentin News* editing class to offer reactions to the Senghor-Winfrey talk. These twenty-somethings were UC Berkeley's best and brightest, and they had all spent at least a semester working closely with inmate writers and editors inside the walls of San Quentin.[7] Was the Oprah Winfrey moment a big deal? Just how different was Winfrey's approach from what had been seen on TV before?

Ahna K. Straube, a *Daily Cal* reporter majoring in political economics from Sonoma, California, wrote this analysis:

Both serving and former prisoners are often only interviewed about their offense and, consequently, their life before and after their conviction is abandoned and is considered unimportant to producers—reflecting that fear and intrigue capture viewers' attention.

In Dr. Phil's 2015 interview, "Teen Convicted of Murdering Mom with Sledgehammer," Zachary Davis sat in uniform and handcuffs and answered logistical questions which included where exactly the teen killed his mother and how heavy the hammer was.

In 2012, Oprah also engaged in a similar type of interview when she questioned Shaquan Duley, a woman who was convicted of killing her two sons. Oprah performed a tearful disdain for Duley and repetitively asked logistical questions about the murder of her sons. When Duley answered that she did not recall whether her children struggled upon death, Oprah became upset and said, "I know you remember it because it's unimaginable to me."

Questions like these do not provide the entire story for formerly incarcerated men and women. Narrow interviews magnify prison stereotypes and dehumanize inmates, making it symbolically ever-more difficult to remove the DOC labeled uniforms once released from prison.

Oprah's interview with Senghor, however, provided a broader depiction of the types of human experiences [that] lead to crime and punishment.[8]

A graduate student from Iceland, Anna Marsibil Clausen, who had more than four years of professional experience writing about the intersection between society and pop culture, provided useful non-American insight into the interview:

> When Oprah tells the world that someone is worth listening to, the world listens. So, when she decides that talking to a convicted murderer was "moving" and that she had been able to "open her heart" to him, it's a big deal.
>
> This was the case in her interview with Shaka Senghor. "Think for a minute of the worst mistake you ever made and imagine that you were forever defined by it," Oprah says in her introduction—pushing the audience to put themselves in Senghor's shoes.
>
> But Oprah, as a stand in for the audience, finds a common ground in how she and her interviewee were raised: without feeling loved. Now, that is something a much larger portion of Americans can identify with. For those that have been luckier, it's still powerful to see that Oprah can relate; that one of the most powerful people on earth can see any part of herself reflected in such a criminal.[9]

Although Senghor's revelations were gripping television, they don't necessarily mean a permanent change in direction, according to another UC student, Chloee Weiner, whose experience included working as a research assistant for the PBS *Frontline* documentary "Stick-Up Kid." She had also worked as an intern in the criminal division of a Washington, D.C., law firm:

> Despite the prevalence of narratives similar to Senghor's, these are still not the stories about prison the average American audience sees on TV. The occasional 60 Minutes interview that dives into the mind of a serial killer or the dramatized Netflix series on the celebrity-obsessed O. J. Simpson trial, for example, are far from Senghor's words in a teary moment of introspection: "How do you re-emerge in a society that's so unforgiving?" Despite the intense American gaze on prisons and prisoners, accounts of genuine change and re-entry are still severely underrepresented. It's this that makes the conversation between Oprah and Senghor significant as a moment that allows the formerly incarcerated to tell their story in their own voice.[10]

IS THIS A BIG DEAL?

Has a paradigm shift taken place? There were clear signs that the wider society of 2018 was softer on incarceration than it had been in 1993. The Marshall Project, a nonprofit news organization that reports on criminal justice, asked in 2015 whether the traditional nomenclature was appropriate for describing people serving penitentiary sentences. "We received more than 200 responses to our callout asking the best way to refer to people behind bars. Of the options we offered, 38 percent preferred 'incarcerated person,' 23 percent liked 'prisoner' and nearly 10 percent supported use of the word inmate. Thirty percent selected 'other' ('person in prison,' 'man or woman,' 'the person's name')."[11]

The Marshall Project initiative was an effort to remove the naming stigma from prisoners when they are mentioned in stories. It was a small step. But the larger problem is that news organizations have a hard time letting go of the idea that releasing felons from prison is risky. Stories about prisoners rarely include efforts by prisoners to reform themselves as a way to get out of the penitentiary. More often news stories dwell on the original conviction and past criminal activity. It is easier to do, because that's all in the clips. It doesn't require any additional reporting.

Crime and punishment are complicated. The CDCR's behavior mirrors the ambiguity the news media feel about people convicted of crime. The policies say one thing, but official implementation is risk-averse. For example, elderly prisoners too feeble to present a danger to anyone stay behind bars, despite the existence of "compassionate release" programs. Other prisoners who are free of any violence in their records and who have completed rehabilitation programs stay locked up because of harsh two-strike and three-strike minimum sentences. Victims' rights groups, district attorneys, and some politicians oppose returning felons to society. Yet the costs of incarceration and court orders have forced the department to trim the inmate population. A CDCR official who was a guest speaker at my class in 2010 suggested that his department should be renamed the Department of Irony.

Miguel Quezada, the onetime managing editor of the *San Quentin News*, is a case in point that the fresh CDCR approach has not yet made its way into media coverage. Quezada was well liked by the prison staff and the inmates and was effective in his job. He was convicted of a homicide he had committed in Stanislaus County when he was sixteen years old. He had served nineteen years of a forty-year-to-life sentence when one day in 2017 a fight broke out on the San Quentin yard and a Mexican inmate was beaten severely.

Quezada, who happened to be nearby, refused to take part. The gang members with whom Quezada was formerly associated did not take his decision lightly. They saw it as an affront. It is part of the unwritten code that when a gang attack is launched against an adversary, everybody lends a hand or a blow. Quezada's refusal made him a marked man. The shot-callers could not tolerate such apparent disrespect. But Quezada had made a courageous personal choice and decided that he wanted no more of the gang life. He valued his job with the newspaper and his rehabilitation program and was determined to stay out of trouble. His *San Quentin News* colleagues applauded his choice.

San Quentin officials decided to take no chances. Quezada first went to the Hole for his own protection and eventually was transferred to Avenal State Prison near Fresno. And about six months later, the parole board found him "suitable" for release. Because he was serving a life term, the governor was allowed a review period and reserved the right to veto a parole.

While Quezada's fate hung in the balance, the local Modesto newspaper published an article reflective of the conventional way the media has treated prisoners.[12] The article displayed a tone of mild alarm that Quezada would ever be free, downplaying the nineteen years he had already served. Instead, it focused on a new law enabling him to be considered for parole because his offense had occurred when he was sixteen. Of course, the story carried no response from the prisoner.

A 36-year-old Modesto man convicted of killing a teenager in an alleged street gang confrontation near Ceres has been found suitable for parole.

A Stanislaus County jury found Miguel Quezada guilty of second-degree murder and three counts of assault with a gun in the 1998 shooting that killed 16-year-old Daniel Reyes.

In October 1999, Quezada was sentenced to 45 years to life in prison. He had served 19 years of his prison sentence on Feb. 6, when he was found suitable for parole, the Stanislaus County District Attorney's Office announced in a news release Friday.

Quezada was 16 years old and a high school dropout when he committed the crime but was prosecuted as an adult. He was not supposed [to] be eligible for parole until 2040, but changes to state law allowed for an earlier parole review.

The *Modesto Bee* story did take note in the final two paragraphs that Quezada had participated in prison programs. It made no mention of his *San Quentin News* role.

Postscript: Quezada was paroled in 2018. On August 29, 2018, I received a handwritten note in my snail-mail box at UC Berkeley: "Hello, Bill. I dropped in to see you. I'll be going back to San Quentin soon to see the guys. I'm enrolling at UC-Berkeley thinking of taking our class. Let's catch up over coffee soon. Miguel Quezada." He went to work as an organizer for a nonprofit, Communities United for Restorative Youth Justice.

PART IV Moving Forward

30 Journalism and Rehabilitation

Functionally illiterate when he came to prison, Curtis (Wall Street) Carroll gained renown for himself by becoming an expert on the stock market, as he served a fifty-four-year-to-life sentence for an Oakland homicide. He taught himself to read by going over issues of the *Wall Street Journal*. Carroll said he had seen a copy of the *Wall Street Journal* in an inmate's cell and asked what it was. "It's where the white people keep their money," he was told.[1] Thereupon, Carroll began to teach himself to read and to understand financial markets. Carroll co-taught a financial literacy class for inmates with a civilian volunteer, Zach Williams, son of the late comedian Robin Williams. Eventually he would share the stage at a TED Talk program with a former US Treasury secretary.

The remarkable accomplishment of Carroll, who later transferred to another prison, is a clue to how rehabilitation works in prison. Journalism played an obvious role in helping Wall Street turn his life around, but the copies of the *Wall Street Journal* were merely a tool. The real change had come from inside him. Practicing journalism can help with that change, but not in the ways you readily expect.

G. K. Chesterton remarked, "Journalism largely consists in saying 'Lord Jones is dead' to people who never knew Lord Jones was alive."[2]

Chesterton's cheeky insult is one of the most frequently quoted put-downs about journalism. The great nineteenth-century writer, biographer, critic, and journalist had a famously jaded view of the craft. Chesterton would likely be dismayed by any claim that practicing journalism would make somebody a better person, or that it should be promoted as a rehabilitation technique for people serving prison sentences. But I'd like to put forward exactly that claim based on what I've seen at the *San Quentin News*.

I believe journalism is an effective tool for rehabilitating people in prison, on the basis, in part, of what members of the *San Quentin News* crew have told me. They have multiple times spelled out the benefits they see in collaborating with me, the other advisers, the many guest speakers, and the student editors I've brought in from UC Berkeley.

SCHOLARLY RESEARCH

But the proof is not just in individual testimonials by the prisoners. Outside researchers have also found that the journalism seems to have a beneficial effect in inspiring prison journalists as well as their readers. Alexandra Stepanov of the University of Central Florida wrote her thesis after doing a content analysis of past issues of the *San Quentin News*. She said the newspaper had been successful not just in providing substantive coverage but in expanding writing programs in the prison that further develop prisoner identity. Here's her analysis:

> SQSP (San Quentin State Prison) incarcerated individuals have written and done segments for Vice Magazine and interviewed with CNN. They have been featured on the "Life of the Law" podcast series. Since the beginning of this project, SQN has remodeled their website to include individual staff writer bios, as well as bios for partnered advisors and volunteers. SQSP is also beginning a podcast series of its own and is working on launching a magazine. These expansions show that this conversation is ever-present and ever-growing. The incarcerated individuals of SQSP are reclaiming their space, voice, and identity through the use of identification processes in multiple mediums with a variety of audiences.[3]

The scholarly record shows that journalism, along with a wide variety of other modes of reflective writing, has effectively helped inmates change their criminal ways. University of San Francisco professor Larry Brewster examined several California arts-in-prison projects and observed that "these programs often provide authentic learning experiences that engage the minds and hearts of the incarcerated. For example, arts education can lead to improved writing skills, greater intellectual agility and creativity, motivation, and enhanced performance in other academic disciplines." He concluded, "Research and experience suggest that prison arts programs have significant benefits and positive outcomes for the incarcerated, their families, the prison environment, and society."[4]

Including journalism among "fine arts" programs may sound like a stretch, but journalists share many attributes with essayists, poets, and fiction writers, and Prisoners who have an interest in journalism often are also involved in creative writing programs. In both fields they write about their experiences. Journalism places an additional burden on writers: What they write must be accurate, true, and above all, fair. And they write under the supervision of an editor.

These social science appraisals don't actually explain what takes place in the convict's mind. Psychologist Shadd Maruna in his book *Making Good* gives a tantalizing hint.[5] The truly reformed criminal, Maruna writes, is often somebody who dreams impossibly big dreams. He "display[s] an exaggerated sense of control over the future and an inflated, almost missionary sense of purpose in life." This description fit Wall Street to a T. It also fit Arnulfo García and many others in the San Quentin Media Center. "They recast their criminal past not as the shameful failings that they are but instead as the necessary prelude to some newfound calling."

On the other hand, the unreconstructed, repeat offender, said Maruna, is the "realist." That's the man who has an accurate assessment of his situation as an ex-convict, knowing how badly the deck is stacked against him. He succumbs to his plight.

The inmates who "make good" on the outside are simply "out of step" with the fate to which the system has sentenced them. They refuse to accept it.

MAKING JOURNALISTS OUT OF PRISONERS

The act of working for a newspaper is a process by which the prisoner is able to build his confidence and nurture his dreams.

First, he gains skills and competence in a craft. I've edited hundreds of stories with prison journalists, almost always sitting side by side with the writer. I've done this work since 2012, when I entered the field of prison journalism to teach two semesters of an Introduction to Journalism course under the auspices of the Prison University Project. Then I became a volunteer adviser to the *San Quentin News*.

Most of the men I've worked with at San Quentin were prison educated, and as a result their grammar and spelling skills were weak. But they were natural storytellers and eager to share. The newspaper was the perfect outlet. Just seeing their names in a byline was a huge boost for their morale. In the editing process, I never hesitated to rewrite their copy. But I did it while they watched. I explained every change I made. Afterward, they looked at the story with awe. Eventually, they caught on to how it was done.

When the newspaper was published, the writers gained status on the prison yard. They were part of a respected crew. And another benefit was that they had regular access to intelligent, educated people from the outside, the UC students and the volunteer editors. A chance to talk to somebody other than prisoners or penitentiary staff was an important perk.

The writing teacher's goal is to help the student develop his or her own "voice." It doesn't matter if the venue is UC Berkeley or San Quentin. My advice in every journalism writing course I've taught in more than thirty years at Berkeley is that journalists need to write the way they talk, and that means reading your copy aloud, moving your lips and passing your creation over your palate. If it sticks on the palate, most likely the reader will struggle. In that sense, journalism is like writing poetry.

That inner voice eventually will tell you the truth about what you've written. You'll know when a sentence is too long, if you run out of breath or if it doesn't track. After years of practice (ten thousand hours, if you believe the popular writer Malcolm Gladwell), seeking that voice allows you to access other parts of your experience. The writer "voice" becomes an inner critic. It also edits the writer's life choices. Through writing, the prison journalist discovers the important difference between what he believes, what he knows, what he can prove, and what his paper will let him publish. These traits of critical thinking begin to permeate the inmate's everyday life.

Furthermore, journalism summons the man outside his cellblock. He's encouraged to exercise curiosity about his surroundings. He must seek out different points of view. He paints pictures with words. Becoming engaged in a world of ideas opens his eyes to other values and other possibilities for his life. He wants to know more. He engages in research, even if it's just interviewing his cellmate or his friends on the yard. He learns to be responsible in his writings, because the guys on the yard will read what he wrote. There could be consequences. A former editor in chief, Kenny Brydon, once told a story about a *San Quentin News* editor who received a beating because somebody disliked what he wrote.

FORMAL TRAINING BEHIND BARS

The staff writers join the newspaper usually after they have done an apprenticeship with the Journalism Guild. It has been the primary training ground for years for aspiring journalists. John Eagan, one of the original advisers, got it going in 2008. Later Yukari Kane, former *Wall Street Journal* reporter and a lecturer at UC Berkeley, took over the Guild. She wrote me this account of her approach to turning raw talent into journalists:

"Journalism behind bars; volunteers needed. No pay unfortunately, but a great group of guys." This was the job ad that I responded to in April 2016.

My job was to teach intro to journalism to men who wanted to write for the newspaper. When I took over in May, my predecessor John Eagan had been teaching the class for about nine years, so the basic class structure was already in place. Some men had been attending for years, and John left me with handouts that he had created.

My challenges in the beginning were two-fold. First, the men came with an extremely wide range of abilities. Some had problems with basic grammar and a few had learning disabilities while others had college and advanced degrees. Secondly, the class was an optional class, which meant that attendance was spotty. I had to review the same material several times, and I couldn't assign homework because many of them showed up only sporadically. But the students were so enthusiastic that they inspired me to take the program seriously.

The first change I made was to create structure and accountability to the class. I needed the men to show up every week, so we could work towards a goal and build toward something. I needed to see their work regularly, so I had a sense of how much they understood, and I wanted to see them practice what they learned. This meant homework, quizzes, and practice articles.

I eventually settled on four to five quizzes, two practice articles and a couple interview and observation exercises as criteria for graduation. Regular attendance and completion of homework was a must. In return, my promise to them was that they would be given regular, personal feedback on everything they turned in. I decided to be flexible about deadlines to accommodate varying abilities and situations. I wanted the men to succeed, and I wanted them to know that I cared about their performance no matter how big the class was. At the same time, I told them that I would pass them only if I thought they were ready to write for the newspaper. We created a certificate of completion, which held little value outside our group but was meant to be an affirmation of the work the men had put in.

Now, I start with newsroom basics and we discuss topics like news judgment and fairness before we start learning practical writing and journalism skills. I use the intro to the intro as a way to get the men to start thinking like journalists and experts.

A big challenge that still exists is the unpredictability of their schedules. I could plan a big lesson only to have the class canceled because the prison was in lockdown due to an incident or heavy fog. Other times, there might be a special event. After a couple semesters of incomplete lessons, we settled on a 26-week semester for a 20-week lesson plan.

My ambition is for the *San Quentin News* and its writers to elevate themselves as key voices in national conversations about criminal justice.

None of these endeavors would have been possible without Marcus Henderson, the chairman of the Journalism Guild. My classes may have started out as a way to train the next-generation of *San Quentin News* writers, but we have also worked in lockstep toward our shared goal to step up our game, improve the curriculum and spread journalism to other prisons.

Every semester, I give the same speech to new students. I tell them that I teach this class because I want to empower their voices and that this is their opportunity to start a new reputation as a journalist. I'm pleased that the word is starting to spread and we've seen more men interested in the program that ever before.[6]

Yukari Kane moved to Chicago in 2018. But the Journalism Guild successfully made the transition to a new instructor.

LOCATION, LOCATION, LOCATION

The journalism practice at San Quentin does not take place in a vacuum. Prisoners are offered a whole menu of self-examination and self-analysis programs. Many programs are devoted to dealing with personality disorders, anger, or addiction. There are several "violent offenders" groups.[7]

These programs seem to work hand in hand with the journalism experience. Aspiring writers have many choices. Besides the *San Quentin News,* they are offered groups on how to become a writer, write a novel, or write poetry. Other volunteers teach yoga, meditation, theater, piano, and guitar.

Even though they are in prison, the inmates have surprisingly busy schedules. One night in February 2018, associate editor Kevin Sawyer sheepishly asked me if I had an assignment for a UC Berkeley student volunteer with whom he was working in the newsroom. It was 7:30 p.m. "I have to go to band practice," said Sawyer, who had been a student in the first Prison University Project class for inmates that I taught in 2012.

The nonprofit Prison University Project, which received a National Humanities Medal from President Obama in 2016, offers qualified prisoners college credit classes and associate of arts degrees for free in a variety of subjects, taught by local university and college faculty.[8] It has 350 students and a long waiting list. Courses include the humanities, math, and science and span topics from neuroscience to world literature.

Sawyer was an unusual PUP student because he was exceptionally well read and held a bachelor's degree from Cal State Hayward (since renamed Cal State East Bay).

SELF-EXAMINATION AND JOURNALISM

No matter how humble their backgrounds, prisoners have big dreams for themselves. And if Shadd Maruna is correct, those dreams might be the passport to success outside prison. I had another prisoner who harbored big dreams for himself. He was a muscular black man from Sacramento with the memorable name of George Burns. His assignments were hand-written in large block letters, and every page was flawless. He used liquid correction fluid to cover any mistakes. Early in the class, I asked each man to write his own obituary. I wanted to see how many had insight into their crimes and how each student would deal with the inevitability of his own death. George Burns's self-written obituary showed his determination to give his life a positive spin.

> George was born in Sacramento November 29, 1971, to Don Weatherspoon and Shirley Smith. He married Cherish Proctor in Sacramento where they lived with their son. Mr. Burns was a student in Patten College where he was trying to achieve his A.A. degree in basic education, also he was a writer for the San Quentin Guild Journalism class.
>
> He was able to make the following achievements in his life. George obtained his high school diploma and completed a course in business. He finished top of his class in janitorial duties, and in computer class.
>
> [M]r. Burns was always trying to find something positive he could do to help others. Mr. Burns early life was rocky he was in and out of jail. He was the founder of the North Highlands Gangsta Crips, which later his gang involvement led him to commit a shooting that landed him in prison for 31 years and 8 months. During this time is when he started changing his ways and attitude towards life. George began to get involved in things that would benefit his future. He enrolled in Patten College, and started writing for San Quentin Guild Journalism class. His going to college and putting articles together for San Quentin newspaper is how he spent his leisure time. . . .
>
> He loved to cook different types of food. He was a very good cook. He enjoyed reading, writing, fishing, fixing up cars, and listening to music. His favorite music was rap, which 2 Pac was his favorite rapper. He was also good at drawing.
>
> Mr Burns funeral will be held June 18, 2012 at 10 a.m. The burial will take place at Sunset Law, 1900 Sunrise Blvd. in Sacramento, California 95678.[9]

As things turned out, George Burns's actual funeral took place a year and three months after he wrote his own obituary. He died in prison of natural causes on October 16, 2013. Every year around ten inmates die in San Quentin, most from natural causes. Other common causes of death are drug overdose and suicide. Homicide is rare. The CDCR records around three hundred deaths from all causes per year.

31 The Campus and the Prison

In March of 2018 the *New York Times* published an opinion piece that posed the challenge, "Turn Prisons into Colleges." The story said, "Imagine if prisons looked like the grounds of universities. Instead of languishing in cells, incarcerated people sat in classrooms and learned about climate science or poetry—just like college students. Or even with them."[1]

In fact, that is what UC Berkeley students have been doing at the *San Quentin News* since 2012. Byrhonda Lyons was a student in the class in 2013.

> Every Friday before I get dressed, I stand in the mirror and go through my mental checklist. No open toe shoes. No cleavage. All black.
>
> Once I realize I've met those requirements, I head for the door, making sure I get to the Journalism School in time to catch my ride. When I get off the bus, I rush to the courtyard, finding Professor Drummond waiting patiently for everyone to arrive. We all pile into his four-door Camry and go across the bridge to one of the most beautiful places in the bay: San Quentin Prison.
>
> When I enrolled in this class, I never knew how much I would learn. Honestly, I was afraid. I had never been to a prison, and I'd never worked with inmates. Yes, I knew it would be different, but I never thought I would learn as much as I did. I never guessed volunteering with the *San Quentin News* would make me a better journalist and a better person.[2]

Lyons confirmed my conviction about what constitutes a successful class. Students learn by doing. Present them with a challenge and see how they respond. If they get in a jam, they come to me for advice. Otherwise, I leave it to them to work it out. When students join the San Quentin editing class, they take a walk into the unknown. It is ominous. Some even find it threatening. They persist and overcome their reservations and insecurity. Amina Wahid went through all those stages and made important discoveries about herself.

> I'm almost certain I've learned more about the intricacies of our criminal justice system in the last five months than if I had decided to go to law school after all. (I also learned how one can make moonshine from behind bars—but I digress.)
>
> By having to sit down with the writers, I was forced to explain my thought process for why I was making the edits I was. By editing the SQ Newspaper, I was also challenged to digest the political and legal jargon that so often pervades these stories, and put them into layman terms.
>
> Beyond my role as a journalist, the *San Quentin News* team also forced me to rethink my role and level of engagement as a citizen residing on the outside. Regardless of which writer I sat with, I realized how little I really knew about the justice system and the politics of prison life. It was humbling, and incredibly eye-opening.
>
> I'll never look at any number of the obstacles this field presents the same way. It would be a disgrace to all that I've learned from the SQ-ers. I'm in awe of the discipline, determination, and passion with which these men get a newspaper printed and distributed every month.[3]

Since 2012, when I first began bringing Cal students to San Quentin, I have noticed that the editing sessions with the prisoners usually go way beyond the content of any particular piece of copy. Prisoners want to know, for example, what the student is learning in college. The students listen in rapt attention, as a lifer talks about the deadly unwritten rules among gangs on the yard. Or as Amina Wahid points out above, how one uses common fruits to brew an alcoholic beverage in one's cell.

When we volunteers as a group walk into the San Quentin newsroom, the prisoners and the students stand around greeting each other and chatting for at least fifteen to twenty minutes before they sit down and begin any work. It is all spontaneous and good-natured.

These conversations represent a melding of cultures that is a by-product and an unintended consequence of the prison-university publishing adventure. The kids from the campus discover the men from the prison. Even the spoken language is a cultural fruit salad. It's where Ebonics meets vocal fry. Another case of "two great peoples divided by a common language," or so George Bernard Shaw would have observed.

In these pages so far I have written that publishing a newspaper in prison was beneficial to the inmate writers, helping them create a positive self-image and giving them motivation to change their lives. I've also argued that the revived newspaper enhanced the ecosystem of rehabilitation at San Quentin and made the once notorious prison a beacon for volunteerism and reform. The newspaper enlisted support in the outside world and helped stem the tide of mass incarceration.

Now I want to argue that as a university class the San Quentin editing project has been singularly successful for the enrolled UC students. I have taught journalism at Berkeley for more than thirty years. I've never witnessed so many "aha" moments. I agree with Amina Wahid: the Cal students learn more from the prisoners than vice versa. Later I will explore another question: If taking students to prison works so well, why isn't everybody doing it?

The San Quentin course began life as an attempt to give journalism students instruction in editing another person's copy. Teaching of editing has vanished from journalism school curricula, largely because news media began shedding copy editor jobs when they began to shrink their staffs. An unintended consequence of having UC students work with inmates on their stories was that students experienced numerous "teachable moments." They had revelations about their own place in the world, about the divisions in society, about personal responsibility, about genuine remorse. None of this was promised in the course syllabus. It became a humanities course instead of a journalism course. Stanford University gives this definition of the humanities: "The humanities can be described as the study of how people process and document the human experience. Since humans have been able, we have used philosophy, literature, religion, art, music, history and language to understand and record our world. These modes of expression have become some of the subjects that traditionally fall under the humanities umbrella. Knowledge of these records of human experience gives us the opportunity to feel a sense of connection to those who have come before us, as well as to our contemporaries."[4] The Cal students received an immersion in contemporary history, and by doing so they came away better people, better citizens, and better journalists for their experience of befriending the inmates, to whom they taught the rules of journalism.

Some friction with the prison rules was inevitable. As a Cal student volunteer in the editing class, Gabriel Sánchez made a big impression on the newspaper staff. He was engaging, smart, and a hard worker. That's why everybody was shocked when the prison suspended his clearance for a month. His initiative and innovation got him in trouble. On one particular night, while he was waiting to go in, Sánchez decided he would interview an interesting volunteer: a retired dentist who regularly visited the Mormon inmates on Death Row. Gabriel was recording when a correctional officer interrupted the interview. The CO said Sánchez had violated prison rules by conducting an unauthorized interview on prison property. Sánchez and the dentist were outside the East Gate across the street from the US Post Office at No. 1 Main Street.

The officer filed a report with the warden's office, and Sánchez was effectively banned from entry for a month.

Gabriel had his teachable moment. His suspension, he said later, was the low point of his San Quentin experience. He later wrote that he had been deeply troubled because he thought he had let the inmate writers and editors down.

> However, I must say that the day I came back there was lots of excitement and made up for the suspension that I was serving.
>
> There were people who hadn't seen me in weeks and it appeared that they were pleasantly surprised to see me enter the room. I walked in the room after the rest of my classmates came in, and when I walked in most of the inmates came out of their seats in order to shake my hand and say hello to me.[5]

The course is an elective. Students often choose to enroll out of curiosity. There's an element of "dark tourism," as criminologist Michael Welch describes it in *Escape to Prison: Penal Tourism and the Pull of Punishment.* "Unsurprisingly, due to their grim subject matter, prison museums tend to invert the 'Disney' experience, becoming the antithesis of 'the happiest place on earth,'" Welch wrote.[6] Was the popularity of the class simply a form of gawking, like a trip to a wax museum? I assigned some students to critique Welch's argument in terms of their own experiences at San Quentin. Sasha Lekatch wrote in 2013 that San Quentin's reputation and the Marin County setting had an "allure."[7]

> But these men are still prisoners, with nearly all their freedom stripped. . . . Their connection to the UC Berkeley Graduate School of Journalism is a big window and outlet to a very different group of people. That's where someone like me comes in: a grad student studying journalism, born and raised in upper middle-class San Francisco, Jewish, white, with no criminal background and privileged in most ways. I would not normally have access to the inside of a prison outside of a special reporting situation (something like a jailhouse interview).

Public information officer Robinson conducts San Quentin tours on a regular basis, and often these include students from surrounding colleges who are studying law or criminal justice. They spend at most three hours on the prison grounds and meet a handful of inmates. The enrollees in the UC Berkeley editing class spend at least a semester. Some have reenrolled multiple semesters and have developed relationships spanning many months. Many of the student volunteers are nonjournalism majors. Rose Oser and Marisa Conroy were Berkeley undergraduates with an interest in theater. Oser took the class and later persuaded Conroy to join her. Conroy did so with misgivings.[8]

> I was so skeptical of this class when Rose first asked me to take it with her at the end of last semester (2013). But it seemed like a once in a lifetime opportunity—a very "only at Cal" experience that you should definitely do in your last semester at Cal. It was an environment in which we were with peers to produce the best final product of an article we could. It also never felt like community service, so my fear of coming across as patronizing was also assuaged upon my first visit to SQ. Primarily it was an extremely humanizing experience. When people asked me what I did in prison, I would say, "Well I spend two hours in the newsroom editing articles with about eight murderers. And they are the loveliest most gentlemanly men you have ever met. And they're quite bright too." Because I enjoyed this program so much, I'm thinking of working with the Madea Project run by Rhodessa Jones. It's a theater program for incarcerated women.

What work did the students actually do with the inmate writers and editors? It was like most newsrooms, said Spencer Whitney. Some writing and a lot of schmoozing:[9]

> When I would visit on Friday afternoons, the newsroom was usually filled with reporters working on their stories for the week or giving a critique on their latest article. I edited Ruben Harper's article on the Basketball game between the San Quentin Kings and The Bittermen who narrowly defeated the visiting team by five points with the final score at 67–62. Mr. Harper and I spoke at length about sports writing and what were important facts about the game to include as well as developing a narrative voice in the story.
>
> When the newspaper was finished, reporters would often inquire about what life is like outside of San Quentin Prison and my opinion on political matters dealing with the prison industrial complex.
>
> Overall, my interactions with these editors and reporters allowed me to gain a deeper understanding of the issues that affect inmates as well as learning about their personal experiences and actions that led them to be incarcerated. The experiences with the editors and reporters have been positive; everyone was respectful, insightful, and ready to work.

The students discovered firsthand an important and unpleasant part of the human experience, incarceration, that is shielded from the eyes of the public. Even the specialized public including law enforcement officers, prosecutors, and judges rarely see it! The students can observe how a correctional institution works from the inmates' standpoint. The California corrections enterprise represents a $7 billion expenditure and has social and political repercussions throughout the state.

Trenise Ferreira, a 2012 University of Southern California grad enrolled in the Berkeley Journalism School, specialized in covering sports. Her only previous exposure to prisons was watching the lurid reality TV show *Lockup*. She had seen San Quentin a couple of times on *Lockup* and was curious enough to enroll in the course.

> I've learned a lot about our justice system, or lack thereof, since being in this class. For example: Many of the guys we work with are in prison under California's old three-strikes law. After hearing their stories and really starting to understand just how flawed the law was, I voted in this most recent election to repeal it. I don't know if I would've had the correct insight to make what I think was the right vote if I had not been in this class.

Working with the guys on the TV and movie reviews project has been the best experience. I love hearing them talk about how pop culture relates to their lives, how their struggles are enacted on the silver screen. I hope that they can keep it going next fall with the new students.

I honestly can't say I have had any bad experiences in San Quentin, and I will always cherish the opportunity to have been a part of this incredible class.[10]

Yes, students at Cal enjoyed the class. Nearly all say it was life-changing and the best experience they had in college.

Why isn't everybody doing this?

THE SIXTY-FOUR-DOLLAR QUESTION

Prisons and universities in California don't mix, but they should. Campuses should be more involved inside penitentiaries. They should be out in front tossing lifelines to incarcerated people yearning for education. They should also be sending students and faculty inside prisons to get a firsthand look at the fruits of thirty years of mass incarceration.

The prison system and UC are two of the oldest institutions in the state, both having been founded in the 1850s. The two institutions, however, have cooperated on few, if any, joint undertakings during the state's plunge into the disastrous mass incarceration policy in the past three decades.

The costs of mass incarceration have left the UC system and the state universities gasping for air. As UC itself reported, in 1970, prisons represented less than 4 percent of state general fund revenue, while the UC and California State University systems combined received nearly 14 percent. Today, the prison system's take is nearly double what higher education gets: 9 percent compared to 5 percent for public higher education.[11]

Nevertheless, even though incarceration funding is crippling higher education, the pipeline to prison has failed to raise an outcry at UC Berkeley, certainly not among administrators or faculty, or strangely, among students. A visit by right-wing provocateur Milo Yiannoupoulos provoked a riot. But one hears only silence in response to the imbalance in allocating state resources. Why is that?

UC Berkeley has had a long and conflicted history with corrections. The Berkeley campus was for decades home to a distinguished school of criminology. Some of the most prominent names in the field of law enforcement served as the school's dean, among them O. W. Wilson and Joseph Lohman, a former sheriff of Cook County, Illinois.

Dean Lohman was especially effective in fund-raising for the criminology school. During his tenure from 1960 until his death in 1968, he raised more than a million dollars. This was a stunning achievement for its time. But the money went to projects that angered many faculty colleagues and students. "Under Lohman's direction, the money flowed in, but there was little concern for the ethical or political implications of the funded research projects." said an editorial in the journal *Crime and Social Justice*.[12] Because of the People's Park incident in May 1970 when a student was killed in a confrontation with police, law enforcement was anathema on the Berkeley campus. But the criminology school welcomed law enforcement. Police officers, jailers, prison guards, FBI agents, and narcs were attending classes on the UC Berkeley campus.

Matters came to a head when in the early 1970s the UC administration shut down the whole criminology school. Even though fifty years have passed, academic memories are long and durable. Tony Platt, a criminologist with firsthand knowledge, wrote me this account of what caused the school to be closed. "There was much debate and fierce argument, but for a while competing viewpoints coexisted: conservative law enforcement, social democratic liberalism, and radicalism. The program ended because the Right, led by Edwin Meese and [then governor Ronald] Reagan, with the active support of the administration, moved to purge the left by closing the school and moving tenured faculty (with the exception of Paul Takagi, the only tenured faculty of color) to the law school and creating a new program."[13] Platt, a scholar with Berkeley's Center for the Study of Law and Society, mentions the demise of the criminology school in his book *Beyond These Walls*.[14]

Since then, the Berkeley campus has preferred arm's-length scholarship and discussions in the safe space of classrooms to exposing its own students and faculty to the reality of the prison yard. Hundreds of inmates who are potential leaders, yearning for the fruits of education, are on the waiting list for the scarce spaces in college-level classes taught at San Quentin by the highly regarded Prison University Project, which is accredited by little Patten University in Oakland.

Meanwhile, San Francisco State's Project Rebound recently celebrated fifty years of success. Since its inception in 1967, Rebound has helped the formerly incarcerated through offers of special admission, counseling, tutoring, lunch vouchers, and financial support. The Rebound concept has spread to seven other CSU campuses.

The only thing comparable on the Berkeley campus is the Underground Scholars Initiative. The goal of USI is recruitment, retention, policy and advocacy. It lacks the institutional support and funding that SF State gives to Project Rebound.

Berkeley students have created several student-initiated classes supporting teaching basic literacy to San Quentin prisoners. Since 2012, I've also taught a School of Journalism editing course in which Berkeley students visit the prison to help with research for the award-winning *San Quentin News*.

It's not just the prisoners who are losing out because of the estrangement between San Quentin and UC. The students are missing out. Allen H. Marshall, a Berkeley student from Santa Rosa who took the San Quentin editing class in 2015, commented, "For all my talking and nice thinking, when faced with reality, I saw that I had many of the judgments and fears of popular culture. Nevertheless, it was only by working with inmates on a weekly basis that I was able to learn this about myself and develop a more nuanced perspective towards criminals and the prison system in America."[15]

32 Is This Scalable?

The *San Quentin News* returned to regular monthly publication in 2008 following a twenty-year hiatus, and two years later the paper had put up a website: sanquentinnews.com. The website was visible to the world, but the prisoners could not see it: the newsroom had no internet because of CDCR policy that banned Wi-Fi and local area connections. Like mobile phones, internet connections were forbidden to prisoners. CDCR officials argued that such links to the outside world might be used for criminal purposes.

Given the absence of internet, the prisoners developed a workaround for the newspaper website, the first of many. Once an issue was published, the design editor turned it into a PDF document and sent it outside the prison on a flash drive to be loaded onto the website. That was an important first step, but the website was crude. It was little more than an electronic page-turner. The PDFs could not be searched. Therefore, issues online were almost useless for serious researchers. Articles, names, or events were unavailable via a Google search.

It was a two-year struggle to overhaul the website so that it could be a portal into the world of incarceration. The new website was the point of entry into the transformation of the *San Quentin News* into a small media company. The story of how the website got overhauled provides insight into the dynamics of the newsroom.

Longtime adviser Steve McNamara built the first website for the *San Quentin News*. He used low-tech software to post snapshots of the newspaper online. He later said in an interview, "What was missing in my primitive version was a search function and a sophisticated design that newspapers have moved to with their web versions."[1]

The inmates redesigned the prison newspaper website in a do-it-yourself collaboration with UC Berkeley. The editors wanted to upgrade the website in 2014, but the work did not begin in earnest until mid-2015. It was a daunting task. Although the *San Quentin News* had PCs, lacking an internet connection they were nothing more than dumb terminals. What needed to be done was to install an up-to-date version of WordPress, the site-creation software, on a prison computer. It had to be done without Wi-Fi or a local area network.

A UC undergraduate from Kenya named Sam Karani who had exceptional web skills agreed to help out, along with Chuck Harris, the UC Berkeley Journalism School's webmaster, who volunteered to help on his own time. Richard Lindsey, the former design and layout editor, who had been released a few years before on parole, also lent a hand.

"What we did, with the help of Chuck, was to make a server of one of the newspaper computers," said Aly Tamboura, an inmate serving a sixteen-year-sentence at the time. Harris and Tamboura loaded the WordPress platform on the server, and Tamboura built a first iteration of the website. They also put a database on the server so they could load the articles dating back to 2008.

If they had had an internet connection, the men at San Quentin could have downloaded the needed WordPress version and the database. Without it, Chuck Harris had to copy parts of the needed software onto flash drives and reassemble them on the computer inside the prison.

That was Step 1. The back issues from 2008 had to be recoded and meta tags had to be added to make the new website searchable. The project stretched into 2016. This tedious chore was carried out by inmates Richard (Bonaru) Richardson, Davontae T. Pariani, Ricky (Malik) Harris, and Tamboura.

When this project began, the prisoners did not know what a "meta tag" was. Most had gone to prison when the internet was in its infancy.

"It took Bonaru, myself, and Davontae about eight weeks to get all of the articles (2008–16) into the database," said Tamboura. He said it took another sixteen weeks to build the entire website.

An ironic sidelight to this project was that UC student Sam Karani and inmate Davontae Pariani were both about nineteen years old when they worked together on this project. Karani was from Kenya, and Pariani was an African American from nearby Marin County, facing a six-year stretch in prison. Pariani was an extraordinarily smart high school student. A local newspaper reported that in his junior year he had been nominated as youth volunteer of the year for his work at a public defender's office.[2]

Nevertheless, Pariani pleaded guilty in 2015 to shooting into two occupied vehicles in Novato in a dispute over drugs. He was charged as an adult. Pariani received a six-year prison sentence, and that's how he came to be in San Quentin. Both nineteen-year-olds were bright and capable, but they were headed in opposite directions.

The jerry-rigged website created by the inmates and the UC people was a brilliant workaround. Later, once the newspaper had secured the grant from the Logan Family Foundation, McNamara enlisted the support of the computer-savvy men in the Last Mile program, which had been teaching inmates to write computer code since 2015. The *San Quentin News* paid $10,000 to Last Mile, and in return inmate Larry Hemphill began creating a new iteration of the website. Hemphill's version allowed the site to make use of more advanced display possibilities than the earlier version created by Aly Tamboura and his group. By that time Last Mile had a live internet connection, and the revisions could be uploaded from inside the prison.

A WINDOW OPENED ONTO MASS INCARCERATION

The rejuvenation of the website proved to be an important benefit not just to the *San Quentin News* but also to the UC Berkeley campus and to social science researchers everywhere.

The nearly one hundred editions of the *San Quentin News* published since 2008 constituted the only firsthand documentation of life inside prison during California's lurch toward mass incarceration. Even though it was subject to censorship, overt as well as de facto, the newspaper had value for future researchers who would try to make sense of what was happening in corrections during this turbulent period. Who else would bear witness from inside the institution?

Those one hundred issues (amounting to nearly two million words, plus photographs) were vulnerable. The paper copies were not being systematically collected or archived. Subscriptions to libraries, including UC Berkeley's, had lapsed back in the 1980s.

In June of 2016 I sent an email to two UC library staff members, Corliss Lee and James Ronnigen:

> Here's the update on *San Quentin News*. The prisoners have been laboriously updating and rebuilding their website. The goal is to meta tag all the stories from the past seven years that are presently PDFs and thus non-searchable. One young man serving a six-year sentence for assault has been assigned this job, and I estimate he might finish the meta tagging before he is released.
>
> In the meantime, the whole inventory of those untagged, unsearchable PDFs of entire issues is now sitting on my computer in north gate hall. Needless to say, the inventory is a big file. Would the Library consider becoming the repository of these PDFs? They would fill the present gap in the Library's collection of copies of the *San Quentin News*.
>
> The past seven years of the *San Quentin News* live on a server outside the prison in somebody's garage. It's not secure. The prisoners asked me to take a copy of the inventory to my office for safe-keeping. I would prefer that it be kept in the Library.

The response from Lee and Ronnigen was enthusiastically supportive. Eventually they both visited the prison and met with the editors. Kevin Sawyer was tasked with handling the project from inside the prison.

By 2016 all of the past one hundred editions were secured. Ever since the project was launched, each new edition of the *San Quentin News* was sent to the UC librarians via flash drive and was added to the UC collection. This would be a boon to interested researchers. I could not have written this book without the searchable database of the prison newspaper.

IS THE *SAN QUENTIN NEWS* A MODEL?

In late 2015, I received an encouraging email from CDCR headquarters. Kristina Khokhobashvili, the information officer who fact-checked and edited the *San Quentin News* in Sacramento, wanted to know if perhaps another prison publishing venture might be set up at Solano State Prison about forty miles to the east up Highway 80:

> As I'm sure you know, the *San Quentin News'* impact is far-reaching. It has inspired inmates at several prisons to start newspapers (including one of our women's facilities!). One of those is CSP-Solano in Vacaville, where Kris Himmelberger transferred. Kris reached out to me when he transferred and started writing for the paper there, the Solano Vision. They are a small but mighty group of writers, two of whom (Kris and Cole Bienek) wrote for the *San Quentin News*. They are struggling to get organized, and while I'm more than happy to help, I know they would be greatly served by working with students and/or journalism professors. I've contacted Solano Community College's student paper and journalism department to try to form a relationship, I'm waiting to hear back from them.

She invited me up to Solano to give a pep talk to the writers and editors there. She wanted me to tell them how the *San Quentin News* had gotten going and how it had gained such recognition. "They would be absolutely overjoyed to see you—and I would love to take you to lunch or coffee and pick your brain as well!" Khokhobashvili wrote. I remembered inmate Kris Himmelberger well. He was a slightly built, soft-spoken inmate who wore a skullcap. He was a regular in the San Quentin newsroom when I arrived in 2012 before he transferred to Solano.

Khokhobashvili's invitation was great news. Having multiple prison newspapers in the state would be a big step in the right direction, I thought. And Solano was the most likely place to establish a beachhead. It's located near the Bay Area on one side and the Sacramento area on the other. A number of respected colleges are nearby. A few ex-newspaper colleagues had retired in the area. They might be recruited, I thought. I enthusiastically accepted the invitation. A few weeks later, in January of 2016 I drove up to Solano State Prison near Vacaville to meet with Khokhobashvili and the crew of the *Solano Vision*.

I had not visited any prison except San Quentin in more than forty years. Solano was a much more secure institution than San Quentin.

The visit to Solano was an eye-opener. Solano was built in 1984 as part of the boom in corrections construction, and like the other twenty-five-odd prisons built in that period, it was overcrowded from the moment it opened. Its design capacity was 2,610. When I pulled into the parking lot, its head count was around 3,700, more than 140 percent of capacity. Solano was considered a medium-security institution, while San Quentin was low security.

In January of 2016, I met with about ten prisoners, Khokhobashvili, and Dr. Kenya Williams, supervisor of the correctional educational programs at the prison. The men expressed keen interest, but I saw at once that they were working under some severe limitations. The *San Quentin News* has always had its own space. The Solano prisoners lacked even a regular meeting room. In addition, the *SQ News* writers held paying clerical jobs as newspaper writers. The pay was miserable, just $1 per day, but that was about average for prison jobs. The Solano inmates working on the newsletter were unpaid.

The men at Solano had occasional access to just one desktop PC. The San Quentin inmates had eight computers at their full-time disposal. In addition, they had a couple of dozen Neo portable word processors. About the size of a laptop, the Neos were used by prisoners to write their stories in their cells, and later they would download the copy into the newsroom PCs. Comparatively, San Quentin was flush with equipment. Generous benefactors had donated the Neos to the SQ newsroom. Solano had no connection with any outside philanthropies.

The bigger limitation on Solano was that it had no dedicated volunteers visiting regularly to train the staff and provide editorial direction. The management at Solano was not chummy with local journalists. Krissi's efforts to generate interest with the student newspaper at Solano Community College produced no results.

The importance of the civilian advisers at San Quentin cannot be overemphasized. Despite the occasional conflicts with the inmate editors over policy, spending, or editorial direction, the advisers were a loyal and supportive bunch and served as a buffer between the inmates and the warden's office when prison officials would occasionally want to tighten up. The relationship had taken years to develop.

The other unique advantage that San Quentin enjoyed was having a nearby journalism school at UC Berkeley that allow students to receive credit for a course that made them in effect editorial assistants in the newsroom. Because of the class, I was able to pay regular visits to the prison. In 2017, I made eighty-three visits to the *San Quentin News*, logging more than 3,700 miles from the campus to the prison and back.[3] I would visit on average twice a week and stay in the newsroom ninety minutes each time.

THE WOMEN'S PRISON WRITING GROUP

During the past thirty years, California's female prison population exploded. From one thousand female inmates in 1980 the population grew to eleven thousand before shrinking back to around eight thousand by 2018. Despite this, coverage of women's issues was largely absent from the *San Quentin News*. The local and national media ignored the women's institutions unless somebody committed suicide.[4] In mid-2016 I was working in the newsroom when PIO Sam Robinson brought in a tour of officials from the CDCR. They were impressed with the buzz and bustle of the newsroom. I made a pitch to one of the visitors that the *San Quentin News* would like to establish an arrangement with the women's institutions and gave him my email address. A few days later I received a message from Denice Green in the Community Resources office at the California Institution for Women in Corona in Southern California. It is the oldest women's institution with around 2,100 inmates (more than 150 percent capacity). Green and I began an email exchange about encouraging female inmates to submit articles for publication in the *San Quentin News*. Green was enthusiastic.

> That is so great!!! thank you!
>   As far as a partnership goes . . . that is new for us, so right now, I'm not sure how or what that looks like or should look like . . . but I am and I'm sure the ladies are, open to suggestions and ideas.

Without having talked about it with the ladies, I would say a lot of what they write about could use a broader audience, and much of what they write about I'm sure is relatable in one way or another to other facilities.

Yes, we have been working with Claremont Colleges for 10+ years and they not only provide handouts/teaching material, they bring in guest authors, poets, and artists who teach different styles and methods of writing.

The *San Quentin News* began publishing articles regularly about the plight of women in the CDCR, some authored by women and some by men. The most ambitious project was an entire issue of *Wall City* magazine devoted just to women's issues.

SOLANO STATE PRISON, PHASE II

The January 2016 visit to Solano broke the ice.

In October of 2017, Elizabeth Rainey, a two-year veteran of the UC Berkeley student editor group, said she wanted to take on the Solano project. Rainey, whose father Jim is a longtime Southern California journalist, had received her BA from Cal the previous May. Nevertheless, she had continued to volunteer at San Quentin. Krissi Khokhobashvili of the CDCR encouraged Rainey to come to Solano. Another Cal student, Adam Iscoe, joined Rainey. On their own they began to make weekly visits to Vacaville to meet with the *Solano Vision* inmates. I gave Rainey various teaching aids, such as syllabi, handouts, and textbooks.

Their project at Solano continued until April of 2018, when Rainey was hired by *Democracy Now,* a daily news program, and left for New York. Adam Iscoe said he would continue the effort.

The student volunteers came with enthusiasm and hope and ran up against the logistical realities of prison security. The problems that the Cal students encountered were endemic to working inside a prison. I reminded them that Rome and the *San Quentin News* were not built in a day. Besides the lack of resources and institutional support, the *Solano Vision* was run like a company newsletter.[5] It had no commitment to journalism. For example, the prisoners were at times forbidden to add personal details about their interview subjects, even things like a person's age or race in an obituary. The prison officials were especially uncomfortable about inmates

writing about their personal experiences while in prison. The prison's education department and Dr. Kenya Williams supervised the *Solano Vision*.
Dr. Williams supported the effort as an educational and rehabilitative
tool. What she lacked was a collection of seasoned journalists at hand who
could explain the prevailing standards in the news industry. Office space
and computer access were major needs. The Cal students did not pack the
necessary heft or credibility. Before her departure, Rainey wrote me this
memo in January 2018 on her six months visiting Solano State Prison,
where establishing a foothold in journalism remained a work in progress:

> I can say without a doubt that my time at Solano has shown me that the San
> Quentin model can and should be reproduced. In my first class with the
> men of the Solano Vision, we talked about why a prison newspaper is impor-
> tant. The journalists in front of me discussed the need for a source of accu-
> rate information within prison walls. They also shared their desire to inform
> readers about sentencing, prison reform and criminal justice. They wanted
> their newspaper to share a wide range of stories about the experience of liv-
> ing at Solano Prison, for both readers on the inside and on the outside. I
> have seen firsthand the way this journalistic work can inspire, encourage
> and promote positive change. I hope that the Solano Vision is given the tools
> and support that it needs to keep doing this work.

THE SECRET INGREDIENT

The student volunteers showed remarkable commitment to the prison
newspaper project, confirming for me the most important discovery I
made in my seven years visiting San Quentin: the power of volunteerism,
which proved to be the secret ingredient that made rehabilitation programs successful and transformed the prison landscape. As opposed to
state employees who see their work in prison as a professional engage-
ment, the volunteers see it as a calling. "I drove past this place a thousand
times," said Carl Gibbs, who had just served as the umpire at a baseball
game on the lower yard inside San Quentin. "I never thought about the
men. Now I had a chance to see into their lives."[6]

Multiply that experience by two thousand (the approximate number
of civilians volunteering at San Quentin). The volunteer-led programs

go way beyond sports. They include everything from yoga classes to Hawaiian hula.[7]

When one of my former UC Berkeley journalism students, Nigel Hatton, later a professor at UC Merced, invited me to join him teaching an introductory journalism course for inmates at San Quentin, I became one of the approximately two thousand volunteers working at San Quentin. The mainline prisoners, approximately two thousand men, more than half of the whole prison population, are the principal beneficiaries of the rehabilitation programs. In effect, they choose among three hundred rehabilitation options. Compared to the more than thirty other California prisons, San Quentin makes available an embarrassment of riches. That's why it has come to be known in the system as a "go home" prison, offering the best chance for access to programs that might lead to parole or commutation. Even though it's the state's oldest prison with crowded, uncomfortable cells, many inmates lobby hard for years to get there.

FUTURE GROWTH

In October of 2018 considerable interest had grown throughout the CDCR about copying San Quentin's success with a newspaper. On the first of that month associate editor Kevin Sawyer sent an email to six different CDCR officials:

> I've noticed an increasing number of inmates and CDCR prison staff expressing interest in starting a newspaper or newsletter. They typically ask us how to get started. I brought this subject up at one of our weekly staff meetings. I suggested inviting those of you on this email list to visit our newsroom on a Tuesday when we hold our weekly staff meetings with our outside volunteers and advisers. Everyone seemed to think it was a good idea.
>
> Wardens and or their PIOs could send delegates here to learn what it is that we do, and how we do it. They can meet our advisers and the *San Quentin News* staff. Since California usually sets the pace, there's no reason why we shouldn't be leading the rest of the nation with journalism. I think a visit to our newsroom would be a good place to start. You can also see what the other groups do inside San Quentin's media center, such as the famous podcast Ear Hustle.

Meanwhile a student prison-support group at UC Davis calling themselves Beyond the Stats began visiting the *San Quentin News* in May of 2018. The year-old group had twelve members on campus, mostly Latinos, and was dedicated to reversing negative stereotypes of prisoners. It published a magazine. Its leaders wanted to set up a support relationship for journalists at Solano State Prison and the newsletter there. It was a hopeful sign.

And in December 2018 a volunteer from the *San Quentin News* visited Corona, California, and met with a volunteer from the California Institution for Women. Molly Kittle, who worked for a marketing firm in the Bay Area, was in Southern California for business. While there, she set up a meeting with Professor Erin M. Runions, chair of the Department of Religious Studies at Pomona College, who teaches a creative writing course at CIW. They discussed concrete ways to get female voices into *Wall City*, the *SQ News* magazine. It was the first time somebody from *SQ News* had had a face-to-face encounter with somebody working directly with a women's prison.

THE MULE CREEK SURPRISE

"What's going on here?" read the text from Aly Tamboura. He included a photograph of himself holding a copy of a newspaper, the *Mule Creek Post*. After leaving prison on parole Tamboura had gone to work for the Chan Zuckerberg Initiative (CZI), the social justice philanthropy project founded by the spouse of the Facebook CEO. Mule Creek State Prison, opened in 1987, houses more than four thousand inmates in Amador County in California's Gold Rush country. Until I received Tamboura's text I had never heard of the *Mule Creek Post*. Copies of the December 2018 edition were sent both to CZI and to San Quentin's Media Center.

After some investigation I discovered that the Mule Creek newspaper represented a collaboration unique in the history of California. The costs of the prison newspaper were paid by the Jackson Rancheria Band of Miwuk Indians.[8] Faculty members from nearby Feather River College were also helping out with the editing and advising.

Jack Mitchell, publisher of the *Ledger Dispatch*, an Amador County community newspaper, also owned by the Miwuk Indians, sent me an email on January 19, 2019, recounting the origins of the Mule Creek prison newspaper:

> I got involved with the *Mule Creek Post* in May of 2018 when [CDCR official] Stella Russell asked me to come speak to the *Mule Creek Post*. As the Publisher of the local newspaper, the *Ledger Dispatch*, I learned that the Mule Creek prison had a newspaper that was being produced on 8.5 X 11 inch paper, folded and distributed, and that the team at the *Mule Creek Post* was hoping to print on real newsprint among other items. It was really more of a newsletter at that time, though the staff members of the *Mule Creek Post*, writers, and their advisors were running the project as a newspaper.
>
> So, in June I started working with Stella and the prisoners to take their layout and pieces and convert it to a newspaper template, and print an actual newspaper. I serve as an advisor, work off the antiquated systems, convert layout to system that works with mine at the *Ledger Dispatch* and print and deliver them back to the *Mule Creek Post* staff that runs and operates their own newspaper. So, I'm an advisor, composing liaison, printer and circulation guide from the outside more than anything.

Joan Parkin, an associate professor at Feather River College, drives three and a half hours each way to reach the prison. She writes a column for the newspaper and helps the inmates develop their story ideas. Parkin points out that, unlike the *San Quentin News,* the *Mule Creek Post* runs on a shoestring and lacks the same stature within the CDCR and the outside media community. "It's basically the warden's baby. Until it gets established and gets political support, it has to really toe the line. They have to be careful with every sentence," she added.

The Miwuk Tribe owns and operates the Jackson Rancheria Casino Resort, as well as Little Oak Learning Center, RV Park, Hotel, and General Store. Mitchell added, "I've covered printing costs through the Jackson Rancheria Band of Miwuk Indians that own the *Ledger Dispatch*. They view the endeavor as a positive influence in the rehabilitation process and hope that inmates interested in journalism find their voice and a profession when they are rehabilitated and released."

33 The Hero with a Thousand Faces

Mythology professor Joseph Campbell created a cultural archetype: the "hero with a thousand faces," a kind of superhero who expresses the cultural yearnings within a people. Arnulfo García fit the bill, even though he was dressed in state-issue blue denim. The Mexican had the power to dream outsized, seemingly impossible dreams and make them happen, overcoming disaster and subduing powerful, implacable forces, using only his shrewd native skills to prevail.

When I first met him, García was another face in the newsroom, a guy with many stories to tell and a friendly, engaging manner. How then did he transform himself into the hero with a thousand faces? As Joseph Campbell describes the mythical protagonist, "A hero ventures forth from the world of common day into a region of supernatural wonder: fabulous forces are there encountered and a decisive victory is won: the hero comes back from this mysterious adventure with the power to bestow boons on his fellow man."[1]

I had seen this before.

It was 1970, and his name was Ruben Salazar, my colleague at the *Los Angeles Times,* forty-two, a veteran newsman who had held posts in

272

Vietnam and later Mexico City. He wrote about the swirling, exciting, unprecedented Chicano awakening in Los Angeles in the late 1960s ("region of supernatural wonder"). He left the security of the *Los Angeles Times* ("common day") to become news director of a local Latino-oriented TV station in 1969. Once there he became a singular voice of Chicano resistance to police power against Latino residents, and because of this he became anathema to Los Angeles law enforcement officials ("fabulous forces," in Campbell's terms). A great battle was fought.

It was a Saturday night, August 29, 1970. An antiwar demonstration took place at a local park. It was staged by the National Chicano Moratorium Day Committee, which was protesting the disproportionate number of Latinos dying in Vietnam. I was assistant city editor, and I got a phone call from Boris Yaro, a *Times* photographer.

"I'm at the Silver Dollar Café on Whittier Boulevard, Bill. There's a dead body inside. They say it's Ruben Salazar," said Yaro in a quavering voice. A Los Angeles County deputy sheriff had fired a teargas projectile into the bar, striking Salazar dead. "If Ruben were dead, the riot on Whittier Boulevard would be much more than just tear gas, burning and looting. It would be an event indelibly marking race relations in Los Angeles for years to come." I wrote that paragraph in an *Esquire* article published about a year afterward.[2] My prediction was correct. In death Salazar became a symbol of the Chicano struggle.

No course on Chicano studies today can be taught without exploring his life and his sacrifice. A great victory had been won. Even folk songs have been written in his honor. The most recent iteration of the Ruben Salazar legend was Phillip Rodriguez's 2014 PBS documentary *The Man in the Middle*.[3] Besides the documentary, three books have been written about Salazar. His work is included in many anthologies. Laguna Park has been renamed Ruben Salazar Park. Scholarships are given in his name. His death accelerated the Chicano renaissance. It was a great victory. In death, Salazar in spirit returned with "the power to bestow boons on his fellow man."

On October 5, 2017, as I drove from Oakland to Santa Clara for Arnulfo García's funeral, I had flashbacks to the September day in 1970 when I drove my VW microbus past the gentle hills near the University of California at Irvine to the cemetery chapel where the Salazar services were held. Inside were public officials and notables, including publisher Otis Chandler of the

Los Angeles Times, who delivered a eulogy. Outside stood a handful of scruffy Latino youngsters wearing brown berets with buttons saying, *"Viva la Raza."*

Enrique Hank Lopez, a friend of Salazar's, wrote at the time, "He was our only established newspaper columnist, the most experienced and articulate Chicano writer in the whole country. Such a loss no community can afford."[4] But nearly fifty years later Latinos have grown in numbers, influence, and recognition in California. They are well represented in the state's media voices. Salazar provided part of the emotional, spiritual uplift for the ensuing social change. His story became the irrepressible cry for Chicano/Latino identity. Fourteen years after his death the *Los Angeles Times* received a Pulitzer Gold Medal for its coverage of Southern California's growing Latino community. Salazar had opened the eyes of the editors.

THE PRISON INCUBATOR FOR SOCIAL CHANGE

No notables or public officials were present to eulogize Arnulfo T. García. After he died I tried to get his obituary into the *Congressional Record,* arguing that he had turned his life around and had a history of good works. Nobody would touch it.

García's name was not a household word, even among Chicanos. The work that he did was undertaken inside the CDCR prisons, not in a public arena. Nevertheless, I would argue that the impact of his journalism might rival Salazar's. The model he developed at San Quentin might become a beacon for leading California out of the mass incarceration mess into which it had descended since 1968. He helped give many men, not just Latinos, swept up in mass incarceration a new, positive identity and a new purpose. His life and death would be a test of Joseph Campbell's idea about the power of myth.

In psychologist Shadd Maruna's definition, García had indeed "made good" and redeemed himself from his life of crime. "If such an enormous life transformation is to be believed, the person needs a coherent narrative to explain and justify his turnaround," wrote Maruna.[5] In chapter 15 of this book I examined García's biography in detail.

García carefully explained and documented his transformation in his voluminous prison writings.

García had visited a land of "supernatural wonder," the dystopic world of incarceration, where he often encountered "fabulous forces" beyond even Joseph Campbell's imagination. Bonaru Richardson, who succeeded García as editor in chief, described one such encounter:

> One day Arnulfo and I was delivering the newspapers to each unit. When we got to the SNY [sensitive needs yard] unit, I was scared because there were stories about SNY inmates attacking general population inmates. I thought we were going to drop the bags off and leave, but when we walked into the building the SNY inmates were outside of their cells everywhere. I immediately dropped the bag on the ground and turned around to get out of there. But as I begin to turn around I noticed Arnulfo shaking hands with them and asking them questions like are they alright, and what can he do for them. I was shocked! Before I knew it, I was shaking hands and talking to them as well. If given an opportunity, Arnulfo would make friends with anyone. That's why I love him because he had a pure soul and a heart filled with divinity.[6]

Latinos are a plurality in California's prison population, but García transcended racial and cultural boundaries. The men in his eyes were united by their bondage and their determination to be better men. An older white lifer, who was convicted in 1990 of an Orange County homicide, said García's friendship helped him change his life.

> "Mr. Arnulfo García was my mentor and best friend, as he was the one who helped me get a job in the *San Quentin News*," said Wesley R. Eisiminger. "While working in the newsroom we were all like a family inside the wall, and we looked after each other. Besides working in the newsroom we both had daughters, and we would take walks around the track and talk about some problems we had; we became even closer as brothers.
>
> I always look up to him as he was like family, and we treated each other that way. I will miss him and will always keep him in my mind and keep his saying "Moving Forward," as he made this paper what it is today. I will do my best to keep it going and make all of his plans for the future come true.[7]

SO MANY BATTLES

The "fabulous forces" were everywhere. They included the prison factions, the correctional officers, and prison bureaucracy, but García never seemed to doubt himself. He imparted that confidence to those who worked with him. He had engaged in a number of battles. Juan Haines told this story about how he and García would have breakfast in the prison mess hall every morning:

> Arnulfo had this huge plastic coffee mug with "Hard Time Cafe" printed on it. He told me that he could only drink about half of the coffee, so I'd always get the other half of the flavorful Taster's Choice brand he liked.
>
> Arnulfo knew I wasn't all right when in 2013, my close friend Lizzie [Buchen], an advisor for *San Quentin News*, left the newspaper abruptly. She was frustrated with the way it was being managed and with how arbitrary some of those management decisions appeared. The administration didn't like her sharp perspective and commentary, and in the end, that was that. Arnulfo could see how disheartened I had become. I couldn't hide it. He knew how her friendship sparked life into me. I felt like I had no support, but how wrong I was.
>
> He took me on walks around the Lower Yard and told me how important Lizzie was. He told me that the kind of changes and directions Lizzie and I wanted had to be approached more cautiously. We were a little too extreme in our ideas. Arnulfo knew how to read the tea leaves far better than I do. He taught me that most people in government really do want a better community and value the work we are doing but can get intimidated by the power of the press, even the little power *San Quentin News* has. Arnulfo figured out how to bring these confrontational issues slowly. He taught me how to engage that way—to bring ideas to the table from all sides without malice. I still feel Arnulfo's presence guiding me to take his approach in doing things important for the betterment of the community.
>
> During breakfast at Table 122, we still talk about the things we used to do when Arnulfo was there. It seems strange that the seat mostly remains empty. Everyone in the chow hall knows that it's Arnulfo's seat and no one is ready to fill it. Eventually, though, someone will take that seat. When they do; I hope they bring something of what Arnulfo brought.
>
> I still arrive at the table with my empty cup. Mike looks at it and says that it's not going to fill itself. He doesn't realize that the spirit of my friend, Arnulfo, fills it every morning.[8]

BESTOWING BOONS ON HIS FELLOW MAN

UC Berkeley student Bo Kovitz, in the inaugural issue of García's brainchild, *Wall City*, wrote this about the late editor: "He appears in my mind when I'm thinking and working as a reporter, telling me to rephrase things, ask different questions. He pulls me out of bed in the morning, guides me through my days. He's still here. He's alive, in all of us."[9]

The volunteers and inmates who worked with García were inspired and devoted to carrying on his vision and his work. But the question remained whether they would be able to sustain the momentum, as time moved on. Would a great victory be won?

The *San Quentin News* crew rebounded after García's death. The staff members could not attend his funeral, so they organized a memorial of their own in the prison. The preparation for the memorial was turned over to Jorge Heredia, a congenial inmate who wrote for the Spanish-language section of the paper. While in prison, Heredia had joined a club that gave him toastmaster's training. I had lent him a copy of Dale Carnegie's classic *How To Win Friends and Influence People*. He took on the planning job as though the weight of the world was on his shoulders.

The next edition of the newspaper was dedicated to the late editor in chief. Of course, it was filled with fulsome tributes from all quarters. I contributed one short paragraph: "I've known many great journalists and great editors. Arnulfo was one of the best. He did more with fewer resources than any of them, and he left a lasting legacy that will change the way Californians think about incarcerated Americans."[10] I did not mention Ruben Salazar. Nobody would have known who I was talking about. But I could easily see some of history repeating itself.

Another believer in García's ability to "bestow boons on his fellow man" was former San Quentin warden Robert Ayers Jr. He spoke at the funeral and later wrote a tribute in the *San Quentin News*:[11]

I believe prison administrations need to constantly search for new ways that inmates may use to help themselves break that cycle. One constant, though, is *success*. And success can be infectious. Arnulfo got infected through his work with the *San Quentin News*. His legacy is that he spread that infection not only to men at San Quentin but to others beyond San Quentin. So, I think that is the underlying reason why I re-started the *San Quentin News*: To present an opportunity for Arnulfo and others like him to taste success, become infected by success and use it as a springboard to break the cycle.

The warden's definition of success was limited to helping him keep the prison running smoothly, but García's vision was much bigger. "While I may have plugged in the lamp, which was the resurrected *San Quentin News*, Arnulfo tweaked it until it became a beacon."[12]

The beacon shone brighter than at any time in the previous forty years.

34 Epilogue

The Atlantic magazine invited me to a roundtable dinner December 13, 2018, at a fancy hotel in San Francisco. The invitees included the criminal justice elite of the city. Next to me sat the San Francisco police chief (a black man named William Scott); across from me sat San Francisco sheriff Vicki Hennessy, and not far away was District Attorney George Gascon.

Twenty or so officials and nonprofit leaders opined for two hours about issues of homelessness, crime, and inequality, as I ate my dinner in silence. I kept asking myself, what am I doing here?

Finally, the moderator, senior editor Ron Brownstein, looked at me: "Professor Drummond, we haven't heard from you. What do the men at San Quentin tell you about how they came to prison?"

Thoughts of the handsome Mexican with the happy eyes those years ago outside the San Quentin educational building crossed my mind. State prison was so far removed from the banquet table with these local leaders. What was the prison truth? I made it short.

"It is common knowledge," I said, "A third of the men in prison are mentally ill. A third have addiction issues. And a third committed a horrible impulsive act, and their rehabilitation sweet spot happened fifteen years ago, but they are still in prison."

The heads around the table nodded like an amen chorus in a Baptist Church. On that note, the moderator Brownstein adjourned the session. I got my coat and walked out onto Geary Street.

Notes

1. OVERVIEW

1. Alyson Brown, "What Has Been Ailing Britain's Prisons?," *History Now, BBC History Magazine*, October 4, 2018.

2. Prior to 2005 it was the Department of Corrections or the CDC. The "R" for Rehabilitation was added as part of a reorganization, thus the CDCR. "A Decade Ago, a New Name Affirmed Mission of CDCR," *Inside CDCR The Department of Corrections and Rehabilitation Newsletter*, August 28, 2015, https://www .insidecdcr.ca.gov/2015/08/a-decade-ago-a-new-name-affirmed-mission-of-cdcr/.

3. Shadd Maruna, *Making Good: How Ex-convicts Reform and Rebuild Their Lives* (Washington, DC: American Psychological Association, 2001).

4. Kevin D. Sawyer, "Few Prisoners Strike at San Quentin," *Bay View: National Black Newspaper*, October 4, 2018, http://sfbayview.com/2018/10 /few-prisoners-strike-at-san-quentin/.

5. *Desistance* is a new term to me in describing penology. I first encountered it in Maruna's book *Making Good*, 22.

6. Richard (Bonaru) Richardson, draft of "San Quentin News Historical Journey," *San Quentin News*, November 15, 2018, https://sanquentinnews.com /san-quentin-news-historical-journey/. This quote was edited out of the editorial before publication.

7. Richard Richardson, draft of "San Quentin News."

8. Richard Hofstadter, *The Age of Reform* (New York: Knopf, 1955).

2. PRISON VOICES HEARD

1. Jessica Pishko, "The *San Quentin News* Seeks to Humanize Inmates," *Columbia Journalism Review*, October 28, 2014, https://archives.cjr.org /behind_the_news/the_san_quentin_news_seeks_to.php.

2. Denise Petski, "'Orange Is the New Black' to End with Season 7 on Netflix," *Deadline Hollywood*, October 7, 2018, https://deadline.com/2018/10/orange-is-the-new-black-to-end-with-season-7-on-netflix-1202484913/.

3. Merrill Barr, "We Finally Know How Many People Watched 'Orange Is the New Black,'" *TV Guide*, June 29, 2016, https://www.tvguide.com/news /nielsen-reveals-orange-is-the-new-black-ratings/.

4. Michelle Alexander, *The New Jim Crow: Mass Incarceration in the Era of Colorblindness* (New York: New Press, 2010).

5. Adam Gopnik, "The Caging of America: Why Do We Lock Up So Many People?," *New Yorker*, January 22, 2012, https://www.newyorker.com/magazine /2012/01/30/the-caging-of-america.

6. Adam Gopnik, "Notes on 'The Caging of America,'" *New Yorker*, February 6, 2012, https://www.newyorker.com/news/news-desk/notes-on-the-caging-of-america.

7. Adam Gopnik, "How We Misunderstand Mass Incarceration," *New Yorker*, April 3, 2017, https://www.newyorker.com/magazine/2017/04/10/how-we-misunderstand-mass-incarceration.

8. Abbie VanSickle, Marshall Project, e-mail to author, October 16, 2018.

9. "Lockup Producer Answers Your Questions," MSNBC, May 30, 2014, http:// www.msnbc.com/lockup/producer-susan-carney-answers-your-questions-0.

10. "'Orange' Creator Jenji Kohan: Piper Was My Trojan Horse," *Fresh Air*, August 13, 2013, NPR, https://www.npr.org/2013/08/13/211639989/orange-creator-jenji-kohan-piper-was-my-trojan-horse%0A.

11. Here are the principal changes in California criminal justice laws signed by Gov. Edmund G. Brown Jr. in 2018:

- Trying Youth as Adults: Senate Bill 1391 (Mitchell and Lara) prohibits children age fourteen and fifteen from being tried as adults in criminal court and being sentenced to time in adult prison.
- Fair and Just Sentencing Reform: Senate Bill 1393 (Mitchell and Lara) restores the court's discretion, in the interest of justice, in deciding whether to impose a five-year sentence enhancement for a prior serious felony conviction.
- Felony Murder Rule: Senate Bill 1437 (Skinner) clarifies that a person may be convicted of first-degree felony murder only if that person intentionally participated in the homicide.
- Setting a Minimum Age for Juvenile Court Prosecution: SB 439 (Mitchell) keeps kids younger than twelve years old out of the juvenile system, and it addresses their offenses as civil matters.

- Recall of Sentence: AB 2942 (Ting) provides prosecutors the discretion to make recommendations for recall and resentencing where the interest of justice so warrants. The recommendation would be made to the sentencing court, which would make the final determination whether a lesser, legal sentence is warranted.
- Exoneree Support: SB 1050 (Lara) requires exonerated people being housed in California prisons to be offered financial support and transitional services, including SSI and CalFresh.
- Pardon and Commutation Reform Act: AB 2845 (Bonta) increases the transparency and accessibility of the pardon and commutation process.
- Resentencing of Cannabis Convictions: AB 1793 (Bonta) requires the Department of Justice to review records in the state summary criminal history database and to identify past convictions that are potentially eligible for recall or dismissal of sentence, dismissal and sealing, or redesignation and to notify the prosecution of all cases in their jurisdiction that are eligible.
- Increasing Police Transparency and Building Community Trust: SB 978 (Bradford) requires local law enforcement agencies to post their manuals and policies, if not exempt from disclosure under the California Public Records Act (CPRA), on their department websites.

12. "Don't Care about Criminals? Maybe You Should Care about What Their Care Is Costing You," editorial, *Sacramento Bee*, November 1, 2018, https://www .sacbee.com/opinion/editorials/article220960000.html?fbclid=IwAR2KDBPjN 1vgRsj8SmmRUJnkIHWNWtKqocIn_MLlLYVJLjC1KgkNdXqn6yo%0A.

3. SOLEDAD BROTHERS

1. Eric Cummins, *The Rise and Fall of California's Radical Prison Movement* (Stanford, CA: Stanford University Press, 1994), 65.
2. Steven Pinker, *The Better Angels of Our Nature: Why Violence Has Declined* (New York: Penguin, 2011), 109.
3. Pinker, *Better Angels*, 115.
4. In addition to Eldridge Cleaver, another famous Black Panther leader was imprisoned during this period. In April 1970 I visited the California Men's Colony (CMC) in San Luis Obispo, where I interviewed Huey P. Newton, cofounder of the Black Panthers, in his cell. Building 2 in A Quad was the cellblock where Newton was imprisoned. CMC was surrounded by cyclone fences and razor wire instead of walls. "I'll resist until my very death if necessary," Newton told me. Newton's resistance efforts had little effect on other CMC prisoners. He was a VIP and was largely removed from the prevalent racial tensions on the yard. He was busy focusing on his strategy to get out of prison, and he had no chance to organize resistance among the other black prisoners. I had brought a pack of cigarettes to break the ice, but Newton said he had stopped smoking. (Many years

later, as a professor at Berkeley, I assigned students to cover the trial of Tyrone Robinson, Newton's confessed murderer.)

5. Cummins, *Rise and Fall*, 93.

6. "1970 Marin County Courthouse Murders," *SFGate*, April 18, 2017, www .sfgate.com/news/slideshow/1970-Marin-County-courthouse-shooting-144014 /photo-12742230.php.

7. The park in the heart of West Oakland was a central location of Black Panther Party social programs in the 1960s.

8. William J. Drummond, "Blue Denim Jungle: Prison Race Trouble," *Los Angeles Times*, August 9, 1970.

9. Jim Stingley, "Revolutionaries Keep San Quentin Tense," *Los Angeles Times*, September 26, 1970.

10. Jim Stingley, "Prison Guards: 24-Hour Day of Fear, Low Pay and Hatred," *Los Angeles Times*, September 6, 1971.

11. Gretel Kauffman, "Attica! Representations of the 1971 Prison Riot in Local and National Journalism" (senior thesis, Notre Dame University, 2016), http:// americanstudies.nd.edu/assets/223714/gretel_kauffman_thesis_.pdf.

12. Stingley, "Revolutionaries."

13. Stingley, "Revolutionaries."

14. Raymond K. Procunier, "Publication Ban," *San Quentin News*, October 22, 1971, https://archive.org/stream/san_quentin_news_1971/san_quentin_ news_1971_djvu.txt.

15. "From the Editor's Desk," *San Quentin News*, October 1, 1971, 2.

16. Philip C. Clark, "Bastille by the Bay," *San Quentin News*, December 24, 1971.

4. KENNEDY TO CLEAVER

1. William J. Drummond, "Black Skin, Kinky Hair, Fleetness of Foot," *Columbia Journalism Review*, Fall 1968, 49–51, https://drive.google.com/file/d /1FJ1FA2PiWeOg68GoCnYMSSr628i6FS13/view?usp=sharing.

2. Next time you watch the film *All the President's Men* or even *The Post*, note the absence of any black faces.

3. Kerner Commission, *Report of the National Advisory Commission on Civil Disorders* (Washington, DC: US Government Printing Office, 1968), https:// www.ncjrs.gov/pdffiles1/Digitization/8073NCJRS.pdf, 2.

5. THE PRIMARY ELECTION

1. Eric Malnic, "Voices—Eric Malnic," *Los Angeles Times*, June 8, 2008, https:// latimesblogs.latimes.com/thedailymirror/2008/06/voices--eric-ma.html.

2. Robert Richardson, "A Taste of What It's Like," *Los Angeles Times,* August 22, 1965, http://documents.latimes.com/taste-what-its/.

3. Eldridge Cleaver, *Soul on Ice* (New York: McGraw Hill, 1968).

4. William J. Drummond, "Eldridge Cleaver: Black Militant Forged by Life: Who Is He? What Is He? And Why?," *Los Angeles Times,* November 29, 1968.

5. Louise Glasscock, personal letter sent to the author, November 29, 1968.

6. W. Drummond, "Eldridge Cleaver."

6. THE JOHNNY CASH MYTH

1. Gayle Thompson, "49 Years Ago Johnny Cash Records 'At San Quentin' Album," J-98 The Boot radio, May 18, 2018. (It went platinum and double platinum on November 21, 1986, and triple platinum on March 27, 2003).

2. Eric Cummins, *The Rise and Fall of California's Radical Prison Movement* (Stanford, CA: Stanford University Press, 1994), 126–27.

3. Allison Griffiths, *Carceral Fantasies: Cinema and Prison in Early 20th Century America* (New York: Columbia University Press, 2016).

4. Michael Darlow, dir., *Johnny Cash in San Quentin* (Granada Television, aired September 6, 1969), www.imdb.com/title/tt0461256/.

5. Haggard saw Cash's first show at the prison in 1958. "Inmate Merle Haggard Hears Johnny Cash Play San Quentin State Prison," History.com, This Day in History, January 1, 1958, n.d., https://www.history.com/this-day-in-history/inmate-merle-haggard-hears-johnny-cash-play-san-quentin-state-prison.

6. Chuck EZ Williams to Aly Tamboura, November 2017, shared with permission.

7. Jacob Simas, *Inside Story: Chronicles the Rise and Fall of Prison Journalism in the United States and the Recent Rebirth of the Prison Newspaper at San Quentin State Prison,* MA thesis film, University of California, Berkeley, 2009, available from Jacob Simas, jsimas@newamericamedia.org.

8. Johnny Cash, "San Quentin [#2][Live] Lyrics," Lyrics.com, https://www.lyrics.com/lyric/813799.

9. Michael Streissguth, *Johnny Cash: The Biography* (Boston: DaCapo Press, 2006), 160.

10. Phil Marsh, "At San Quentin," *Rolling Stone,* July 1969, https://www.rollingstone.com/music/music-country/at-san-quentin-189370/.

11. Boston Woodard, "Johnny Cash: Prison Reform Advocate," *San Quentin News,* March 13, 2013, https://sanquentinnews.com/johnny-cash-legendary-prison-reform-advocate/.

8. THE LEE COMMISSION AND THE "TOUGH-ON-CRIME" ERA

1. Kerner Commission, *Report of the National Advisory Commission on Civil Disorders* (Washington, DC: US Government Printing Office, 1968), https://www.ncjrs.gov/pdffiles1/Digitization/8073NCJRS.pdf.

2. William J. Drummond, "'Black Skin, Kinky Hair, Fleetness of Foot,'" *Columbia Journalism Review*, Fall 1968, 49, https://drive.google.com/file/d/1FJ 1FA2PiWeOg68GoCnYMSSr628i6FS13/view?usp=sharing.

3. "Blaxploitation: The Controversial 1970s," Separate Cinema Archive, n.d., accessed April 13, 2019, www.separatecinema.com/exhibits_blaxploitation.html.

4. Brad Dharma, "The 50 Best Blaxploitation Movies of All Time," IMDb, last updated May 22, 2014, www.imdb.com/list/ls058887687/.

5. This claim was dubious at best. See Bryan J. Cook, American Council on Education, "More Black Men in Prison Than in College? Think Again," *The Presidency,* Fall 2012, https://www.acenet.edu/the-presidency/columns-and-features/Pages/By-the-Numbers-More-Black-Men-in-Prison-Than-in-College-Think-Again-.aspx.

6. William J. Drummond, "Media," chap. 9 in California Commission on the Status of African-American Males, *African-American Males: The Struggle for Equality. Final Report* (Sacramento, CA: The Commission, 1996).

7. Ishmael Reed, "The Black Pathology Biz," *Nation,* November 20, 1989; reprinted in *Nation,* February 12, 2002, https://www.thenation.com/article/black-pathology-biz/.

8. Daniel Patrick Moynihan, *The Case for National Action: The Negro Family,* Report for the Office of Policy Planning and Research, US Department of Labor (Washington, DC: US Government Printing Office, 1965).

9. Full disclosure: Pat Moynihan and I became friends in India in 1971 when he arrived as ambassador. He was an important mentor to me in my career. We never discussed black pathology. He began life as a poor boy from a dysfunctional family in Hell's Kitchen. I was a poor boy from Oakland who grew up in a dysfunctional family. We had common ground. I was the *L.A. Times* correspondent in India from 1971 to 1974.

10. Quoted in Drummond, "Media," 174.

11. J.J. McIntyre and J.J. Teevan, "Television Violence and Deviant Behavior," in *Television and Social Behavior,* vol. 3, *Television and Adolescent Aggressiveness,* ed. G.A. Comstock and E.A. Rubinstein (Rockville, MD: National Institute of Mental Health, 1972), cited in California Commission, *African-American Males,* 175.

12. William Shakespeare, *The Tempest* 1.2.517–18.

13. Roy K. Procunier, "Christmas Messages," *San Quentin News,* December 24, 1971, 2, https://sanquentinnews.files.wordpress.com/2010/09/san-quentin-news-dec-24–1971.pdf.

14. California Commission, *African-American Males*, 115–17.

15. "CDCR is the 3rd largest law enforcement in the United States behind the U.S. Customs and Border Protection (CBP) which is an arm of Dept of Homeland Security (DHS), and the New York City Police Department, which employ approximately 66,000 federal officers and 42,000 police officers respectively. CDCR correctional officers are sworn law enforcement officers with peace officer powers." Cal Poly Center for Innovation and Entrepreneurship, "Correction Captain Study," June 1, 2019.

16. Steven Pinker, *The Better Angels of Our Nature: Why Violence Has Declined* (New York: Penguin, 2011), 121.

17. Pete Wilson, "State of the State Address," Sacramento, January 5, 1994, http://governors.library.ca.gov/addresses/s_36-Wilson04.html.

18. Michael G. Wanner, Jim Mayer, and Faizah Alim, "Most Drug Abusers Are White—but Blacks Fill Jail Cells Here," *Sacramento Bee*, December 16, 1990.

19. California Commission, *African-American Males*, 115–17.

20. William J. Drummond, "LA Crime Rate Could Collapse Justice System, Computer Says. Overloaded Jails Seen as Threat If Trend Persists," *Los Angeles Times*, September 13, 1970.

21. Paige St. John, "As More Inmates Are Released from Prison, More Parolees Return," *Los Angeles Times*, December 27, 2014, https://www.latimes.com/local/california/la-me-ff-pol-lifer-parole-20141228-story.html.

9. THE *SAN QUENTIN NEWS*

1. Clinton Duffy, "Warden Duffy Tells How He Started the San Quentin News," *San Quentin News*, July 2010, https://archive.org/stream/san_quentin_news_2010/san_quentin_news_2010_djvu.txt.

2. Eric Cummins, *The Rise and Fall of California's Radical Prison Movement* (Stanford, CA: Stanford University Press, 1994), 14.

3. James McGrath Morris, *Jailhouse Journalism: The Fourth Estate behind Bars* (Jefferson, NC: McFarland, 1998), 171.

4. Morris, *Jailhouse Journalism*, 174.

5. Morris, *Jailhouse Journalism*, 174.

6. Morris, *Jailhouse Journalism*, 177.

7. Procunier v. Martinez, 416 U.S. 396 (1974), Supreme.justia.com, https://supreme.justia.com/cases/federal/us/416/396/case.html.

8. Procunier v. Martinez.

9. Procunier v. Martinez.

10. Bailey v. Loggins, 32 Cal.3d 907, SCOCAL, https://scocal.stanford.edu/opinion/bailey-v-loggins-30569.

11. Laura Fraser, "State's Prison Press Sentenced to Silence," MediaFile, April 1985, published monthly by Media Alliance. Photocopy sent to me by the author.

12. Fraser, "State's Prison Press."

13. Wilbert Rideau, "Can a Free Press Flourish behind Bars?," *Nation*, June 25, 2014, www.thenation.com/article/can-free-press-flourish-behind-bars/.

14. Raymond K. Procunier, "Publication Ban," *San Quentin News*, October 22, 1971, https://archive.org/stream/san_quentin_news_1971/san_quentin_news_1971_djvu.txt.

15. Jacob Simas, *Inside Story: Chronicles the Rise and Fall of Prison Journalism in the United States and the Recent Rebirth of the Prison Newspaper at San Quentin State Prison*, MA thesis film, 2009, available from Jacob Simas, jsimas@newamericamedia.org.

16. Robert Ayers, "Retired Warden Robert Ayers Honors Late Arnulfo Garcia," *San Quentin News*, October 2, 2017.

17. Michael Taylor, "San Quentin Inmate Newspaper Fills Need to Know," *San Francisco Chronicle*, March 28, 2009.

18. Simas, *Inside Story*.

19. Kenny Brydon, email to author, December 11, 2018.

20. Brydon, email to author.

21. Brydon, email to author.

22. Fraser, "State's Prison Press."

23. Simas, *Inside Story*.

24. Simas, *Inside Story*.

10. THE FOUNDING FATHERS

1. Kenneth Brydon, email to author, December 26, 2018. Earlier in the year Brydon had been paroled after serving forty years.

2. Ryan Masters, "How $107 Million of West Coast Rap King Suge Knight's Money Got Divvied Up in a Monterey Courtroom," *Monterey County Weekly*, April 27, 2006, www.montereycountyweekly.com/news/local_news/how-million-of-west-coast-rap-king-suge-knight-s/article_d46629ee-59f2-585b-acc1-838c44e0dedf.html.

3. "Closing the Print Shop," inmate-produced video, February 2010, in the author's collection.

11. MEDIA RECOGNITION

1. Megan Hansen, "San Quentin's Inmate-Run Newspaper Suspended over Photo Controversy," *Marin Independent Journal*, February 10, 2014.

2. Tommy Winfrey, "San Quentin and Marin Shakespeare Collaborate on Play Inspired by *Merchant of Venice*," *San Quentin News,* December 2013, https://sanquentinnews.com/s-q-and-marin-shakespeare-collaborate-on-play-inspired-by-merchant-of-venice/.

3. The bond between Lindsey and the *SQ News* staff continued even after his release, and he continued to visit the prison weekly through 2018 on his own time to provide outside research for their articles.

4. Chris Magerian, "San Quentin Inmate-Run Newspaper Honored, Suspended," *Los Angeles Times,* February 7, 2014, http://articles.latimes.com/2014/feb/07/local/la-me-pc-san-quentin-news-honored-suspended-20140207.

5. Krissi Khokhobashvili, email to author, October 27, 2017.

6. Jarvis JuVan Clark, "Officer Hauwert's Thoughts concerning Gender Identification," *San Quentin News,* November 30, 2014, https://sanquentinnews.com/officer-hauwerts-thoughts-concerning-gender-identification/.

7. Lindsey Bever, "California Prison Ordered to Grant Inmate's Sex Change Surgery," *Washington Post,* April 3, 2015, https://www.washingtonpost.com/news/morning-mix/wp/2015/04/03/california-prison-ordered-to-grant-inmates-sex-change/?utm_term=.fee9121980e2.

8. Mark Berman, "Five Things I Learned Reading the *San Quentin News,*" *Washington Post,* May 21, 2014, https://www.washingtonpost.com/news/post-nation/wp/2014/05/21/five-things-i-learned-reading-the-san-quentin-news/?utm_term=.85afb21d0384.

12. SAM ROBINSON

1. "Firsts," *Ear Hustle* podcast, season 2, March 14, 2018, https://static1.squarespace.com/static/5bd0d552e8ba44146721bb3c/t/5cab9984e79c703b55bae8f8/1554749836311/Firsts+transcript.pdf.

2. "A Day in the Life of a Public Information Officer," *Inside CDCR: The Department of Corrections and Rehabilitation Newsletter,* March 14, 2013.

13. RACE IN THE PRISON NEWSROOM

1. Jesse Vasquez, "One Prison Taught Me Racism. Another Taught Me Acceptance," *Washington Post,* October 1, 2018, https://www.washingtonpost.com/outlook/2018/10/01/one-prison-taught-me-racism-another-taught-me-acceptance/?utm_term=.2f6c8ca8a9d7.

2. Octavio Paz described this phenomenon back in 1950: "Since the *pachuco* [Mexican street gang member] cannot adapt himself to a civilization which, for its part, rejects him, he finds no answer to the hostility surrounding him except

this angry affirmation of his personality. Other groups react differently. The Negroes, for example, oppressed by racial intolerance, try to 'pass' as whites and thus enter society. They want to be like other people. The Mexicans have suffered a less violent rejection, but instead of attempting a problematical adjustment to society, the *pachuco* actually flaunts his differences." Octavio Paz, *The Labyrinth of Solitude* (New York: Grove Press, 1961), 14.

3. Armenian nationalist Harry Sassounian, serving a life sentence for the assassination of a Turkish official in Los Angeles, led a decades-long fight to get Armenian felons removed from the "other" category and classified as "white."

4. Juan Haines, "Home after Two Decades of Prison and Accomplishments," *San Quentin News,* July 1, 2017, https://storage.googleapis.com/sqn-archives /PDF/SQN-Edition-94-July-2017.pdf.

5. Haines, "Home after Two Decades."

14. THE KEY PLAYERS

1. "Coyote Point Productions Biographies," inmate-written autobiographies, San Quentin, 2014. As explained later in the chapter, inmates wrote these to provide background for their characters in a reality show in the prison that was proposed but never happened.

2. The email was sent to Jon Michael Spurlock of the Haas School of Business team but was copied to me as well.

15. ARNULFO GARCÍA

1. Arnulfo T. García, "The Life of Arnulfo Timoteo García," unpublished manuscript, 2012.

2. García, "Life."

3. García, "Life."

4. García, "Life."

5. García, "Life."

6. García, "Life."

7. García, "Life."

8. Carmelita Vargas, email to author, September 2017.

9. Arnulfo T. García, "The Tour," unpublished manuscript, 2008.

10. García, "Tour."

11. García, "Tour."

12. Professor Hatton's father and I had attended McClymonds High School together in Oakland, along with William A. Christmas, who would die with Jonathan Jackson in the ill-fated hostage-taking incident in 1970 at the Marin Civic Center, an event described elsewhere in this book.

13. "Behind Bars: The California Convict Cycle," http://berkeley.news21.com
/behindbars/, produced by my UC Berkeley class "News 21: Reporting on a
Changing America," Summer 2010.

16. GLENN BAILEY

1. My brother Jack died in 2005.
2. Tammerlin Drummond, "Years after Leaving San Quentin, Men Return
with Message of Hope," *Oakland Tribune,* June 9, 2017.
3. T. Drummond, "Years after Leaving."
4. T. Drummond, "Years after Leaving."
5. Juan Haines, "Former Lifer at Large in Community," *Wall City* magazine,
Spring 2019.
6. Sam Hurwitt, "A Life behind Bars Unfolds on Stage in Oakland," *San Jose
Mercury-News,* January 9, 2018.
7. Ayodele Nzinga, *Lifer,* 2017, unpublished copy of the play's production
script. A video of a performance by the Lower Bottom Playaz at Flight Deck in
Oakland, CA, can be seen on Vimeo at https://vimeo.com/261563845, uploaded
in 2018.
8. Hurwitt, "Life behind Bars."
9. Nzinga, *Lifer,* 30.
10. Nzinga, *Lifer,* 32.
11. J. Haines, "Former Lifer ."
12. Nzinga, *Lifer,* 42.
13. Nzinga, *Lifer,* 50.

17. JUAN HAINES

1. Lila LaHood, "2017 Excellence in Journalism Award Winners," Society of
Professional Journalists, Northern California, press release, October 23, 2017,
https://spjnorcal.org/2017/10/23/2017-excellence-in-journalism-award-winners/.
2. Alissa Greenberg, "Prisons Need Newspapers for the Same Reason the
Public Needs Newspapers," *Pacific Standard,* December 7, 2018, https://psmag
.com/social-justice/prisons-need-newspapers-interview-with-juan-haines-at-san-
quentin-news?fbclid=IwAR3TgqYppLHTDjbE-veq7p2E7mVa2KxsJR4HWAJI
VU3VKUFBM9A1NvrsvFY.
3. " Coyote Point Productions Biographies," inmate-written autobiographies,
San Quentin, 2014.
4. "Coyote Point Productions Biographies."
5. The text of Haines's speech is in my personal possession.

18. RAHSAAN THOMAS

1. "Coyote Point Productions Biographies," inmate-written autobiographies, San Quentin, 2014.
2. "Behind These Walls," episode of *United Shades of America*, CNN, aired May 1, 2016, transcript, http://transcripts.cnn.com/TRANSCRIPTS/1605/01/se.01.html.
3. "Coyote Point Productions Biographies."
4. "Coyote Point Productions Biographies."
5. "Coyote Point Productions Biographies."
6. "Coyote Point Productions Biographies."
7. "Coyote Point Productions Biographies."

19. RICHARD (BONARU) RICHARDSON

1. "Coyote Point Productions Biographies," inmate-written autobiographies, San Quentin, CA, 2014.
2. Esmeralda Bermudez, "A Prison Newsroom Mourns Its Former Editor in Chief, Recently Released and Then Killed in a Crash," *Los Angeles Times*, October 8, 2017, www.latimes.com/local/california/la-me-san-quentin-20171008-htmlstory.html.
3. "Coyote Point Productions Biographies."
4. "Coyote Point Productions Biographies."
5. "Coyote Point Productions Biographies."
6. "Coyote Point Productions Biographies."

20. WATANI STINER

1. Jessica Pishko, "The Curious Case of Prison Publishers," *Narratively*, August 22, 2014, http://narrative.ly/the-curious-case-of-the-prison-publishers/.
2. Pishko, "Curious Case."
3. "Coyote Point Productions Biographies," inmate-written autobiographies, San Quentin, 2014.
4. "Coyote Point Productions Biographies."
5. Robin Abcarian, "A Young Man in Oakland Has Captured the Wisdom of His Elders on a Blog and in a Book," *Los Angeles Times*, April 9, 2017, www.latimes.com/local/abcarian/la-me-abcarian-og-harshaw-20170409-story.html.

21. KEVIN SAWYER

1. Eric Cummins, *The Rise and Fall of California's Radical Prison Movement* (Stanford, CA: Stanford University Press, 1994).

2. "Coyote Point Productions Biographies," inmate-written autobiographies, San Quentin, 2014.

3. Allen Marshall, term paper written for Journalism 298 class at University of California, Berkeley, May 8, 2015.

4. "Coyote Point Productions Biographies."

5. "Coyote Point Productions Biographies."

6. "Coyote Point Productions Biographies."

7. "Coyote Point Productions Biographies."

8. "Coyote Point Productions Biographies."

9. "Coyote Point Productions Biographies."

10. Sawyer v. Chappell et al., Case No. 15-cv-00220-JD, https://www.leagle.com/decision/infdco20150730831.

22. ASIANS IN THE NEWSROOM

1. "Coyote Point Productions Biographies," inmate-written autobiographies, San Quentin, 2014. Mr. You calls himself "Sane" in the biographies.

2. "Coyote Point Productions Biographies."

3. Juan Haines, "San Quentin Hosts Fourth D.A. Forum," *San Quentin News*, August 2, 2017, https://sanquentinnews.com/?s=San+Quentin+hosts+fourth+D.A.+forum.

4. Chris Megerian, "Inmates Writing Their Own Obits Reveal Regrets, Failed Dreams," *Los Angeles Times*, March 4, 2015, http://graphics.latimes.com/prison-obits/.

5. Joel Christie, "'I'm Here Because I Took a Life—When I Leave This World, I Would Love to Save Someone': Prison Inmates Pen Their Own Moving Obituaries as Part of Class Assignment," *Daily Mail Online*, March 8, 2015, www.dailymail.co.uk/news/article-2984813/I-m-took-life-leave-world-love-save-Prison-inmates-pen-moving-obituaries-class-assignment.html.

6. John Lam, "Stateless: A Massacre, a Murder and Now Free," *San Quentin News*, January 31, 2017, https://sanquentinnews.com/stateless-massacre-murder-free/.

7. J. Haines, "San Quentin Hosts."

8. Rahsaan Thomas, "Exploring Injustices in Mass Incarceration," *San Quentin News*, August 1, 2015, https://sanquentinnews.com/exploring-injustices-in-mass-incarceration/.

9. "The Last Mile Transforms San Quentin Inmates into Tech Entrepreneurs," KPIX-TV, April 1, 2015, https://sanfrancisco.cbslocal.com/2015/04/01/the-last-mile-turns-san-quentin-inmates-start-ups-tech-pitch-ideas-silicon-valley-entrepreneurs/.

10. Associated Press, "Man Sentenced to 50 Years to Life for Killing L.A. Musician," January 17, 2006, https://groups.google.com/forum/#!topic/alt.obituaries/duOWWMyyiMs.

11. From Jonathan Chiu's letter to Governor Brown asking for commutation of his sentence, April 3, 2013.

12. Chiu to Brown, April 3, 2013.

13. Jonathan Chiu, "Marathon Man: A Lifer Takes Up Running to 'Earn Back' His Life," Marshall Project, May 11, 2017, https://www.themarshallproject.org/2017/05/11/marathon-man.

23. ALY TAMBOURA

1. "Aly Tamboura, Former Staff—Served Sentence," *San Quentin News*, May 17, 2016, https://sanquentinnews.com/staff/aly-tamboura/. Aly Tamboura never completed the autobiography requested for Coyote Point Productions. So what I know about him is based on our conversations going back to 2012.

2. Kevin D. Sawyer, "A Look Back at Aly Tamboura's Legacy and Accomplishments," *San Quentin News*, October 26, 2016, https://sanquentinnews.com/a-look-back-at-aly-tambouras-legacy-and-accomplishments/.

3. Jacob Simas, *Inside Story: Chronicles the Rise and Fall of Prison Journalism in the United States and the Recent Rebirth of the Prison Newspaper at San Quentin State Prison*, MA thesis film, 2009, available from Jacob Simas, jsimas@newamericamedia.org, 2009.

24. LITTLE NICK'S STORY

1. Sexual relations in prison are a criminal offense under state and federal law. Yet San Quentin dispenses condoms for free. Inmates may have no more than three in their possession at any time.

2. Regina Graham, "Women Who Risked Everything for Love with Prisoners," *Daily Mail*, April 5, 2018, www.dailymail.co.uk/news/article-5582019/Women-resist-dating-prisoners-risk-love.html?ito=facebook_share_article-home.

3. Lynn Bartels, "Free to Kill," in *Crime on Deadline*, ed. Lisa Beth Pulitzer (Brooklyn, NY: Boulevard Books, 1996), 236. Bartels went on to work for years in Denver, where she became a journalism icon at the *Rocky Mountain News* and later the *Denver Post*. She retired in 2015 and became a communications director for the secretary of state.

4. Marcus Henderson, "Project Avary Raises Money for Incarcerated Kids," *San Quentin News*, October 1, 2017.

25. HE CAME TO ME IN A DREAM

1. Arnulfo T. García, "Editor-in-Chief Steps Aside to Pursue Other Dreams," *San Quentin News*, March 1, 2016, https://sanquentinnews.com/?s=steps +aside+to+pursue.

2. Esmeralda Bermudez, "A Prison Mourns Its Former Editor-in-Chief, Recently Released and Then Killed in a Crash," *Los Angeles Times*, October 8, 2017, www.latimes.com/local/california/la-me-san-quentin-20171008-html-story.html.

26. THE PRESS IN PRISON

1. Adam Liptak, "Justices, 5-4, Tell California to Cut Prison Population," *New York Times*, May 24, 2011, https://www.nytimes.com/2011/05/24/us/24scotus .html.

2. Kitty Calavita and Valerie Jenness, *Appealing to Justice: Prisoner Grievances, Rights and Carceral Logic* (Oakland: University of California Press, 2015), 6.

3. Marshall Project, "The Catalyst: Thelton Henderson Transformed California's Criminal Justice System," April 23, 2018, https://www.themarshallproject .org/2018/04/23/the-catalyst.

4. David Marsh, "California Officials Openly Defy Federal Judge," *San Quentin News*, November 1, 2008, https://sanquentinnews.com/california-officials-openly-defy-federal-judge/.

5. Crystal Haines, "'This Isn't Just Numbers It's Lives': Half of Americans Have Family Members Who've Been Incarcerated," *USA Today*, December 6, 2018, http://bit.ly/2PuVZl7.

6. "CACorrections—About," Facebook, n.d., accessed April 18, 2019, https:// www.facebook.com/pg/cacorrections/about/?ref=page_internal.

7. Congresswoman Speier attended a *San Quentin News* forum. About a dozen inmates described their experiences in prison and their hopes for their lives after they got out.

8. "California Prison Info and Support—About," n.d., accessed 2018, https:// www.facebook.com/groups/Californiaprisoninfo/about/.

9. "Prison Reform Movement—About," n.d., accessed 2018, https://www .facebook.com/groups/PrisonReformMvt/about/.

10. Carole Leonard, emails to author, 2018.

11. Marcia Reynolds, "Why Is *Orange Is the New Black* So Popular?" *Huffington Post,* December 6, 2017, https://www.huffingtonpost.com/marcia-reynolds /why-is-orange-is-the-new-black-so-popular_b_7576698.html.

12. Reynolds, "Why."

13. Amber Healy, "Ear Hustle's Remarkable Success in Podcasting from Prison," *It's All Journalism,* February 1, 2018, http://itsalljournalism.com /remarkable-success-prison-podcast/.

14. Tana Ganeva, "Ear Hustle: How Two Inmates Created First Prison Podcast," *Rolling Stone,* July 10, 2017, https://www.rollingstone.com/culture/features /ear-hustle-how-inmates-created-enthralling-prison-podcast-w491292.

15. "Ear Hustle—About, Press," n.d., accessed April 18, 2019, https://www .earhustlesq.com/ about/#press.

16. See "Bud Abbott—Biography," IMDB, n.d., accessed April 18, 2019, https:// www.imdb.com/name/nm0007941/bio.

17. "Getting a Date," *Ear Hustle* podcast, season 1, episode 10, October 25, 2017, transcript, https://static1.squarespace.com/static/591a00ae197aea4b603d 2762/t/5a00c09f8165f51d9ed03a93/1509998751875/10_Ear+Hustle_transcript_ Getting+a+Date.pdf.

18. "Getting a Date."

19. Olga R. Rodriguez, "'Ear Hustle' Host Is Freed, but Prison Podcast Will Go On," Associated Press, January 2, 2019, https://www.apnews.com/cb78634a 65524494a74e10714660c2c8.

20. "Theme: Life Revealed," TEDx San Quentin, January 22, 2016, https:// www.ted.com/tedx/events/13459.

21. Curtis (Wall Street) Carroll, "How I Learned to Read and Trade Stocks in Prison," TEDx Talk, January 2016, https://www.ted.com/talks/curtis_wall_ street_carroll_how_i_learned_to_read_and_trade_stocks_in_prison.

22. Juan Haines, "San Quentin Hosts First TEDx," *San Quentin News,* February 1, 2016, https://sanquentinnews.com/san-quentin-hosts-tedx/.

23. Jeffrey Richardson, answer to the question "Which Prisons Are Safer and Better (UK Prisons or US Prisons)?" *Quora,* June 10, 2017, https://www.quora .com/Which-prisons-are-safer-and-better-UK-prisons-or-US-prisons.

24. Analytics came from CDCR public information officer Kristina Khokho-bashvili in an April 30, 2018, email to the author.

25. "Go behind the Walls of San Quentin for Facebook Live Q&A," *Inside CDCR,* January 24, 2018, https://www.insidecdcr.ca.gov/2018/01/go-behind-the-walls-of-san-quentin-for-facebook-live-qa/; Khokhobashvili e-mail to author, April 30, 2018.

26. Kevin D. Sawyer, "2011 Realignment Had Modest Impact on Recidivism," *San Quentin News,* April 19, 2018, https://sanquentinnews.com/2011-realignment-modest-impact-recidivism-inmates-slightly-higher-rate-recidivism-released-ab-109/.

27. PHILANTHROPY

1. Jody Lewen, email to author, June 2015.

2. Jonathan Logan Family Foundation, "About," n.d., accessed 2018, https://jonathanloganfamilyfoundation.org/about/.

3. Jody Lewen, email to author, February 7, 2018.

4. Jon Spurlock, email to author, July 21, 2014, including a copy of the McNamara letter to Professor Silver.

5. Spurlock, email to author, July 21, 2014.

28. THE FORUMS

1. Supreme Court of the United States, Brown, Governor of California, et al. v. Plata et al., 2011, Legal Information Institute, https://www.law.cornell.edu/supct/html/09-1233.ZS.html.

2. Arnulfo García, memorandum to *San Quentin News* staff, April 8, 2017, in author's collection.

3. Juan Haines, "Santa Clara County D.A. Attends Forum with S.Q. Inmates," *San Quentin News,* April 2014, https://storage.googleapis.com/sqn-archives/PDF/SQN_Edition_55_April_web.pdf.

4. Juan Haines, "Santa Clara D.A. Discusses Solutions to Crime," *San Quentin News,* April 26, 2018, https://sanquentinnews.com/santa-clara-countys-head-da-discusses-solutions-crime/.

5. Juan Haines, "Congresswoman Jackie Speier Given New Insights into Prison Rehab," *San Quentin News,* August 1, 2015.

6. Juan Haines, "Santa Clara County D.A. Attends Forum with S.Q. Inmates," *San Quentin News,* April 24, 2014.

7. Juan Haines, "San Quentin News Hosts Nationwide DA Forum," *San Quentin News,* February 28, 2017, https://sanquentinnews.com/sq-news-hosts-nationwide-da-forum/.

8. Juan Haines, "Prosecutors Visit SQ News Seeking Public Safety," *San Quentin News,* January 31, 2017, https://sanquentinnews.com/prosecutors-visit-sq-news-public-safety/. Melendez was paroled in 2018.

9. Haines, "Prosecutors Visit."

10. Juan Haines, "Prosecutors Visit."

11. Juan Haines, "San Quentin Hosts 4th DA Forum," *San Quentin News,* August 2, 2017, https://sanquentinnews.com/san-quentin-hosts-fourth-da-forum/.

12. The author's notes from a July 2015 meeting.

13. Haines, "Congresswoman Jackie Speier."

14. Juan Haines, "SQN Forum Welcomes Appellate Judge J. Anthony Kline," *San Quentin News,* September 1, 2016.

29. A NEW NARRATIVE

1. Jesse Lau, "Incarceration to Convocation," *Daily Californian,* May 10, 2015, www.dailycal.org/2015/05/10/incarceration-to-convocation/.

2. "Pelican Bay," *60 Minutes,* September 12, 1993, CBS News, https://www.cbsnews.com/video/from-the-archives-60-minutes-first-pelican-bay-report/.

3. "Pelican Bay," *60 Minutes,* January 19, 2018, CBS News, https://www.cbsnews.com/video/pelican-bay/.

4. Magnus Lofstrom, Mia Bird, and Brandon Martin, "California's Historic Corrections Reforms," Public Policy Institute of California, September 2016, www.ppic.org/content/pubs/report/R_916MLR.pdf.

5. "The Letter That Transformed Shaka Senghor's Life," *Super Soul Sunday,* March 13, 2016, OWN, www.oprah.com/own-super-soul-sunday/the-letter-that-transformed-shaka-senghors-life.

6. "Shaka Senghor's Life-Changing Epiphany," *Super Soul Sunday,* season 7, episode 1, March 13, 2016, OWN, www.oprah.com/own-super-soul-sunday/shaka-senghors-life-changing-epiphany.

7. Final papers written for my Journalism 298, San Quentin Editing Class, 2018, University of California, Berkeley.

8. Final papers.

9. Final papers.

10. Final papers.

11. Blair Hickman, "Inmate. Prisoner. Other. Discussed," Marshall Project, April 3, 2015, https://www.themarshallproject.org/2015/04/03/inmate-prisoner-other-discussed?utm_medium=social&utm_campaign=share-tools&utm_source=twitter&utm_content=post-top.

12. Rosalio Ahumada, "Modesto Man Convicted in Deadly Gang Fight. Now, He's Eligible for Parole," *Modesto Bee,* February 20, 2018.

30. JOURNALISM AND REHABILITATION

1. Catey Hill, "Murderer Turned Stock Picker Is 'Oracle of San Quentin,'" MarketWatch, July 13, 2014, https://www.marketwatch.com/story/murderer-turned-stock-picker-is-oracle-of-san-quentin-2014–07–10.

2. G. K. Chesterton, "The Purple Wig," in *The Wisdom of Father Brown* (London: Cassell, 1914), 164.

3. Alexandra Stepanov, "Prison Newspapers: Identification Prison Settings," honors thesis, University of Central Florida, Orlando, 2017.

4. Larry Brewster, "The Impact of Prison Arts Programs on Inmate Attitudes and Behavior: A Quantitative Evaluation," *Justice Policy Journal* 11, no. 2 (Fall 2014), www.cjcj.org/uploads/cjcj/documents/brewster_prison_arts_final_formatted.pdf.

5. Shadd Maruna, *Making Good: How Ex-convicts Reform and Rebuild Their Lives* (Washington, DC: American Psychological Association, 2001), 9.

6. Yukari Kane, email to author, April 23, 2018.

7. Assessing the effectiveness of these groups is beyond my competence and beyond the scope of this book. A documentary titled *The Work* examines a novel therapeutic group therapy approach at New Folsom Prison that has been widely praised. Gary Goldstein, "Documentary 'The Work' Goes inside Prison Group Therapy, Where Inmates Drop Their Masks," *Los Angeles Times*, October 24, 2017, www.latimes.com/entertainment/movies/la-et-mn-the-work-review-20171024-story.html.

8. "President Obama Awards Prison University Project National Humanities Medal," Prison University Project, September 16, 2016, https://prisonuniversity project.org/news/national-humanities-medal/.

9. Self-written obituaries for a class assignment in 2012 under the auspices of the Prison University Project. In the author's collection.

31. THE CAMPUS AND THE PRISON

1. Elizabeth Hinton, "Turn Prisons into Colleges," *New York Times*, March 6, 2018, https://www.nytimes.com/2018/03/06/opinion/prisons-colleges-education .html.

2. Byrhonda Lyons, term paper submitted for Journalism 298, San Quentin Editing Class, 2013, University of California, Berkeley.

3. Amina Wahid, term paper submitted for Journalism 298, San Quentin Editing Class, 2013, University of California, Berkeley.

4. "What Are the Humanities?," Stanford Humanities Center, n.d., accessed April 22, 2019, http://shc.stanford.edu/what-are-the-humanities.

5. Gabriel Sánchez, term paper, submitted for Journalism 298, San Quentin Editing Class, 2013, University of California, Berkeley.

6. Michael F. Welch, *Escape to Prison: Penal Tourism and the Pull of Punishment* (Berkeley: University of California Press, 2015).

7. Sasha Lekatch, term paper, submitted for Journalism 298, San Quentin Editing Class, 2013, University of California, Berkeley.

8. Marisa Conroy, term paper, submitted for Journalism 298, San Quentin Editing Class, 2013, University of California, Berkeley.

9. Spencer Whitney, term paper, submitted for Journalism 298, San Quentin Editing Class, 2013, University of California, Berkeley.

10. Trenise Ferreira, term paper, submitted for Journalism 298, San Quentin Editing Class, 2013, University of California, Berkeley.

11. "Don't Care about Criminals? Maybe You Should Care about What Their Care Is Costing You," editorial, *Sacramento Bee*, November 1, 2018, https://www .sacbee.com/opinion/editorials/article220960000.html.

12. "Berkeley's School of Criminology, 1950–1976," editorial, *Crime and Social Justice*, no. 6 (Summer 1976), https://www.socialjusticejournal.org/SJEdits/06Edit-1.html.

13. Tony Platt, email to author, January 21, 2019.

14. Tony Platt, *Beyond These Walls: Rethinking Crime and Punishment in the United States* (New York: St. Martin's Press, 2019).

15. Allen H. Marshall, term paper, submitted for Journalism 298, San Quentin Editing Class, 2015, University of California, Berkeley.

32. IS THIS SCALABLE?

1. Kevin D. Sawyer, "SQN Launches a New Web Site," *San Quentin News*, October 1, 2017, https://sanquentinnews.com/sqn-launches-sanquentinnews-com/.

2. Glen Klein, "Prep School to Brink of Prison," *Marin Independent Journal*, January 22, 2016, https://www.mercurynews.com/2016/01/22/prep-school-to-brink-of-prison-marin-shooters-sentencing-delayed/.

3. Kevin Sawyer, the inmate business manager of the newspaper, keeps a log of all visits by volunteers to the newsroom.

4. Rina Palta, "Suicides in California Prisons Due to Lack of Leadership, Oversight," Southern California Public Radio, August 17, 2017, https://www.scpr.org/news/2017/08/17/74775/auditor-suicides-in-ca-prisons-caused-by-lack-of-l/.

5. Krissi Khokhobashvili, "Inmate Newspaper Developing a 'Vision' at CSP-Solano," *Inside CDCR*, July 24, 2015, https://www.insidecdcr.ca.gov/2015/07/inmate-newspaper-developing-a-vision-at-csp-solano/.

6. Marcus Henderson, "Old Fashioned Baseball Revived in the Lower Yard," *San Quentin News*, December 25, 2018. https://sanquentinnews.com/old-fashion-baseball-revived-on-the-lower-yard/.

7. Nathalie Basha, "Hula Dancing Is Being Taught in San Quentin State Prison for Reform—and It's Working," *Circa*, January 10, 2019, https://www.circa.com/story/2019/01/10/crime-justice/hula-dance-is-being-taught-in-san-quentin-state-prison-for-reform-and-its-working.

8. California law refers to Indian reservations as "rancherias."

33. THE HERO WITH A THOUSAND FACES

1. Joseph Campbell, *The Hero with a Thousand Faces* (1968; repr., Novato, CA: New World Library, 2008), 23.

2. William J. Drummond, "Death of a Man in the Middle," *Esquire*, April 1972, 74.

3. Phillip Rodriguez, dir., *Ruben Salazar: Man in the Middle,* PBS.org, April 29, 2014, www.pbs.org/program/ruben-salazar-man-middle/.

4. Quoted in W. Drummond, "Death."

5. Shadd Maruna, *Making Good: How Ex-convicts Reform and Rebuild Their Lives* (Washington, DC: American Psychological Association, 2001), 85.

6. Juan Haines, an editor at *San Quentin News,* in October 2017 collected several staff reminiscences of Arnulfo García and sent them to Sean Webby, an assistant in the Santa Clara County District Attorney's Office. Webby was writing an obituary for a county publication. This is an excerpt.

7. Richard "Bonaru" Richardson, "Remembering Arnulfo T. García," *San Quentin News,* October 5, 2017, https://sanquentinnews.com/remembering-arnulfo-t-garcia/.

8. Richard Richardson, "Remembering."

9. Bo Kovitz, "Implementing Arnulfo García's Vision for an Outstanding Inmate-Run Magazine," *Wall City* 1, no. 1 (Spring 2018).

10. Richard Richardson, "Remembering."

11. Robert Ayers, "Retired Warden Robert Ayers Honors Late Arnulfo Garcia," *San Quentin News,* October 2, 2017, https://sanquentinnews.com/retired-warden-robert-ayers-late-arnulfo-garcia/.

12. Esmeralda Bermudez, "A Prison Newsroom Mourns Its Former Editor in Chief," *Los Angeles Times,* October 8, 2017, www.latimes.com/local/california/la-me-san-quentin-20171008-htmlstory.html.

Bibliography

Abcarian, Robin. "A Young Man in Oakland Has Captured the Wisdom of His Elders on a Blog and in a Book." *Los Angeles Times*, April 9, 2017. www .latimes.com/local/abcarian/la-me-abcarian-og-harshaw-20170409-story .html.

Ahumada, Rosalio. "Modesto Man Convicted in Deadly Gang Fight. Now, He's Eligible for Parole." *Modesto Bee*, February 20, 2018.2Alexander, Michelle. *The New Jim Crow: Mass Incarceration in the Era of Colorblindness*. New York: New Press, 2010.

Associated Press. "Man Sentenced to 50 Years to Life for Killing L.A. Musician." January 17, 2006. https://groups.google.com/forum/#!topic/alt.obituaries /duOWWMyyiMs.

Ayers, Robert. "Retired Warden Robert Ayers Honors Late Arnulfo Garcia." *San Quentin News*, October 2, 2017.

Barr, Merrill. "We Finally Know How Many People Watched 'Orange Is the New Black.'" *TV Guide*, June 29, 2016. https://www.tvguide.com/news/nielsen-reveals-orange-is-the-new-black-ratings/.

Bartels, Lynn. "Free to Kill." In *Crime on Deadline*, edited by Lisa Beth Pulitzer. Brooklyn, NY: Boulevard Books, 1996.

Basha, Nathalie. "Hula Dancing Is Being Taught in San Quentin State Prison for Reform—and It's Working." *Circa*, January 10, 2019. https://www.circa .com/story/2019/01/10/crime-justice/hula-dance-is-being-taught-in-san-quentin-state-prison-for-reform-and-its-working.

Bermudez, Esmeralda. "A Prison Newsroom Mourns Its Former Editor in Chief, Recently Released and Then Killed in a Crash." *Los Angeles Times,* October 8, 2017. www.latimes.com/local/california/la-me-san-quentin-20171008-htmlstory.html.

"Blaxploitation: The Controversial 1970s." Separate Cinema Archive, n.d. Accessed April 13, 2019. www.separatecinema.com/exhibits_blaxploitation.html.

Brewster, Larry. "The Impact of Prison Arts Programs on Inmate Attitudes and Behavior: A Quantitative Evaluation." *Justice Policy Journal* 11, no. 2 (Fall 2014). www.cjcj.org/uploads/cjcj/documents/brewster_prison_arts_final_formatted.pdf.

Brown, Alyson. "What Has Been Ailing Britain's Prisons?" *History Now, BBC History Magazine,* October 4, 2018.

Brown, Patricia Leigh. "Inmates' Newspaper Covers a World behind San Quentin's Walls." *New York Times,* May 20, 2014. https://www.nytimes.com/2014/05/21/us/inmates-newspaper-covers-a-world-behind-san-quentins-walls.html.

Calavita, Kitty, and Valerie Jenness. *Appealing to Justice: Prisoner Grievances, Rights, and Carceral Logic.* Oakland: University of California Press, 2015.

California Commission on the Status of African-American Males. *African-American Males: The Struggle for Equality. Final Report.* Sacramento, CA: The Commission, 1996.

Campbell, Joseph. *The Hero with a Thousand Faces.* 1968. Reprint, Novato, CA: New World Library, 2008.

Carroll, Curtis (Wall Street). "How I Learned to Read and Trade Stocks in Prison." TEDx Talk, January 2016. https://www.ted.com/talks/curtis_wall_street_carroll_how_i_learned_to_read_and_trade_stocks_in_prison.

CBS News. "Pelican Bay." *60 Minutes,* September 12, 1993. https://www.cbsnews.com/video/from-the-archives-60-minutes-first-pelican-bay-report/.

CBS News. "Pelican Bay." *60 Minutes,* January 19, 2018. https://www.cbsnews.com/video/pelican-bay/.

Chiu, Jonathan. "Marathon Man: A Lifer Takes Up Running to 'Earn Back' His Life." Marshall Project, May 11, 2017. https://www.themarshallproject.org/2017/05/11/marathon-man.

Christie, Joel. "'I'm Here Because I Took a Life—When I Leave This World, I Would Love to Save Someone': Prison Inmates Pen Their Own Moving Obituaries as Part of Class Assignment." *Daily Mail Online,* March 8, 2015. www.dailymail.co.uk/news/article-2984813/I-m-took-life-leave-world-love-save-Prison-inmates-pen-moving-obituaries-class-assignment.html.

Clark, Phillip. "Bastille by the Bay." *San Quentin News,* October 1, 1971. https://archive.org/stream/san_quentin_news_1971/san_quentin_news_1971_djvu.txt.

Cleaver, Eldridge. *Soul on Ice.* New York: McGraw Hill, 1968.

CNN. "United Shades of America: Behind These Walls." Aired May 1, 2016. Transcript. http://transcripts.cnn.com/TRANSCRIPTS/1605/01/se.01 .html.

"Coyote Point Productions Biographies." Inmate-written autobiographies, San Quentin, 2014.

Crime and Social Justice. "Berkeley's School of Criminology, 1950–1976." Editorial. No. 6 (Summer 1976). https://www.socialjusticejournal.org/SJEdits /06Edit-1.html.

Cummins, Eric. *The Rise and Fall of California's Radical Prison Movement.* Stanford, CA: Stanford University Press, 1994.

Darlow, Michael, dir. *Johnny Cash in San Quentin.* Granada Television. Aired September 6, 1969. www.imdb.com/title/tt0461256/.

Dharma, Brad. "The 50 Best Blaxploitation Movies of All Time." IMDb, last updated May 22, 2014. www.imdb.com/list/ls058887687.

Drummond, Tammerlin. "Years after Leaving San Quentin, Men Return with Message of Hope." *Oakland Tribune,* June 9, 2017.

Drummond, William J. "'Black Skin, Kinky Hair, Fleetness of Foot.'" *Columbia Journalism Review,* Fall 1968, 49–51. https://drive.google.com/file/d /1FJ1FA2PiWeOg68GoCnYMSSr628i6FS13/view?usp=sharing.

———. "Blue Denim Jungle: Prison Race Trouble." *Los Angeles Times.* August 9, 1970.

———. "Death of a Man in the Middle." *Esquire,* April 1972, 74.

———. "Eldridge Cleaver: Black Militant Forged by Life. Who Is He? What Is He? And Why?" *Los Angeles Times.* November 29, 1968.

———. "LA Crime Rate Could Collapse Justice System, Computer Says. Overloaded Jails Seen as Threat If Trend Persists." *Los Angeles Times,* September 13, 1970.

———. "Media." Chap. 9 in California Commission on the Status of African-American Males, *African-American Males: The Struggle for Equality. Final Report.* Sacramento, CA: The Commission, 1996.

Duffy, Clinton. "Warden Duffy Tells How He Started the San Quentin News." *San Quentin News,* July 2010. https://archive.org/stream/san_quentin_news_ 2010/san_quentin_news_2010_djvu.txt

Ear Hustle podcast. "Firsts." Season 2, March 14, 2018, transcript. https:// static1.squarespace.com/static/5bd0d552e8ba44146721bb3c/t/5cab9984e 79c703b55bae8f8/1554749836311/Firsts+transcript.pdf.

———. "Getting a Date." Season 1, episode 10, October 25, 2017, transcript. https://static1.squarespace.com/static/591a00ae197aea4b 603d2762/t/5a00c09f8165f51d9ed03a93/1509998751875/10_Ear+Hustle_ transcript_Getting+a+Date.pdf.

Fraser, Laura. "State's Prison Press Sentenced to Silence." MediaFile, April 1985.

Ganeva, Tana. "Ear Hustle: How Two Inmates Created First Prison Podcast." *Rolling Stone*, July 10, 2017. https://www.rollingstone.com/culture/features /ear-hustle-how-inmates-created-enthralling-prison-podcast-w491292.

García, Arnulfo T. "Editor-in-Chief Steps Aside to Pursue Other Dreams," *San Quentin News*, March 1, 2016. https://sanquentinnews.com/?s=steps+aside +to+pursue.

———. "The Life of Arnulfo Timoteo García." Unpublished manuscript, 2012.

———. "The Tour." Unpublished manuscript, 2012.

Goldstein, Gary. "Documentary 'The Work' Goes inside Prison Group Therapy, Where Inmates Drop Their Masks." *Los Angeles Times*, October 24, 2017. www .latimes.com/entertainment/movies/la-et-mn-the-work-review-20171024- story.html.

Gopnik, Adam. "The Caging of America: Why Do We Lock Up So Many People?" *New Yorker*. January 22, 2012. https://www.newyorker.com/magazine/2012 /01/30/the-caging-of-america.

———. "How We Misunderstand Mass Incarceration." *New Yorker*, April 3, 2017. https://www.newyorker.com/magazine/2017/04/10/how-we- misunderstand-mass-incarceration.

———. "Notes on 'The Caging of America.'" *New Yorker*, February 6, 2012. https://www.newyorker.com/news/news-desk/notes-on-the-caging-of- america.

Graham, Regina. "Women Who Risked Everything for Love with Prisoners." *Daily Mail*, April 5, 2018. www.dailymail.co.uk/news/article-5582019/Women- resist-dating-prisoners-risk-love.html?ito=facebook_share_article-home.

Greenberg, Alissa. "Prisons Need Newspapers for the Same Reason the Public Needs Newspapers." *Pacific Standard*, December 7, 2018. https://psmag.com /social-justice/prisons-need-newspapers-interview-with-juan-haines-at-san- quentin-news?fbclid=IwAR3TgqYppLHTDjbE-veq7p2E7mVa2Kxs- JR4HWAJIVU3VKUFBM9A1NvrsvFY.

Griffiths, Allison. *Carceral Fantasies: Cinema and Prison in Early 20th Century America*. New York: Columbia University Press, 2016.

Haines, Crystal. "'This Isn't Just Numbers It's Lives': Half of Americans Have Family Members Who've Been Incarcerated." *USA Today*, December 6, 2018. http://bit.ly/2PuVZl7.

Haines, Juan. "Congresswoman Jackie Speier Given New Insights into Prison Rehab." *San Quentin News*, August 1, 2015.

———. "Former Lifer at Large in Community." *Wall City* magazine, Spring 2019.

———. "Home after Two Decades of Prison and Accomplishments." *San Quentin News*, July 1, 2017. https://storage.googleapis.com/sqn-archives /PDF/SQN-Edition-94-July-2017.pdf.

————. "Prosecutors Visit SQ News Seeking Public Safety." *San Quentin News*, January 31, 2017. https://sanquentinnews.com/prosecutors-visit-sq-news-public-safety/.

————. "San Quentin Hosts First TEDx." *San Quentin News*, February 1, 2016. https://sanquentinnews.com/san-quentin-hosts-tedx/.

————. "San Quentin Hosts Fourth D.A. Forum." *San Quentin News*, August 2, 2017. https://sanquentinnews.com/?s=San+Quentin+hosts+fourth+D.A.+forum.

————. "San Quentin News Hosts Nationwide DA Forum." *San Quentin News*, February 28, 2017. https://sanquentinnews.com/sq-news-hosts-nationwide-da-forum/.

————. "Santa Clara County D.A. Attends Forum with S.Q. Inmates." *San Quentin News*, April 24, 2014. https://storage.googleapis.com/sqn-archives/PDF/SQN_Edition_55_April_web.pdf.

————. "Santa Clara D.A. Discusses Solutions to Crime." *San Quentin News*, April 26, 2018. https://sanquentinnews.com/santa-clara-countys-head-da-discusses-solutions-crime/.

————. "SQN Forum Welcomes Appellate Judge J. Anthony Kline." *San Quentin News*, September 1, 2016.

Healy, Amber. "Ear Hustle's Remarkable Success in Podcasting from Prison." *It's All Journalism*, February 1, 2018. http://itsalljournalism.com/remarkable-success-prison-podcast/.

Henderson, Marcus. "Old Fashioned Baseball Revived in the Lower Yard." *San Quentin News*, December 5, 2018. https://sanquentinnews.com/old-fashion-baseball-revived-on-the-lower-yard/.

————. "Project Avary Raises Money for Incarcerated Kids." *San Quentin News*, October 1, 2017.

Hickman, Blair. "Inmate. Prisoner. Other. Discussed." Marshall Project, April 3, 2015. https://www.themarshallproject.org/2015/04/03/inmate-prisoner-other-discussed?utm_medium=social&utm_campaign=share-tools&utm_source=twitter&utm_content=post-top.

Hill, Catey. "Murderer Turned Stock Picker Is 'Oracle of San Quentin.'" Market-Watch, July 13, 2014. https://www.marketwatch.com/story/murderer-turned-stock-picker-is-oracle-of-san-quentin-2014-07-10.

Hinton, Elizabeth. "Turn Prisons into Colleges." *New York Times*, March 6, 2018. https://www.nytimes.com/2018/03/06/opinion/prisons-colleges-education.html.

Hofstadter, Richard. *The Age of Reform*. New York: Knopf, 1955.

Hurwitt, Sam. "A Life behind Bars Unfolds on Stage in Oakland." *San Jose Mercury-News*, January 9, 2018.

Inside CDCR: The Department of Corrections and Rehabilitation Newsletter. "A Day in the Life of a Public Information Officer." March 14, 2013.

————. "A Decade Ago, a New Name Affirmed Mission of CDCR." August 28, 2015.https://www.insidecdcr.ca.gov/2015/08/a-decade-ago-a-new-name-affirmed-mission-of-cdcr/.

————. "Go behind the Walls of San Quentin for Facebook Live Q&A." January 24, 2018. https://www.insidecdcr.ca.gov/2018/01/go-behind-the-walls-of-san-quentin-for-facebook-live-qa/.

Kauffman, Gretel. "Attica! Representations of the 1971 Prison Riot in Local and National Journalism." Senior thesis, Notre Dame University, 2016. http://americanstudies.nd.edu/assets/223714/gretel_kauffman_thesis_.pdf.

Kerner Commission. *Report of the National Advisory Commission on Civil Disorders*. Washington, DC: US Government Printing Office, 1968. https://www.ncjrs.gov/pdffiles1/Digitization/8073NCJRS.pdf.

Khokhobashvili, Krissi. "Inmate Newspaper Developing a 'Vision' at CSP-Solano." *Inside CDCR: The Department of Corrections and Rehabilitation Newsletter,* July 24, 2015. https://www.insidecdcr.ca.gov/2015/07/inmate-newspaper-developing-a-vision-at-csp-solano/.

Klein, Glen. "Prep School to Brink of Prison." *Marin Independent Journal,* January 22, 2016. https://www.mercurynews.com/2016/01/22/prep-school-to-brink-of-prison-marin-shooters-sentencing-delayed/.

Kovitz, Bo. "Implementing Arnulfo García's Vision for an Outstanding Inmate-Run Magazine." *Wall City,* Spring 2018.

KPIX-TV. "The Last Mile Transforms San Quentin Inmates into Tech Entrepreneurs."April1,2015.https://sanfrancisco.cbslocal.com/2015/04/01/the-last-mile-turns-san-quentin-inmates-start-ups-tech-pitch-ideas-silicon-valley-entrepreneurs/.

Lam, John. "Stateless: A Massacre, a Murder and Now Free." *San Quentin News,* January 31, 2017. https://sanquentinnews.com/stateless-massacre-murder-free/.

Lau, Jesse. "Incarceration to Convocation." *Daily Californian,* May 10, 2015. www.dailycal.org/2015/05/10/incarceration-to-convocation/.

Liptak, Adam. "Justices, 5–4, Tell California to Cut Prison Population." *New York Times,* May 24, 2011. https://www.nytimes.com/2011/05/24/us/24scotus.html.

Lofstrom, Magnus, Mia Bird, and Brandon Martin. "California's Historic Corrections Reforms." Public Policy Institute of California, September 2016. www.ppic.org/content/pubs/report/R_916MLR.pdf.

Malnic, Eric. "Voices—Eric Malnic." *Los Angeles Times,* June 8, 2008. https://latimesblogs.latimes.com/thedailymirror/2008/06/voices--eric-ma.html.

Marsh, David. "California Officials Openly Defy Federal Judge." *San Quentin News,* November 1, 2008. https://sanquentinnews.com/california-officials-openly-defy-federal-judge/.

Marsh, Phil. "At San Quentin." *Rolling Stone*, July 1969. https://www.rollingstone.com/music/music-country/at-san-quentin-189370/.

Marshall Project. "The Catalyst: Thelton Henderson Transformed California's Criminal Justice System." April 23, 2018. https://www.themarshallproject.org/2018/04/23/the-catalyst.

Maruna, Shadd. *Making Good: How Ex-convicts Reform and Rebuild Their Lives*. Washington, DC: American Psychological Association, 2001.

Masters, Ryan. "How $107 Million of West Coast Rap King Suge Knight's Money Got Divvied Up in a Monterey Courtroom." *Monterey County Weekly*, April 27, 2006. www.montereycountyweekly.com/news/local_news/how-million-of-west-coast-rap-king-suge-knight-s/article_d46629ee-59f2-585b-acc1-838c44e0dedf.html.

Megerian, Chris. "Inmates Writing Their Own Obits Reveal Regrets, Failed Dreams." *Los Angeles Times*, March 4, 2015. http://graphics.latimes.com/prison-obits/.

Morris, James McGrath. *Jailhouse Journalism: The Fourth Estate behind Bars*. Jefferson, NC: McFarland, 1998.

Moynihan, Daniel Patrick. *The Case for National Action: The Negro Family*. Report for the Office of Policy Planning and Research, US Department of Labor. Washington, DC: US Government Printing Office, 1965.

MSNBC. "Lockup Producer Answers Your Questions." May 30, 2014. http://www.msnbc.com/lockup/producer-susan-carney-answers-your-questions-0.

NPR. "'Orange' Creator Jenjii Kohan: Piper Was My Trojan Horse." *Fresh Air*, August 13, 2013. https://www.npr.org/2013/08/13/211639989/orange-creator-jenji-kohan-piper-was-my-trojan-horse%0A.

Nzinga, Ayodele. *Lifer*. Video of performance by the Lower Bottom Playaz at Flight Deck in Oakland, CA, 2017. Vimeo, uploaded 2018, https://vimeo.com/261563845.

OWN. "The Letter That Transformed Shaka Senghor's Life." *Super Soul Sunday*, March 13, 2016. www.oprah.com/own-super-soul-sunday/the-letter-that-transformed-shaka-senghors-life.

———. "Shaka Senghor's Life-Changing Epiphany." *Super Soul Sunday*, season 7, episode 1, March 13, 2016. www.oprah.com/own-super-soul-sunday/shaka-senghors-life-changing-epiphany.

Palta, Rina. "Suicides in California Prisons Due to Lack of Leadership, Oversight." Southern California Public Radio, August 17, 2017. https://www.scpr.org/news/2017/08/17/74775/auditor-suicides-in-ca-prisons-caused-by-lack-of-l/.

Petski, Denise. "'Orange Is The New Black' to End with Season 7 on Netflix." *Deadline Hollywood*, October 7, 2018. https://deadline.com/2018/10/orange-is-the-new-black-to-end-with-season-7-on-netflix-1202484913/.

Pinker, Steven. *The Better Angels of Our Nature: Why Violence Has Declined.* New York: Penguin, 2011.

Pishko, Jessica. "The Curious Case of Prison Publishers." *Narratively,* August 22, 2014. http://narrative.ly/the-curious-case-of-the-prison-publishers/.

———. "San Quentin News Seeks to Humanize Inmates." *Columbia Journalism Review,* October 28, 2014. https://archives.cjr.org/behind_the_news/the_san_quentin_news_seeks_to.php.

Platt, Tony. *Beyond These Walls: Rethinking Crime and Punishment in the United States.* New York: St. Martin's Press, 2019.

Procunier, Raymond K. "Christmas Messages." *San Quentin News,* December 24, 1972. https://sanquentinnews.files.wordpress.com/2010/09/san-quentin-news-dec-24–1971.pdf.

———. "Publication Ban." *San Quentin News,* October 22, 1971. https://archive.org/stream/san_quentin_news_1971/san_quentin_news_1971_djvu.txt.

Pulitzer, Lisa Beth. *Crime on Deadline: Police Reporters Tell Their Most Unforgettable Stories.* New York: Boulevard Books, 1996.

Reed, Ishmael. "The Black Pathology Biz." *Nation,* November 20, 1989; reprinted in *Nation,* February 12, 2002. https://www.thenation.com/article/black-pathology-biz/.

Reynolds, Marcia. "Why Is *Orange Is the New Black* So Popular?" *Huffington Post,* December 6, 2017. https://www.huffingtonpost.com/marcia-reynolds/why-is-orange-is-the-new-black-so-popular_b_7576698.html.

Richardson, Richard (Bonaru). "Remembering Arnulfo T. García." *San Quentin News,* October 5, 2017. https://sanquentinnews.com/remembering-arnulfo-t-garcia/.

———. "San Quentin News Historical Journey." *San Quentin News,* November 15, 2018. https://sanquentinnews.com/san-quentin-news-historical-journey/.

Richardson, Robert. "A Taste of What It's Like." *Los Angeles Times,* August 22, 1965. http://documents.latimes.com/taste-what-its/.

Rideau, Wilbert. "Can a Free Press Flourish behind Bars?" *Nation,* June 25, 2014. https://www.thenation.com/article/can-free-press-flourish-behind-bars/.

Rodriguez, Olga. "'Ear Hustle' Host Is Freed, but Prison Podcast Will Go On." Associated Press, January 2, 2019. https://www.apnews.com/cb78634a65524494a74e10714660c2c8.

Rodriguez, Phillip, dir. *Ruben Salazar: Man in the Middle.* PBS.org, April 29, 2014, www.pbs.org/program/ruben-salazar-man-middle/.

Sacramento Bee. "Don't Care about Criminals? Maybe You Should Care about What Their Care Is Costing You." Editorial. November 1, 2018. https://www

.sacbee.com/opinion/editorials/article220960000.html?fbclid=IwAR2KDBP jN1vgRsj8SmmRUJnkIHWNWtKqocIn_MLlLYVJLjC1KgkNdXqn6yo%0A.

San Quentin News. "Aly Tamboura, Former Staff—Served Sentence." May 17, 2016. https://sanquentinnews.com/staff/aly-tamboura/.

————. "From the Editor's Desk." October 1, 1971, 2.

Sawyer, Kevin D. "Few Prisoners Strike at San Quentin." *Bay View: National Black Newspaper.* October 4, 2018. http://sfbayview.com/2018/10/few-prisoners-strike-at-san-quentin/.

————. "A Look Back at Aly Tamboura's Legacy and Accomplishments." *San Quentin News,* October 26, 2016. https://sanquentinnews .com/a-look-back-at-aly-tambouras-legacy-and-accomplishments/.

————. "SQN Launches a New Web Site." *San Quentin News,* October 1, 2017. https://sanquentinnews.com/sqn-launches-sanquentinnews-com/.

————. "2011 Realignment Had Modest Impact on Recidivism." *San Quentin News,* April 19, 2018. https://sanquentinnews.com/2011-realignment-modest-impact-recidivism-inmates-slightly-higher-rate-recidivism-released-ab-109/.

SFGate. "1970 Marin County Courthouse Murders." April 18, 2017. www.sfgate .com/news/slideshow/1970-Marin-County-courthouse-shooting-144014 /photo-12742230.php.

Simas, Jacob. *Inside Story: Chronicles the Rise and Fall of Prison Journalism in the United States and the Recent Rebirth of the Prison Newspaper at San Quentin State Prison.* MA thesis film, University of California, Berkeley, 2009. Available from Jacob Simas, jsimas@newamericamedia.org, 2009.

Stepanov, Alexandra. "Prison Newspapers: Identification Prison Settings." Honors thesis, University of Central Florida, Orlando, 2017.

Stingley, Jim. "Prison Guards: 24-Hour Day of Fear, Low Pay and Hatred." *Los Angeles Times,* September 6, 1971.

————. "Revolutionaries Keep San Quentin Tense." *Los Angeles Times,* September 26, 1970.

St. John, Paige. "As More Inmates Are Released from Prison, More Parolees Return." *Los Angeles Times,* December 27, 2014. https://www.latimes.com /local/california/la-me-ff-pol-lifer-parole-20141228-story.html.

Streissguth, Michael. *Johnny Cash: The Biography.* Boston: DaCapo Press, 2006.

Taylor, Michael. "San Quentin Inmate Newspaper Fills Need to Know." *San Francisco Chronicle,* March 28, 2009.

TEDx San Quentin. "Theme: Life Revealed." January 22, 2016. https://www .ted.com/tedx/events/13459.

Thomas, Rahsaan. "Exploring Injustices in Mass Incarceration." *San Quentin News,* August 1, 2015. https://sanquentinnews.com/exploring-injustices-in-mass-incarceration/.

Thompson, Gayle. "49 Years Ago Johnny Cash Records 'At San Quentin' Album." J-98 The Boot radio, May 18, 2018.

Vasquez, Jesse. "One Prison Taught Me Racism. Another Taught Me Acceptance." *Washington Post,* October 1, 2018. https://www.washingtonpost.com /outlook/2018/10/01/one-prison-taught-me-racism-another-taught-me-acceptance/?utm_term=.2f6c8ca8a9d7.

Welch, Michael F. *Escape to Prison: Penal Tourism and the Pull of Punishment.* Oakland: University of California Press, 2015.

Wilson, Christopher P. *Cop Knowledge: Police Power and Cultural Narrative in Twentieth-Century America.* Chicago: University of Chicago Press, 2000.

Wilson, Pete. "State of the State Address." Sacramento, January 5, 1994. http:// governors.library.ca.gov/addresses/s_36-Wilson04.html.

Woodard, Boston. "Johnny Cash: Prison Reform Advocate." *San Quentin News,* March 13, 2013. https://sanquentinnews.com/johnny-cash-legendary-prison-reform-advocate/.

Index

Page references including *"fig."* refer to photos.

Founded in 1893,
UNIVERSITY OF CALIFORNIA PRESS
publishes bold, progressive books and journals
on topics in the arts, humanities, social sciences,
and natural sciences—with a focus on social
justice issues—that inspire thought and action
among readers worldwide.

The UC PRESS FOUNDATION
raises funds to uphold the press's vital role
as an independent, nonprofit publisher, and
receives philanthropic support from a wide
range of individuals and institutions—and from
committed readers like you. To learn more, visit
ucpress.edu/supportus.